# JAMES DAKIN, ARCHITECT

*Longitudinal section of St. Patrick's Church, New Orleans, by James Dakin. (Courtesy Louisiana State Museum)*

# JAMES DAKIN, *Architect*

## *His Career in New York and the South*

Arthur Scully, Jr.

Louisiana State University Press

BATON ROUGE

ISBN 0–8071–0213–X
Library of Congress Catalog Card Number 72–89897
Copyright © 1973 by Louisiana State University Press
All rights reserved
Manufactured in the United States of America

Designed by Dwight Agner. Set in Hermann Zapf's
Linofilm Palatino by Southwestern Typographics Inc.,
Dallas, Texas. Printed and bound by Halliday Lithograph Corp.,
West Hanover, Massachusetts. Color inserts printed by
Kingsport Press, Kingsport, Tennessee.

*To* KATHYRINE REGAN

# CONTENTS

# LIST OF ILLUSTRATIONS

# ACKNOWLEDGMENTS

THE AUTHOR IS INDEBTED TO MANY PERSONS IN THE PREPARA-
tion of this book and would like to gratefully acknowledge
that debt here.

In New Orleans, Mrs. Dorothy Whittemore, Humanities
Reference Department, Tulane University, Howard-Tilton
Memorial Library; Mr. Boyd Cruise, Director, and Mrs.
Edith Long, Librarian, Historic New Orleans Collection;
Mr. Collin Hamer and Mr. Ernest Brin, of the Louisiana
Department, New Orleans Public Library; Mrs. Connie
Griffith and her staff, especially Mr. William Cullison, at the
Archives Department, Tulane University Library; Miss
Kathyrine Regan, Mrs. Blanche Hyatt King, and Mrs. Beryl
Trenchard Patin—all Dakin descendants, for their gener-
osity with original material; Mrs. Mary Oalmann, Librarian,
Louisiana National Guard Library, Jackson Barracks; and
last, but most importantly, Mr. Samuel Wilson, Jr., F.A.I.A.,
first a teacher, then a friend, whose pioneering research on
New Orleans architectural history is the foundation for
everyone who has come after him.

In Baton Rouge, Mr. Powell Casey and Mrs. James Thom,
who found Charles Dakin's grave in 1967; and the staff of
the late Virgil Bedsole, of the Archives Department, Louisiana State University Library.

In Mobile, Mr. Caldwell Delaney, Curator of the Mu-
seums of the City of Mobile; Mr. John Mandeville, Clerk of
Court, Mobile County Courthouse; and Mrs. Josephine Dix,
Secretary, Christ Church Episcopal.

In Louisville, Dr. Samuel Thomas, Archivist, Jefferson
County Courthouse; and to the staff of the Filson Club.

In New York, Mr. Adolph Placzek, Librarian, Avery Architecture Library, Columbia University; Mrs. Jane Davies
of Columbia University, the A. J. Davis expert, for her
generous sharing of Davis information, but whom I exoner-
ate from any errors in judgment I may have made in its use;
the staff of the New-York Historical Society; Dr. James
Grote Van Derpool, Director, New York Landmarks Preservation Commission and his research specialist, Miss Regina
Kellerman; Miss Elfreida Kraege, archivist of the Fifth Avenue Presbyterian Church (formerly Duane Street Church);
and Professor Lawrence Wodehouse, Pratt Institute.

In Washington, D.C., Miss Virginia Daiker, Prints Division, Library of Congress; Mr. Edwin Flatequal and the staff
of the National Archives and Records Service; and Mr.
Denys Peter Myers of the National Park Service.

To all the above and the many others who supplied
information for this book, the writer expresses his gratitude.

Arthur Scully, Jr.

New Orleans, Louisiana

# INTRODUCTION

THIS IS THE STORY OF A MAN AND HIS WORKS. AMONG THE major American architects of the early nineteenth century, James H. Dakin was the only one who practiced extensively in both the North and the South. After contributing to the development of the Revival movements—Greek, Gothic, and Egyptian—in New York with Town and Davis, he left these roots in the East and brought his skill to the South, where he literally changed the faces of New Orleans, Mobile, Baton Rouge, and other important southern cities. Their skylines still reflect his architectural genius.

It was with good reason that Talbot Hamlin, one of America's most noted architectural historians, described Dakin as "brilliant," "forceful," and "original." Nurtured for four years in the fertile soil of the Town and Davis firm in New York, Dakin emerged in 1833 as a full-fledged practitioner of his art. He continued on his own in New York for but a few years more before moving to New Orleans.

James Dakin arrived in the South at the right time with the right talents. In 1835, the South's "Golden Era," the boom period between 1830 and the start of the Civil War, was just beginning. This era of prosperity and progress lacked only someone to focus these elements into the visible sign which architecture provides society to help it express the feelings of the times. The Greek Revival had already found its way to New Orleans by the 1830s, but it was at the hands of James Dakin (and, to a somewhat lesser extent, his brother Charles, and James Gallier) that it would receive its ultimate fulfillment in the Deep South.

Greek Revival was the style which pervaded American architecture in this period. In the years just preceding the 1830s, the United States had begun erecting its great federal buildings, and the ancient Greek principles of architecture contained the elements which attracted America: dignity, good taste, and a feeling of permanence which the new country wished for itself. New Orleans and the Deep South shared the common mood of the country, and the Greek Revival flourished there as well.

The career of James H. Dakin can readily be divided into two parts: his early days in New York with Town and Davis, at that time the most influential architectural firm in the country, and the post-1835 or southern phase. A separate story could be written on his early career, but that is beyond the scope of this work because it is so closely intertwined with the Town and Davis firm, a highly complex subject in itself. The New York phase of Dakin's career is treated here only to the extent that it gives perspective to the whole.

At a time when there was a hazy area between the roles of builder and architect, James Dakin, Alexander Jackson Davis, William Strickland, Isaiah Rogers, and others were attempting to elevate their work to the level of a profession. In 1835, they founded the American Institution of Architects, the forerunner of the American Institute of Architects, which, though it did not function widely or actively, did make a beginning toward raising standards badly in need of uplifting.

James Dakin was a controversial man. His fist fight with a contractor on the walls of the Louisiana Capitol over bad bricks, the arguments with St. Patrick's Church, and the problems over the New Orleans Custom House all evidence this aspect of his personality. Even the means by which, up to now, we knew something of his career, is subject to dispute. Some of James Gallier's statements about the Dakins in his autobiography are reevaluated here.

The accomplishments of James Dakin (and of his younger brother and sometime partner, Charles Dakin) are formidable. If only a brief list were made of them as of the time of James's death in 1852, it would have to include: one of only two Gothic Revival state capitols—the capitol of Louisiana at Baton Rouge, by James H. Dakin; the tallest structure in New Orleans and the Deep South—St. Patrick's Church, by Dakin and Dakin, completed by Gallier; the earliest serious proposal to use cast iron extensively in a major American building—the New Orleans Custom House (the largest building in the United States, excluding the national Capitol)—supervised in part by James H. Dakin; the first major "Collegiate Gothic" building in America—New York University in New York City, by James H. Dakin, Alexander Jackson Davis, and Ithiel Town; the highly imaginative Bank of Louisville, Louisville, Kentucky, by James H. Dakin; the first campus of Tulane University at New Orleans, by James Dakin; the two largest hotels in the United States—the St. Charles Hotel, by Gallier and Charles Dakin, and the United States Hotel in Mobile, by Dakin and Dakin; the largest hotel in the central Mississippi Valley—the Gayoso House Hotel, Memphis, Tennessee, by James Dakin; the first permanent public school building in Alabama—Barton Academy in Mobile, by Gallier and Charles Dakin, completed by Dakin and Dakin. These buildings, as well as many others described later, place James Dakin in the top rank of American architects.

# JAMES DAKIN, ARCHITECT

# 1
## WITH TOWN AND DAVIS
## IN NEW YORK

### THE EARLY YEARS

JAMES HARRISON DAKIN WAS BORN IN NEW YORK STATE ON August 24, 1806, in the Township of Northeast, which comprises the upper corner of Dutchess County near the Connecticut border. His younger brother, Charles Bingley Dakin, was born at the same place on May 24, 1811. They were the sons of James and Lucy Harrison Dakin. Three other children survived to maturity, including another son, Edgar.[1]

The Dakin family has a long history in America, tracing back to Thomas Dakin of Concord, Massachusetts, who was born about 1624, probably in England, and is definitely placed in Concord by 1652.[2] James Dakin's grandfather, Simon Dakin, Jr., participated in the Revolutionary War—first as a member of the Continental Association of Dutchess County, Northeast Precinct, in 1775, and later as a member of the Sixth Regiment, Dutchess County Militia, Millerton, New York.[3]

The Dutchess County vicinity in which the Dakin boys grew up is a very hilly area, almost mountainous; the chief livelihood was farming, although there were craftsmen in the villages. The occupation of the Dakins' father is not known, but it is certain that he died when James was thirteen and Charles eight years old. Their mother had great difficulty keeping her family together after the death of her husband, and soon she was forced to send young James off to live with his father's sister Phebe and her husband, Herman Stoddard of Hudson, New York. Charles Dakin was sent to live with a "Waterman" family, probably also related to the Dakins.[4]

Two letters from James Dakin's mother, written to him in Hudson when he was about fifteen years old, have fortunately been preserved. The second, in particular, is a very touching one, revealing how painful was this dispersion of the Dakin family:

Well, Harrison, we are moved to Rhinebeck [N.Y.]. We have a very pleasant house and I hope we shall do well. Julia [Dakin's aunt] has a very nice shop and I think we shall have work plenty. . . .

I sent Charles to Mr. Waterman. Do, for pity's sake, make him take him—I want him to take, clothe and board him until he is twenty one. You must come and see us soon.[5]

And the other letter:

Dear Child:

I received your letter of the 16th. and now sit down to answer it. I returned last evening from Wethersfield [Connecticut] and have been gone three weeks. Our friends are all well in that place. My health is better than it has been, but am not all well yet. I don't think that I have enjoyed my health since I have been here and think that is one reason that I have not been more contented, but I am much better than I have been and I hope I shall soon be well.

. . . . . . . . . . . . . . . . . . .

I don't think I can have my children here with me, Harrison. I know it is impossible, but I want to live where I can see them often—I should never had all those feelings if I had stayed in my little home in Northeast. There, I was at home. Do you remember how you felt when you lived with Mr. Holmes? If you do, you know what I have experienced since I have lived in Rhinebeck. I hope I shall be more content than I have been and will try at all events. I hope, if I live, and my children, that I shall have another little home where I can sometimes be alone. Yes, Harrison, I often think how thankful I had ought to be that my children are all steady, and doing well. I have not one of them to find fault with in the least—and if it were not for my unpleasant thoughts and low spirits that you say I am apt to indulge, I should enjoy myself, but I can't help it.

Edgar [Dakin's brother] wrote me some time ago. He tried to comfort me as well he could. Oh—Harrison, you don't know the feeling I have for my children. It seems they are left alone in the world like their mother, to take care of themselves, but I hope Heaven will bless us with health and strength to bear the trial of

*Portrait of Alexander Jackson Davis. (Courtesy Avery Library)*

life with fortitude. I will try my best to feel more contented. And I think when I get my health, I shall be.

.   .   .   .   .   .   .   .   .   .   .   .   .   .   .   .   .   .

I will write you again, You must not be concerned about my health for I am getting better fast. I was taken with something of an alarming symptom, a raising blood. It was done by a strain. I was very much frightened. It left me weak and feeble. But I have never raised any but once, and I think I shall get entirely over it. I am happy to learn of your health. There is not more to enjoy when we are deprived of it. I know by experience. Write me soon.

Wishing you every blessing in this life, and happiness in the world to come, I subscribe myself, your affectionate

Mother [6]

What a simple, ingenuous letter this is! It is moving, not only for the anguish so thinly concealed, but for the straightforward manner of expression of this mother separated from her children. It also serves to remind us of the charity of the early inhabitants of our country, who, in times of tragedy, took into their homes the children of others and reared them as their own.

Lucy Dakin's apprehension about her health was well founded, for just a few years after writing the letters, she died, at the age of forty-two, on Christmas Day, 1826.[7] James was then nineteen and Charles fifteen. The self-reliance which the Dakin brothers were thus forced to develop was to hold them in good stead later in life.

James Dakin's guardian, Herman Stoddard, was a carpenter, and we may presume that it was from him young James learned the trade of carpentry and thereby acquired his love for architecture. Dakin apparently remained with the Stoddards until the late 1820s; by 1829, he was ready for the great metropolis down the river from Hudson. In an amazingly short period of time, he was to find himself established as a well-known architect of New York City.

## DAKIN'S APPRENTICESHIP WITH TOWN AND DAVIS

In New York, in February of 1829, Ithiel Town, forty-four years old, urbane, well traveled, and already established as an architect, engineer, and inventor (of the Town truss used for bridge construction), joined in partnership with a new associate after splitting with Martin Thompson. Town's partner in the new venture was Alexander Jackson Davis.[8]

Davis was only twenty-six, but he was already noted as an artist, draftsman, and budding architect. His talents developed rapidly, and eventually he would overshadow his partner—indeed, virtually every other architect of his time. The Town and Davis firm, off to a running start with principals of such stature, was to attract and develop other men of ability; one of these was James Dakin.

In that year of the formation of Town and Davis, 1829, James Dakin became associated with the firm. Then only twenty-three, he was apprenticed to A. J. Davis. In the same year Dakin married; his wife was Georgianna (she preferred to use Georgianna, although her real name was Joanna Belcher Collard. She had been widowed about 1826 by the death of her first husband, George Collard, a young actor from Port Gibson, Mississippi, who was killed in a stage coach accident. Georgianna, at thirty-one, was eight years Dakin's senior. However, theirs was to be a long and happy marriage and would bear the fruit of several children.[9]

In just a short time, the Town and Davis firm was to become the most influential in the country. To describe all of the accomplishments of Town and Davis would require another book, but a brief survey of their innovations will help demonstrate their creativity and show the influence that went into the development of James Dakin. Skeptics of the creativity of the Greek Revival period in America

*Portrait of Ithiel Town, by Nathaniel Jocelyn. (Courtesy National Academy of Design)*

architecture need only examine closely the work of Town and Davis for examples of something new.

One of the earliest examples of this striving for something new is the Greek Revival villa originated by Town. It has been described by Vincent Scully as part of American architecture's attempt to break out of the boxlike form to which 1820s-held-over Georgian architecture had limited itself. With the Bowers house in Northampton, Massachusetts, of the late 1820s, Town gave the country villa a new cast. His addition of a pair of low wings with a colonnade across the front, repeating on a smaller scale the theme of its full Greek portico, altered the old boxy forms into a new interplay of masses, while giving the whole a sense of great power.[10]

From the firm flowed another idea, for which a word has been coined: "pilastrades." Mrs. Jane Davies points out that Greek Revival architects were faced with the problem of how to preserve the feel of a Greek templelike building and yet admit light into the interior, while at the same time eliminating the costly peripteral columns. Town and Davis solved this problem with their use of rows of massive projecting square pilasters down the flanks which produce a feel of rhythm, light, and shadow similar to that of a fully colonnaded building.[11]

This, in turn, generated another innovation, a new window shape, which Davis himself named "Davisean." The spaces between the new "pilastrades" could now be opened up with massive windows to let in light and air. Town and Davis frequently designed them to fill the *entire* space between pilasters, running two stories or more in height.[12]

Another Town and Davis reorchestration of Greek themes was the invention of the granite pier storefront.

Talbot Hamlin expressed his doubts about its origination with Town and Davis; but if Davis can be believed, it was Ithiel Town who developed the type into the style we know today with his early 1830s design for the Tappan store on Wall Street. Basically, it consisted of massive square granite columns at the ground floor, almost always with *antae* capitals. There was a heavy granite entablature above and little or no decoration, perhaps a course of moulding at most. This design spread rapidly all over the country, In the depths of lower Manhattan can still be found examples of these interesting buildings, now, alas, fugitives from wrecking crews. Boston (where a prototype by Alexander Parris was introduced), Mobile, and New Orleans are also known to have many survivors of this style.

The practical value of this storefront cannot be gainsaid. Hamlin observed that "the rhythmical regularity of their openings give a pleasant harmony and unity to the streets they border. The best of these buildings are simple, useful, unostentatious, human in scale and restrained and delicate in detail."[13] Thus Town and Davis answered partially the complaint of John Kouwenhoven that a dichotomy frequently existed in America between the professional architect and the vernacular. The granite pier store was the creation of the most professional architects in the United States of the time; and they gave it acceptable aesthetic qualities, yet made it simple enough for the practical builder to utilize cheaply.[14]

Finally, laurels are due Town and Davis for developing the *distyle in antis* floor plan for church architecture. Church congregations in this early period of America's growth were rich in spirit but poor in funds; few could afford a Greek building with a full colonnade across the front, much less around all sides. Town and Davis developed, with economy

*Drawing of New York by James Dakin, from Fay's* Views in New York. (*Courtesy Library of Congress*)

uppermost in mind, the *in antis* church plan which, though relatively inexpensive, did no damage to the Greek aesthetics in architecture. The first generally known Town and Davis church in this style was the Carmine Street Presbyterian Church in New York City, built in 1831.[15] The essence of the Town and Davis design was its facade which consisted of two free-standing columns in a recessed portico and *antae* pilasters at the corners. Especially important was the fact that its portico, unlike the full porch of the ancient Greek *in antis* buildings, usually occupied only about one third of the front facade. The remaining space was taken up with blank walls, unornamented except for pilasters; the deployment and treatment of these lent opportunity for great variety within the limits of the plan. The Town and Davis design for the flanks of their churches usually consisted of pilastrades with Davisean windows between. The total result of the plan was the elimination of the expensive fully columned porch and the imparting of a monumental quality to the building.

While Town and Davis did not invent the *in antis* floor plan, they did carry its development far beyond those structures found in ancient lands. Professor Jacob Landy, searching for antecedents of the Town and Davis design, located several in England dating from the Revival period which might have inspired the Americans' plan.[16] But those that this author have examined bear little resemblance to the Town and Davis design. The English prototypes seem rather timid and unprepossessing in comparison with the monumental American creation.

Kouwenhoven's [17] other major point about American architecture of this period—that what sets it off from contemporary European work is the "plane surface"—applies especially to the designs of Town and Davis. Their work is discernible almost at a glance by their persistent use of

unadorned surfaces. They combined these plane surfaces with massive pilasters and huge two-story windows to produce buildings of great power. Their exterior ornamentation, always in judicious scale, was used sparingly: a wreath here, a course of anthemia there. Their byword was restraint.

Thus, it may seem paradoxical to say that a firm working mostly in the Greek Revival idiom was "original," but we believe the observations just made have shown this to be so. In evaluating these early Revival architects, it should be remembered particularly that they were working in the era before reinforced concrete and steel, before elevators and electricity, indeed even before gas light. It was not to be until the technological breakthroughs of the last half of the nineteenth century that entirely new forms in architecture would evolve through the application of new technology.

It was in this stimulating milieu of the Town and Davis office that young James H. Dakin matured as an architect. He was to evolve with the two principal partners and acquire many of their characteristics: imagination, originality, and a great sense of restraint and refinement of detail. He studied drafting under Alexander Jackson Davis and in a short period of time came to full flower.

Dakin, having begun with Town and Davis in 1829, just two years later was known as an architect of repute. In 1831, he was prominent enough to be credited as the illustrator for one of the first picture books of New York, *Views in New York* by Theodore Fay. The book's frontispiece reads: "Drawings taken on the spot, expressly for this work, by Dakin, Architect." Oddly, although Dakin received title page credit for the drawings, other artists also contributed to the book, including A. J. Davis, who is not mentioned in the credits. Dakin's drawings number eight in all and they display a highly advanced technique.[18]

*Drawing of City Hall by James Dakin, from Fay's* Views in New York. *(Courtesy Library of Congress)*

*Drawing of Bowling Green by James Dakin, from Fay's* Views in New York. *(Courtesy Library of Congress)*

*Drawing of Philip Hone's home by James Dakin, from Fay's* Views in New York. *(Courtesy Library of Congress)*

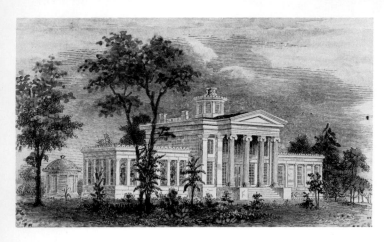

Perry House, the first building known to have been designed by James Dakin. (Courtesy Avery Library)

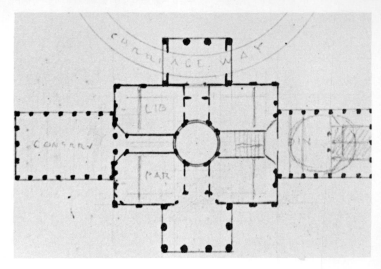

Floor plan of Perry House. (Courtesy Avery Library)

Indeed, Dakin's drafting ability was phenomenal. Davis is considered by some to be the best *artist* of all American architects of the past. Yet, so excellent is Dakin's work that it is almost indistinguishable from Davis'. In a competition for a building, Dakin's great technique must have disheartened many a fellow architect challenging for the job; yet Dakin himself decried the use of artistic prettying-up of a drawing purely to "sell" a design.

It is possible to identify several buildings done by James Dakin when he was with Town and Davis; however, his early work is so closely intertwined with that firm that exhaustive research on Town and Davis would be necessary to extricate all of his activities. This is clearly beyond the scope of this book.

The earliest known building by Dakin is the J. W. Perry house in Brooklyn, New York, dating from 1832 (now destroyed). It was a palatial Greek Revival mansion, patterned after the Ithiel Town prototype, the Bowers house, insofar as the facade was concerned. It was two stories high, with a large Ionic columned portico and one-story wings at either side. These latter were colonnaded all around with square, engaged pilasters. Atop the house was an octagonal tower crested with a row of anthemia similar in feeling to the Choragic Monument of Lysicrates. The floor plan shows a central hallway with a central rotunda directly beneath the tower. In the original drawing, it appears that an elliptical ceiling was penciled in over the dining room which was located in the right wing. In the rear, a carriage-way of the same dimensions as the front portico balanced off the whole composition.[19]

Minard Lafever's *Modern Builder's Guide* contains a drawing, Plate 75, by Lafever, as well as a frontispiece by James Gallier, of a "Country Residence" which is very similar to this house type. However, Lafever's book was not published until 1833, after both Dakin and Gallier had left Town

and Davis; Gallier, in fact, was still in England when Town designed the Bowers house about 1826. It is probably no coincidence that this frontispiece by a former Town and Davis man resembles Town's villa.

Also interesting is the fact that the Greek Revival mansion Gaineswood, at Demopolis, Alabama, about one hundred miles above Mobile where Charles and James Dakin had a practice in the 1830s, is similar to the Perry house. The architect of Gaineswood is unknown; he is assumed to be the original owner (who was not an architect), but the similarity of the Perry house and the Alabama mansion points to the possible influence of the Dakins.

### TOWN, DAVIS, AND DAKIN

On May 1, 1832, Messrs. Davis and Town took in James Dakin as a full partner, and the name of the firm was changed to Town, Davis, and Dakin, Architects. This was undoubtedly, in part, because both Davis and Town expected to be away from New York during the next several months, and it was considered necessary to compensate Dakin for his increased responsibilities as head of the New York office. The partnership's financial records reveal that Dakin had the largest interest of the three men, 40 percent for Dakin and 30 percent for each of the others.[20]

During the Town, Davis, and Dakin period, Dakin designed one of the largest buildings he was ever to erect, the Rockaway Marine Pavilion, a hotel at Rockaway Beach, Long Island. Built on a small promontory overlooking the Atlantic, the main building of the Pavilion had a front footage of 230 feet, plus wings and a broad piazza. This huge two-story Greek Revival hotel had a colonnaded porch across the front, consisting of twenty-four square Doric columns and a six-columned portico projecting from the

*Rockaway Marine Pavilion, Rockaway, Long Island. Designed by
James Dakin, 1833. (Courtesy New-York Historical Society)*

center. Six square pilasters at each side repeated the rhythm of the front colonnade. It was surmounted by a two-tiered cupola, having much the same feeling as the later one by Davis for the Ohio State Capitol of 1839 with its "drum-without-a dome" motif. Rockaway's was much more handsome, however, and unlike the other had two tiers and a small dome to top it off.

The hotel was conceived by a former mayor of New York, Philip Hone, whose diary forms a valuable chronicle of New York life. In 1833, he organized a group of seventy wealthy men to subscribe to the cost of the hotel, which came to $45,000. The Town, Davis, and Dakin records show a payment to Dakin of $508.00 in 1833 for the plans. The hotel was begun that year; by May, 1834, it was nearing completion.[21]

Hone planned the hotel as a place where New Yorkers, tired of the bustle of the city (it was hectic even then), could slip away for the peace of the seashore. He believed it would receive a large and fashionable patronage. Hone himself was entranced by it, for an entry in his diary for September 1, 1835, reads: "At 11:00 PM I returned to my room, lighted a cigar and seated myself at the front window. The view was unspeakably grand. The broad red moon, setting over the tops of the mountains of Nevarsink [N.J.], threw a solemn light over the unruffled face of the Ocean, and the lofty columns of the noble piazza, breaking the silver streams of light into dark and gloomy shadows, gave the edifice the appearance of some relic of classical antiquity."[22]

James Early, writing in his *Romanticism and American Architecture,* has properly used this passage as an example of historical suggestiveness. He says: "Such historical reveries stimulated by revivalist architecture constituted an important element in its appeal. Much of the attraction of classical architecture had, since the Renaissance, been due to its connection with the admired Roman past, but in the nineteenth century, the dependence upon historical associations became extreme."[23]

As evocative as the Pavilion was to Hone, he was never to see it succeed as fully as he had envisioned. It was not a money-maker; and by May, 1836, Hone and his friends sold it for $30,000. The hotel continued to operate with moderate success until June 25, 1864, when it was destroyed by fire.[24]

A plan for a very interesting and original building has turned up in the Dakin collection at the New Orleans Public Library called simply, "Design for a Hotel, 1832." It is unsigned, but obviously by Dakin; the lettering is definitely his. The drawing is the prototype for a huge hotel he and his brother Charles were to build in Mobile five years later. The hotel is basically Greek Revival, but as transformed by Dakin. It is an extraordinarily fine plan, particularly coming at a fairly early period of James Dakin's development. The hotel is flat roofed, with four great Ionic columns standing in the center of a recessed portico, these in turn being flanked by five massive square pilasters on either side. A low dome sits atop the roof, ringed by a course of anthemia fixed at the point on the drum where each rib of the dome meets its support. Davisean windows extend between the pilasters for the top two floors, split by mullions which are in reality small pilasters with *antae* caps repeating on a smaller scale the large ones on the facade. The executed version of this design will be discussed later in the chapter on Charles Dakin in Mobile, but it should be made clear that the germ of the idea began in New York five years earlier.

During the Town, Davis, and Dakin era, the great Lafayette Terrace was begun in New York. Originally twelve row

*"Design for a Hotel, 1832," drawing probably by James Dakin*

*La Grange Terrace, New York City, plate by James Dakin, from Fay's* Views in New York. *The architect for the building is unknown, but the interior details were designed by James Dakin and A. J. Davis, ca. 1832. (Courtesy Library of Congress)*

houses united in a common facade, only four now remain. This facade consisted of an elongated recessed porch without a pediment; supporting the entablature were twenty-eight huge Corinthian columns commencing above a rusticated first floor. There may have been some influence on its design by Regent Park York Gate in London, by John Nash. This English building employs the Ionic order instead of Corinthian, but the recessed porch with colonnade above a rusticated first floor is basic to both the Terrace and York Gate. Because of the enormous Town and Davis library (discussed by Landy in his Lafever book) and because Town was himself a traveler of Europe, we may be assured that the firm was aware of Nash's work.

The author of Lafayette Terrace is uncertain, but it appears that Town, Davis, or Dakin, separately or together, may have had a hand in it. What *has* been demonstrated is that the Town, Davis, and Dakin firm did do some interior detailing for the Terrace. And James Dakin did a superb drawing of the row for Fay's *Views in New York.* The building was erected by Seth Geer, a New York builder, but it is not believed to have been designed by him. Perhaps someday we will know for certain who the architect of this great row was, but this writer feels that Town, Davis, and Dakin did more than the interior.[25]

### EARLY TOWN, DAVIS, AND DAKIN WORK IN NEW ORLEANS

The first buildings that James Dakin did in New Orleans were done in absentia. These were designed in New York at the Town, Davis, and Dakin office and the plans brought back to New Orleans by contractors or merchants to be executed by local builders. This helped place Dakin's name before the public in New Orleans even before he moved there.

The most important of these New York-designed buildings is the "Thirteen Sisters" (Plate 1), a row dwelling on Julia Street, between Camp and St. Charles, on the uptown side of Julia. They extend the entire block and are still standing. No documentary evidence has yet been located to prove that Dakin designed the row, but both his son and daughter have stated that he was the architect.[26]

A very credible theory which agrees with this attribution by Dakin's children has been advanced by the well-known New Orleans architect Samuel Wilson, Jr. He believes that Dakin may have designed the row at the request of A. T. Wood, a one-time New Yorker, then (1833) a builder and "architect" in New Orleans. Wilson's theory has since been supported by his discovery in the succession of George Clarkson, also a New York builder, that in 1832, Wood and Clarkson entered into a partnership in New York whereby Clarkson would go to New Orleans and commence some buildings there for "The Company of Architects of New Orleans"; Wood was to follow later. These records also show that payments were made to Dakin for plans, and there is an entry in the Town, Davis, and Dakin records showing a payment made to them between August 15, 1833, and October, 1833, for "Drawings for Mr. Wood, N. Orleans $140.00."[27]

Furthermore, during this same period, Wood did work for the group of entrepreneurs who built the row, the New Orleans Building Company. Later, in 1847, Wood was to write of Dakin that he had "sixteen years acquaintance with that gentleman," indicating that he had known him since 1831 when Dakin was still in New York. Thus, there seems little doubt that Dakin designed this very fine row.[28]

The New Orleans Building Company, which developed the row, was chartered by the Louisiana legislature on February 28, 1828, with Samuel Livermore, Samuel Kohn, and George A. Waggaman the chief organizers. In April, 1832, they assembled all the various parcels of land on Julia Street into one property and commenced to build their row. By May, 1833, it was substantially finished, at least at the Camp Street end, and they commenced to sell the individual segments, completing the rest of the block as they went along. The builder was Daniel Halstead Twogood, an excellent local builder whose name appears in the acts of sale of the segments. In all probability, A. T. Wood supervised the construction, using Dakin's plans.[29]

The individual units are very narrow, as were most contemporary row units in New Orleans, where land was at a premium. Each is 26.3 feet across and 135 feet in depth. They stand three stories high, with the original wrought iron balcony railing still intact on the second floor. The ends of the building have the typical eastern gabled ends with twin chimney stacks linked by a square course of brick between. Just below these chimneys are two round arched windows with very fine wooden fans in the arch.

The doorways are what make the row seem surely the work of an architect rather than a builder. They are somewhat typical Georgian doorways of the late 1820s, early 1830s style, with round arch above and twin Ionic columns supporting a finely moulded entablature. However, much richer than these elements of the doorway are the fan lights in the transoms. A floral motif radiates from the lower center of the fan, in a fernlike manner, and the intrados of the arch is detailed with extremely fine and delicate motifs. Interestingly, these fans match almost identically that of the Tredwell house in New York City dating from about the same year.

The side lights flanking the twin Ionic columns are excellently conceived. They consist of three ellipses of glass, set in a kind of vermiform panel. However, the vermifica-

"Thirteen Sisters" doorway, New Orleans, 1832. (Courtesy Samuel Wilson, Jr., F.A.I.A.)

tion is not random, but instead radiates from a bow device set between each elliptical light. It will be noted repeatedly that Dakin loved the ellipse form and its use here further supports the attribution of the Thirteen Sisters to him.

Eliza Ripley, writing in her *Social Life in Old New Orleans,* devotes several pages to the Thirteen Sisters. Many personalities associated with the row are of only parochial interest to New Orleanians, but some are more national in importance. One resident of the row was Henry Buckner, whose daughter married James B. Eustis, a United States ambassador to France. A daughter of another resident, Dr. William Kennedy, married a son of the prominent Mississippi politician, Sargent Prentiss. But Mrs. Ripley's father's home in the row was the most important of all for its associations. Henry Clay was a frequent visitor, as were General E. P. Gaines and his wife, Myra Clark Gaines, the central character in one of the most involved lawsuits in southern history. And the esteemed Maunsel White lived across the street from the Sisters.[30]

Looking at the row today, one can hardly envision its halcyon days. Cut into many small rooms and apartments, the row is inhabited now by men living on the fringes of society. Only one of the original thirteen doorways remains intact. Some minor alterations have changed parts of the bottom floor arrangements; but, amazingly, this row survives after 135 years, still basically intact, still occupying an entire block front, and hopefully, ripe for restoration.

Besides this row, other New Orleans buildings were designed in New York by either Dakin or the Town, Davis, and Dakin firm. It is not known whether the owners themselves or the contractors who were to build them purchased the plans, except for A. T. Wood, as just noted. The earliest entry for such a transaction in the Davis records was made on August 4, 1830: "Plan and elevations for three stores with 15 doors; corner lot of Magazine and Canal Streets, New Orleans, with drawings of mouldings, full size—for W. W. Montgomery $25.00 paid."[31]

Montgomery was a heavy investor in real estate in New Orleans at that time. It is not known if his plan from Town and Davis was ever executed, but a drawing by Davis, labeled "Stores for W. W. Mortimer [*sic*], New Orleans," is undoubtedly for the same building. It depicts a granite pier type building; and its date would make it almost certainly the first granite pier structure in New Orleans, for it had been just a year or so earlier that Ithiel Town did the first one, his Tappan store building.[32]

Another entry, dated June 6, 1832 reads: "Design. Two stores for Mr. Anthony Rasch, New Orleans $15.00 paid Mr. Davis." Rasch's store still stands in the Vieux Carre at 313-15 Chartres Street, but its erection from this plan is questionable, for it has round arches and paneled lintels, both being examples of a style more typical of the late 1820s than the 1830s. The outmoded lintels could, of course, have been some supplier's leftovers, used simply because they were available presumably at a cheaper price. The present cast iron gallery was obviously added at a much later date.[33]

Finally, the last New Orleans entry in the Town, Davis, and Dakin records is "September, 1833. Mr. Florence [*sic*]—a dwelling house $15.00," and "Perspective view of buildings, New Orleans Mr. Florence. Stores for New Orleans $50.00." The "stores" aspect remains clouded, but Jacob Florance did build a beautiful house not long after the entry date at the corner of South and Camp Streets, facing Lafayette Square. What makes it probable that it was done from these Town, Davis, and Dakin plans is the fact that the building contract, dated January 27, 1834, was signed between Florance and A. T. Wood, who has been mentioned in connection with the Thirteen Sisters.[34]

*Unidentified drawing by James Dakin, exemplifying the* di *style in* antis *design popularized by Town and Davis and a superb example of Dakin's technique.*

"*Design for a Prison at Havanna* [sic], *Isle of Cuba,*" *by Town, Davis, and Dakin, Architects, 1833. Drawing by James Dakin*

The Florance house was of brick, three stories high, its stairs lighted by a "very handsome dome immediately over them." And "all rooms in the second story . . . have a very rich centre piece in each." The plan was to have been attached to the notarial act where this information is located, but, by mutual consent, was removed and given to A. T. Wood. A notation in the act says that the cistern is to be identical to the houses "built by the New Orleans Building Co. on Julia St." This virtually establishes Dakin's connection with the Thirteen Sisters and Wood's acting as the connecting link.[35]

### THE LAST YEARS WITH TOWN AND DAVIS

A splendid example of the Town, Davis, and Dakin *distyle in antis* church type was the Washington Street Methodist Episcopal Church in Brooklyn (Plate 3), designed by Dakin about 1832. It stood between Tillary and Concord Streets. For this Greek Revival church, Dakin used an unadorned triangular pediment, with two Ionic columns in the recessed portico, set between twin square *antae,* the pilasters running down the flanks with Davisean windows in between, forming a pilastrade. A very large door opened onto the porch, this time not in the usual Greek "ear" motif, but very rectangular, with an austere entablature and slightly overhanging cornice. An interesting adjunct to the original drawing, signed "J. H. Dakin, Architect and Delineator," is the background filled in behind the church for illustrative purposes. This "throw-away" device is rather interesting in itself, for it depicts a Doric colonnade, but with massive square columns supporting a heavy entablature with wreaths on the frieze and a flat roof. The feel of these square columns is startlingly like those at Ashland planatation below Baton Rouge, Louisiana, built for Duncan Kenner

about 1839. As we will see later, there was considerable connection between Kenner and Dakin in the 1830s and 1840s.

The Washington Street Church survived until about 1892, when it was demolished, probably for work on an approach for the Brooklyn Bridge. The congregation had already disbanded in 1891, helping to seal its doom.[36]

The Egyptian Revival was also in the repertory of James Dakin as early as his New York period. A very interesting drawing found in his collection, labeled "Design for a Prison at Havanna [sic], Isle of Cuba," originated in the Town, Davis, and Dakin period, for it is mentioned in the partnership's records between August 15, 1833, and October, 1833.[37]

The prison's main gate consists of two pylons similar to those at Edfu, and a portico, with battered walls, standing in front of the pylons. At either end of the prison walls stands a pylonlike tower, more squat than the center pylons. A cavetto cornice runs all around the perimeter of the walls and pylons. Adding to the distinctiveness of this design is the placing of crenellation atop the two center and end pylons—a Gothic motif—and the use of two Greek Revival columns with *antae* capitals, related to the Doric order, set *in antis* in the portico. As hodgepodge as this may seem, it comes off rather nicely, leaving the impression of a well-integrated design. The records do not show whether this plan was paid for, and because of the political situation now prevailing in Cuba, it was impossible to learn anything more about this fascinating plan.

The Town, Davis, and Dakin partnership records show a payment to Dakin for $550 for plans for the building for New York University at Washington Square. This building has been described as the first important example of "Colle-

In the third and fourth stories of the south wing are the Library and Reading Room, connected by a winding central stair.

In the centre of the edifice, fifty feet wide, rising from the ceiling of the second story to the top, and running through from front to rear, is the chapel. As a work of art, this room is far in advance of any other in our country, a specimen of the pointed architecture of the age of Henry VII, the golden age of that style. It is florid, but not gaudy; rich, but not over-wrought. All the parts are bold, prominent, and dignified. It carries the spectator back about three centuries, and nothing reminds him of the present but the arms of the nation, the state and the city, displayed on the flat of the ceiling. The great window in the west end is 24 by 50 feet, glazed with painted and stained glass. . . . The whole was executed in this city. And the entire work is highly creditable to the two architects, who designed the exterior and interior of the edifice — Mr. Dakin and A. J. Davis, who has his studio and library in the north wing.[41]

From the Dakin letters to Davis, we may conclude that the idea of using Gothic for NYU originated with the university rather than with Town, Davis, and Dakin. Dakin, obviously unhappy with the first plan, calls it "half barbarous," but in the second letter he seems pleased with himself for bringing it up to his standards — "it will do quite well."

A. J. Davis, in his diary, sketched in a front elevation and floor plan, beneath which he wrote "Town, Davis, Dakin and Douglass, Architects, 1836." The floor plan matches identically that which Dakin drew in his letter to Davis in 1833. The allusion by Davis to "Douglas" was undoubtedly to Professor Davis B. Douglass, an instructor at NYU in natural philosophy and civil engineering. Davis said of his own part in the building, that he "had a hand" in designing the university, with support in the selection of the Gothic style from Reverend Cyrus Mason, who was the most

*Interior of the Chapel of New York University, by Dakin and Davis. Unsigned watercolor, probably by James Dakin or A. J. Davis. (Courtesy New-York Historical Society)*

energetic promoter of the new school. Mason had been educated at Cambridge University in England and was undoubtedly influenced by his memories of that school.[42]

From Cambridge University obviously came the inspiration for the exterior of NYU. King's College Chapel was the basis for the huge window, flanked by the pair of octagonal towers. However, the similarity becomes less and less apparent as one examines the details of both buildings. At Cambridge, the towers are topped off with pinnacles bristling with crockets; but a look at Dakin's sketch in his letters shows that he topped the towers off with battlements. He also added as an entrance a three-sided bay instead of the recessed doorway at King's College. The similarity between the buildings ends entirely at either side of the twin towers. At NYU, the school extended out, terminating at the ends in matching square towers, castellated like the central towers, but on a smaller scale.

A large unsigned watercolor of the interior of NYU provides the best early representation of the chapel. This view has been attributed to Davis, but the style appears to be as close to that of Dakin. The two men, it has been mentioned, had very similar styles of drawing and painting. This interior, it has been correctly pointed out by Patton, is based on the choir of Oxford Cathedral. Supporting this influence on Dakin is a lithograph of an interior view of Oxford found in Dakin's personal collection of engravings.[43]

Again, however, as we examine the details, the similarity to the European antecedent fades more and more. Both employ lierne vaulting, forming a starlike effect. But at NYU, the stars are different and set in a different rhythm. Under the clerestory vaulting in both buildings, the intrados is identical, employing Perpendicular paneling topped off with trefoil cusping. On the other hand, the imposts of the fan vaulting at Oxford land in line with the moulding under the clerestory windows, while at NYU the imposts are at some distance below this level. In addition, there was suspended from the center of the ceiling at NYU a massive fan-shaped pendant.

Adding to the dissimilarity is the make-up of the large stained glass window. The treatment at NYU is completely different from that of King's College. On the exterior, NYU has a return on the dripstone which lines up with the string course of moulding on the flanking octagonal towers. No return is even possible at Cambridge, for the window is sandwiched between and touches its towers. Both windows employ Perpendicular "Y" tracery, but the similarity almost ends there. NYU employs two transoms, Cambridge one. The mullions continue up to the intrados at Cambridge, but they are diverted by a "Y" in New York. The overall feeling of the tracery is really more curvilinear there; Oxford could only be described as Perpendicular. For NYU, Dakin and Davis had used two European models as a source of inspiration, but they created an almost new building.

NYU was not completed until 1837, the dedication taking place on May 20 of that year. Patton describes its white marble construction as apparently intended to "endure for all time." Indeed, it might well have, but for the wreckers. In 1894, NYU moved uptown, as does everything else in that city, and the school was demolished. Patton quotes the lament of Henry James, on that sad occasion, that "any . . . form of civic piety [in New York is] inevitably and forever absent." [44]

Before departing from the NYU project, it should be noted that several facets of Dakin's personality are revealed in his letters to Davis. Here is the first glimmer of a trait which was destined to make his career as an architect more difficult: his intemperate expression. A candid approach to what he thought was right, or in good taste, is demon-

strated by his allusions to the "Gothic gentry" and their "half barbarous" and "half savage Gothic." He also says somewhat scornfully that he is "happy to learn that the Philadelphians are more attracted to the magnificence of Mr. Walter's designs than the severe simplicity of Girard's will," a reference to the Girard College competition, in which severe limitations were imposed on the architect. Finally, he irreverently refers to a church congregation as being "either poor or roguish and I am not sure which."

But Dakin's career was just beginning at this time. He was ready to work more independently now.

# 2
# ON HIS OWN
# IN NEW YORK

ON NOVEMBER 1, 1833, JAMES DAKIN WITHDREW FROM THE Town, Davis, and Dakin partnership. The reason is unknown, but Dakin obviously felt his time had come, that he was now fully prepared to stand on his own as an architect. With Dakin gone from the association with Davis, records become sketchier than previously, when the Davis diaries and account books provided some insight into their activities. While this lack has made research more difficult on Dakin's work from 1833 to 1835 when he left for New Orleans, his original drawings have provided us with a glimpse of his output during that period.

Among the structures definitely known to have been designed by James Dakin after his leaving Town and Davis is the First Presbyterian Church at Troy, New York. Besides his original drawings, Dakin is also verified, by a bill for one hundred dollars, as the architect for the plans found in the church archives and dated December 9, 1834.[1] Much more archeological than most Dakin buildings, the church at Troy is in the style of the Hephaisteion (Thesion), with a Doric colonnade of six fluted columns in front and the usual Doric accoutrements: triglyphs, mutules, and a triangular pediment. But Dakin designed it amphiprostyle, plus two return columns. And the flanks are out of the Town, Davis, and Dakin book, with seven massive square pilasters down the side. Somewhere between the design and the execution, the rear porch was deleted. Marble was supplied by the firm of Frazee and Launitz of New York City, both men renowned sculptors.[2]

The most imposing feature of the interior is a round coffered dome in the ceiling. At the base of this dome stands a row of anthemia, set alternatingly large and small in the ring. Indirect lighting behind the anthemia produces a very pleasing effect, pointing up their presence and illuminating the coffers. A small lantern pierces the top

*James H. Dakin's business card*, ca. 1833. *(Courtesy Miss Kathyrine Regan)*

*Interior, windows, of First Presbyterian Church, Troy, New York, designed by James Dakin, 1834. (Courtesy Rensselaer County Historical Society)*

towards a skylight. The existence of this domed ceiling is not detectable from outside the church.

Below the dome, in the sanctuary, huge pilasters project slightly from the walls, as if in answer to their counterparts outside making up the "pilastrade." These inner pilasters were imaginatively designed in a doubled style—that is, two superimposed one on the other, a device seen sometimes in Renaissance architecture. The inner pilaster is rather wide, with a capital comprised of three rows of fascias resembling an architrave. The outer pilaster resembles an Ionic column, complete with the appropriate capital, but flattened, as if it had been a round column that had been neatly sliced to leave its surface flat. This column-pilaster is the more effective for its entasis, designed in true column fashion.

How much of this interior is Dakin's is uncertain, for the inside of the church was remodeled in 1873. At that time, balconies which once stood on either side of the sanctuary were removed entirely, and the choir and organ were moved to the front. It would seem certain that the dome, so integral a part of the fabric of the building, would not have been redone, nor would the super-imposed pilasters, for they are in a very strict Greek Revival style and devoid of any Victorian embellishments common to the 1873 period.[3]

Despite its archeological overtones, the First Presbyterian Church at Troy, thanks to its Town and Davis pilastrade, ranks as one of the finest surviving examples of this feature. The fact that the church still exists at all gives it the distinction of being one of the few Dakin buildings left anywhere in this country. It has been well cared for by a congregation which is still using it after 130 years and, hopefully, will continue to use and care for it.

A huge painting on canvas by Dakin indicates that he apparently entered the competition for a Washington

*Interior, dome, of First Presbyterian Church, Troy. (Courtesy Rensselaer County Historical Society)*

*Exterior view of First Presbyterian Church, Troy*

monument in New York. This competition was given an excellent and thorough study by Dr. Jacob Landy, but he was unable to locate any reference to Dakin. It is possible that the New York Monument Association, managers of the project, did not record his competition entry or that the records are now incomplete. The painting is undated, but the association was formed in 1833, so that the painting was probably done shortly after that.[4]

Dakin's plan is based on—indeed, is almost a copy of—the Choragic Monument of Lysicrates. A circular colonnade of Corinthian columns stands atop a square pedestal. The roof, with its row of anthemia, is identical to the Choragic Monument, but the top is crowned by a graceful American eagle. The center of the colonnade is open, and standing in it is a figure which is clearly recognizable as Washington. Dakin, like Greenough and a few other sculptors, clothed Washington in a Roman toga, holding a fasces. It was a concept worthy of the classical medium Dakin worked in. Like his contemporaries, Dakin visualized Washington's statue in republican terms, symbolizing the then-prevailing conception of the Romantic period with its idealization of supposed democratic Roman rule.[5]

Compared to various other plans for the monument project, Dakin's design seems, first of all, very rational, and more importantly, feasible. Many of the other competition schemes, while interesting, are so grandiose as to make them impossible to build. Dakin's plan, though derivative, had a simple elegance lacking in most of the others. The overbloated ideas expressed in these plans were matched by the backers of the project: it never came off.

The finest building Dakin was to design in the period after leaving Town and Davis—and one of the two or three best of his career—was the Bank of Louisville. It has for years been attributed erroneously to Gideon Shryock of Kentucky, without any documentation that this writer could find other than an attribution made by his niece. Ironically, this writer did find the only documentary evidence linking Shryock with the building, but *not* with its design.[6]

What sets the building apart from almost all other Greek Revival structures is its facade. Dakin, calling upon his knowledge of the Egyptian style, conceived for it a massive, powerful facade, employing two *in antis* Ionic columns, but set in a portico with battered walls, thus giving a pylonlike feeling. As the slant of these walls leads the eye upward, the apex of the unpedimented roof culminates in a beautiful acroterion, a fanlike anthemion of large proportion. This acroterion motif is continued beneath it, where loops of honeysuckle swirl about, and to either side, with curls of the vine turning up and inward toward the center of the roof. This is one of the least archeological buildings ever designed by a Greek Revival architect.[7]

Talbot Hamlin praises the creativity of the architect, crediting Shryock, and says, "The bank facade . . . has, in its battered side walls, a distinct departure from the typical Greek antae, and the whole front, because of this refinement, is unusually alive. In addition, the cresting, with its refined scroll pattern, is anything but archeological. Here, one may trace, perhaps, certain ideas from Lafever; both this, at least and some of the Lafever plates show the same kind of creative modifications of Greek ideas. The charm of the bank front lies not in its archeological quality, but in its proportion and in these new and fresh touches."[8]

Clay Lancaster, equally impressed, said: "The facade was not so much directly influenced by antiquity as by [the architect's] own times." He also credits Shryock with the building and mentions an influence of Lafever's *Beauties of Modern Architecture*.[9]

*Bank of Louisville, Louisville, Kentucky, designed by James Dakin.*
*Drawing by James Dakin, 1834.*

*Ceiling plan of Bank of Louisville.*

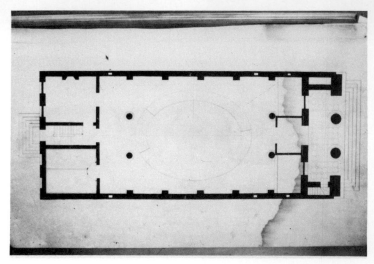

*Floor plan of Bank of Louisville.*

The allusions to the Lafever book and to Shryock by both Hamlin and Lancaster were, of course, made before the discovery of Dakin's drawings. Significantly, the drawings date from 1834 and the Lafever book a year later. It is not lightly that this writer takes credit from Shyrock for this great Greek Revival building and gives it to Dakin. But the evidence is overwhelming that it came from Dakin's hand. Besides a drawing in the Dakin collection signed "Plan of the ceiling for the Bank of Louisville, 1834," which matches the elliptical coffered ceiling perfectly, there are other drawings of the bank in the collection. They are unidentified and unsigned, but clearly the work of Dakin, verifiable by comparison with the almost two hundred other drawings in the collection, and easily recognized as the bank drawings. One is the floor plan, which matches the existing building and its interior column and doorway arrangement perfectly, and two front elevations which match in the minutest detail the Louisville building. This includes a tiny patera under the acroterion in the pocket formed by the swirl of the vine.

The Ionic forms used in the bank do not seem to derive from any one ancient source. The architrave utilizes the three-coursed mouldings like the Erechtheion as well as the typical Ionic row of dentils along the soffit of the cornice. But, unlike the Erechtheion's columns, there is no necking band below the volutes of the capitals. Instead, Dakin has placed in the balteus of each capital, in line with the center of the column, a delicate anthemion above a swirl of honey-suckle, which repeats the theme of its larger brother on the roof.

The interior of the bank makes as much of an impression as the facade. Dakin gave the main banking room an elegant elliptical ceiling, with deep coffers, each of which contains a rosette. In the oculus, two bands of moulding, separated by a more pronounced one in the center, lead up to where once

was located a stained glass skylight. Three Greek "ear" doorways, decorated with patera, open the main banking room to smaller ones in the rear.

A contemporary description of the ceiling, by Gideon Shryock, reads:

The panels are about 3 feet by 3 feet and sunk about 8 inches. The stiles and rails between the panels are divided by a large bead moulding 3 inches in diameter at the bottom and 1½ inches at the top; each panel is finished with mouldings in the angles and roseate ornaments in the center. . . .
The rosettes are handsome and executed in bold relief. The moulding in the angle of the panel is formed of square annulets, which are as difficult to execute as they would have been if the section of this moulding was circular. The ceiling is divided laterally into three parts by an architrave extending across the room. The frieze and cornice in the central part of the room are elliptical, supporting the base of the dome above. The plan of the dome is an ellipse, the conjugate diameter of the base is 32 feet and the transverse diameter is 40 feet. The dome has an elliptical skylight in the centre of 10 feet by 17 feet. The ceiling of the dome is divided into three horizontal courses of sunk panels, each course containing 26 panels.[10]

Further establishing Dakin's connection with the bank is a lawsuit recorded in New Orleans in 1836–37.[11] The file includes letters from its first president, John S. Snead. Snead apparently went to New York in 1834 to obtain drawings for his bank, a kind of trip frequently made by others, as we have seen in the case of A. T. Wood, Anthony Rasch, and others. He probably went not long after his bank received its charter from the Kentucky legislature on February 2, 1833. Work on the bank appears to have begun in the summer or fall of 1835, for an entry in the Minute Books of the Louisville Board of Administrators dated April 27, 1835, reads: "Council rejects the request of the President and Directors of the Bank of Louisville to extend the steps of their Bank five feet eight inches on the sidewalk; it is

*Ceiling photo of Bank of Louisville. (Photograph by Jim Blue)*     *Interior view of Bank of Louisville. (Photograph by Jim Blue)*

considered unreasonable and the same is rejected." The surveyor probably finished his work of laying out the building soon after this rejection.[12]

Dakin himself probably supervised the construction for a short period late in 1835, for a letter from Snead to Dakin reads:

Mr. Thurston, our Cashier, has just returned from New Orleans without having the pleasure of seeing you as he wished.

He admired very much the Horizontal skylight in the New Exchange and thinks that such a one would suit our Bank. If you think so, please make out a drawing.

Mr. Thurston thinks the Glass is painted as he saw it in New Orleans and that the same thing may be done here.

Please give us early information as to both of these matters.

It is with regret that I have to inform you of the death of Mr. Rogers. He died about a month ago, and I fear the completion of our work will be impaired by his successor. Your presence on your return to New York will be the more desirable on this account.[13]

At the time this letter was written, Dakin had begun supervision of the Merchants Exchange on Royal Street where Mr. Thurston had missed seeing him. Snead's letter suggests that Dakin had previously been involved in the construction of the bank. Obviously, Dakin had known Rogers, the carpenter for the job, or Snead would not have informed Dakin of his death. Dakin, however, did not return to Louisville but remained in New Orleans. The bank then turned to Gideon Shryock to be its supervising architect after he returned to Louisville in 1835 after his work in constructing the Kentucky capitol in Frankfort.[14]

The bank was apparently completed in the summer of 1837, for in June, the plastering contractors sued the bank over the price of their contract. Only $688 separated the two parties, but we should be appreciative of this difference, for the suit has provided some contemporary comments on the magnificent bank building. One fact that emerges from this file is that Dakin's coffered elliptical ceiling was the most elaborate ever done up to that time in Louisville. Joseph Irwin, the City Measurer, said that "The plain [plastering] work is common and the price fixed. There has been no such work as the stucco work done in Louisville and consequently no fixed prices." Another plasterer, a disinterested witness from Baltimore, went so far as to say, "Such expensive work has never been done in Baltimore."[15]

Shryock then gave his own comments regarding the plastering: "I believe there has not been any other work of the same description done in Louisville.... The commissioners for rebuilding the Capitol at Frankfort in their contract for plastering agreed that the ornamental parts of the work should be paid at the Baltimore prices.... By comparing the work in the Bank with that in the State House, having had the direction of the work in both cases, I was enabled to affix ... a fair value...."[16] Shryock's comments appear to have been decisive in settling the case.

In addition to the plasterers' suit, Dakin himself filed suit against the bank on February 27, 1837, for $576.13 due him for the skylight requested by Snead, which he built in New Orleans and had shipped upriver to Louisville. It was built by Doyle and May of New Orleans, with some carpentry work by William Gott, a name which recurs often in Dakin's story.

After Dakin replied within two weeks of Snead's first letter (of February 29, 1836), Snead wrote Dakin again on April 6. By September 6, 1836, the bank was progressed far enough to require the skylight, for Snead wrote Dakin: "We need now the sash and light . . . as without it, the light will be too intense." It was shipped by the steamer Havana about December 27, 1836, the date of the drawing of a bill of exchange on the bank by Dakin.[17]

The bank, in reply to the suit, said it had not money to

*Exterior view of Bank of Louisville. (Photograph by Jim Blue)*

pay the judgment, but some funds were found on deposit with a New Orleans bank, and were attached by the court. So, in the lean year of the Panic of 1837, Dakin finally got his fees for the skylight.

The Bank of Louisville remained in use, under various names, until 1930. It was left vacant during the early 1930s and was in danger of demolition. Then, in 1937, the Louisville Credit Men's Association purchased it and restored it to its former state, the architects being Otis and Lea. At that time, they added the rear portion of the existing building. Dakin's bank still stands today in excellent condition, its future safety now assured by its acquisition by the Actors Theatre of Louisville.

Because of all the supposed influence of Lafever's books on Shryock and thereby, on the Bank of Louisville, which was really by Dakin, it will be worthwhile to examine the probable interrelationship between Dakin and Lafever. The author of the recent (1970) book on Lafever and his architecture, Dr. Jacob Landy, has gone no further on this subject than to leave the question of influence as wide open as ever. He says, "Still problematical is the extent to which Lafever's influence inspired the work of Gallier and the Dakins in the South, as compared with the possibility that the increasing refinement of Lafever's own work, from the *Young Builder's General Instructor* to *The Modern Builder's Guide,* was stimulated to some degree by James Dakin and Gallier." [18]

In this writer's opinion, the influence was greater in the direction of Dakin to Lafever than conversely. In addition, James Gallier, another ex-Town and Davis man, seems to have been a conscious or unconscious transmitter of Town, Davis, and Dakin concepts to Lafever. Lafever's first book of consequence was *The Modern Builder's Guide,* published in 1833, followed by his second major book, *The Beauties of Modern Architecture.* It was Plate 25 of this second book which was supposed to have been a possible inspiration for the facade of the Bank of Louisville. However, as mentioned above, the book was published in 1835, a year *after* Dakin prepared his plans for the bank. This plate owes most of its interest to its acroterion and honeysuckle swirls a-la-Bank of Louisville. An examination of several other plates in the *Beauties* reveals the substantial influence of Dakin's bank facade.[19]

Another plate in the *Beauties*, Number 32, Details of Ionic Capital, was specifically credited by Lafever to Dakin. He says in the text: "This capital is not of any particular specimin of antique productions, but partakes of several, as well as of fancy. The composition is a departure from the strict, perfect and arbitrary rules of design. Notwithstanding, it will be admitted that it, as a modern combination of parts, presents rather a pleasing effect. . . . The method of describing this volute was invented and reduced to practice by Mr. James H. Daken [*sic*] whose talents, taste and ideas are of the first order, and by the writer held in very high esteem." [20]

Furthermore, many of the plates in *The Modern Builder's Guide* were prepared and signed by Dakin. Indeed, the 1969 Dover reprint of this book uses for its cover illustration a design for a doorway by Dakin. Of the forty plates in the book which depict whole buildings or architectural details, as contrasted with schematic or constructional details, ten are by Dakin and one by Gallier. Lancaster has noted the "remarkable artistic advance" in Lafever's books. This is due, in no small part, to Dakin's plates.

Some of these plates by Dakin have been copied and executed almost exactly as in the book. Lancaster has found a doorway in Charleston, at the Miller-Kerrison house, 138 Wentworth Street, which duplicates almost exactly Plate 63 of *The Modern Builder's Guide* (Plate 2). And Hamlin has told us of the next plate, Number 64, having been copied by an architect in Painesville, Ohio, for use in his own house. Undoubtedly, many more remain to be discovered.[21]

Clearly, then, Dakin influenced the Lafever books rather than being guided by them. Not only did Dakin contribute a number of plates to the book, his influence is seen in the many plates which were either based on or inspired by his Bank of Louisville. Lafever's acknowledgment of Dakin in the book suggests an even larger influence—that which Dakin had upon contemporary architecture. Dakin's philosophy of making his own "modern combination of parts," adding his personal flights of "fancy," was perhaps his most significant influence. The result was that, through the Lafever books, Dakin helped to promote a greater creativity among architects while still working in the Greek Revival style.

Another post-Town, Davis, and Dakin building that James Dakin was to design was the Duane Street Presbyterian Church in New York (Plate 4), done in 1834. It was a very handsome Greek Revival church in the Ionic style, parts of which follow the Temple on the Ilissus (illustrated so well by Stuart and Revett, in their *Antiquities of Athens*) and partly on the Erechtheion. Although not exceedingly lavish, it provoked an outburst from Dakin's erstwhile mentor, Alexander Jackson Davis.

The congregation, now known as the Fifth Avenue Presbyterian Church, began as the Cedar Street Church in 1808. Then later, as the members moved farther and farther north of the church's location, it was decided to move the church nearer its members. This was a typical theme in Manhattan, a trend toward moving uptown which continued throughout the century.[22]

On December 20, 1833, "The trustees met at Mr. Dakin's room, Clinton Hall" to begin the decision-making process

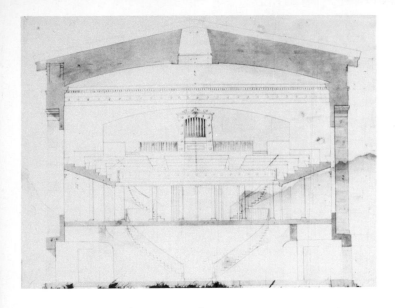

*Duane Street Presbyterian Church, New York, designed by James Dakin, 1834. Drawing by Dakin shows that the organ cover has the same acroterion motif as the Bank of Louisville facade.*

of selecting suitable plans. By March 20, 1834, Dakin had them ready for approval, and on May 17, 1834, the session of the church signed a contract with one John Heath to build a new church on a lot 116 feet by 100 feet, at the corner of Duane and Chapel (later Church) Streets, to cost $35,000, with "Plans drawn by J. H. Dakin." His drawings have been found, with one signed "New York, June 24, 1834, J. H. Dakin, Architect," and the others readily identifiable as the Duane Street Church.[23]

On May 30 of that year, the trustees passed a resolution "that Mr. James H. Dakin, the architect, be allowed as a compensation for his services in drawing the Plan of the New Church and Superintending the erection of the Building to its completion the sum of Five Hundred Dollars."[24]

The portico employed six columns across the front, and two "return" columns, just behind each end column. A square vestibule projected into the porch, its front in line with the return columns. The capitals were adapted from the Temple on the Ilissus, no doubt, because of its simplicity of detail. The entire pediment of the church, and most of its detail, is likewise rather simple. An exception was the cornice of the pediment, where Dakin added just enough interest to brighten up an otherwise somber facade. He adapted from the Erechtheion its cavetto moulding containing a course of anthemia, but without copying these exactly. On this occasion, Dakin did not employ the pilastrade principle down the sides of the church, but used smooth sides instead, pierced only by three long rectangular windows.[25]

The interior featured twin winding stairways leading to the galleries, towering above which is an organ cover in a Greek "ears" motif. A most important feature of this cover ʦ an acroterion decoration like that of the Bank of Louis- ──, that is, the crest with the swirls turning inward

toward the acroterion and two whorls beneath the crest. It is well to remember that this was in early 1834, long before Lafever's *Beauties of Modern Architecture* appeared containing this motif. The chancel arch is decorated with a row of patera, tastefully scaled and placed. The apse apparently included a *trompe l'oye* decoration behind the pulpit for this is penciled in on the original drawing which is otherwise ink and wash. The painting (?) on this rear wall shows a circular row of square pilasters which support a domed ceiling.

A. J. Davis was furious over this design for the church. He wrote a strong letter to Reverend Cyrus Mason, the church's pastor, excoriating the plan for being too elaborate. This was the same Cyrus Mason who deserves much of the credit for the erection of NYU; it was surely through Dakin's friendship with Mason over this project that he obtained the job for the Duane Street Church. Davis had obviously sought the work himself, but was rejected in favor of Dakin and his plan. Davis wrote Mason in March, 1834:

In adopting a design for your church, with a portico of eight Ionic columns, you subject yourselves to an unnecessary and wasteful expenditure, or you build with a mean and perishable material.

The expenditure will be wasteful, as the front bears no proportion to the depth, and the right flank must have dwelling houses of the common awkward description towering in their height, abutting upon it, tending to destroy the chaste elegance which the style you are adopting would, in other circumstances, present. It is therefore a false economy to adopt a portico of the hexastyle species with "return columns" where one more simple, tasteful and characteristic of its uses, might be chosen.

Mr. Dakin has done well, and I am far from attributing this error to any want of judgment on *your* part. . . .

A noticeable space in the letter follows here, and the handwriting, slightly different, obviously written at a later time, follows:

*Drawing by James Dakin of proposed alterations for Wall Street Presbyterian Church, New York, 1834. Exterior.*

I delayed sending them to you, but it is necessary to inform you, before the building is commenced, that I have a design, which I made last summer for your church, *and which I intend to publish as one rejected by you,* where the ancient prostyle temple is exhibited in its true proportion, and which presents a character of grave solemnity; more appropriate in a *sacred* edifice than the comparatively gay and ostentatious style before you. . . .

This design I cannot now, *on any solicitation,* grant even a view of, but, with a mind adverting to the golden rule of social virtue, and with the greatest respect for the eminent in every enobling quality, though with the utmost contempt for ignorance and self-sufficiency, wherever they may be found, I remain,

Most respectfully yours,
A. J. Davis [26]

Aside from being an interesting example of stilted nineteenth-century verbosity, this letter shows Davis to be capable of great vehemence and intemperateness of expression. This characteristic could hardly work to his benefit, and in this case, it didn't. Dakin's plan was accepted over his.

But more than this, the letter smacks of the "poor loser." The most Davis could bring himself to say kindly of Dakin's design was that "Mr. Dakin has done well." All the barbs against Dakin's design are, of course, undeserved, for a glance at Dakin's drawings show it to be quite handsome and restrained, hardly "gay and ostentatious," as Davis would have us believe.

Construction of the church began in 1834, and by January 3, 1836, it was opened for its first services. The congregation was happy here for a while, but the population's relentless move uptown and the instrusion of commerce into former residential neighborhoods forced another move. The propensity to move uptown which had worked to make the construction of Dakin's church necessary was now to lead to its sale and ultimate destruction.[27]

By 1849, the move was inevitable, and in April, 1851, the congregation began construction of a new edifice on Fifth Avenue and 19th Street. Dakin's building was sold for $32,000 on January 8, 1851, and presumably demolished in the nineteenth century.[28]

Another Presbyterian church plan by Dakin has been found, dating from 1834; this was his proposed project for rebuilding the Wall Street Church, which had burned that year. Dakin submitted a set of drawings for its reconstruction. He obviously failed to sell the congregation on his plans, for the church was instead rebuilt much along the same lines as before.[29]

But Dakin's drawings for the Wall Street Church are interesting, and had they been executed, the church would have been a most handsome building. The style was Corinthian, the portico having six columns with capitals influenced by the Choragic Monument of Lysicrates. The pediment was topped off by a cavetto moulding and anthemia therein, very similar to Dakin's Duane Street Church. This, as noted before, was based on the Erechtheion. The apse was exceedingly attractive. Dakin placed the podium in a hemisphere, ringed at the rear with ten free-standing columns, with capitals freely based on the Tower of the Winds. The wall area behind the ring was absolutely stark, resulting in a very chaste appearance.

The ceiling of this apse was one of Dakin's finest inventions. It consisted of octagonal coffered panels, with moulding setting them off from little triangular coffers between. Over the nave, the ceiling, in the form of a flat dome, was also very handsome. Instead of the coffered ceiling one might expect, Dakin complimented the coffered apse by giving the nave ceiling concentric rows of patera separated by moulding, forming rectangles radiating up

*Drawing by James Dakin of proposed alterations for Wall Street Presbyterian Church, New York, 1834. Interior.*

ward toward a skylight. It is unfortunate that this design was not executed, for it is possibly Dakin's finest in the Corinthian order.

Still another church for the Presbyterians was at least planned by Dakin; the question of its execution is yet in doubt. Three drawings by him, dated 1833, have turned up, described as the "Chambers St. Church." Because a transverse section through the portico shows return columns, we may reasonably assume that they are not from the Town, Davis, and Dakin period, in view of Davis' vehement letter about the Duane Street Church.[30]

The section indicates an Ionic building, typically pedimented with a projecting vestibule similar to the Duane Street Church. The only other existing drawings are for two types of roof trusses, one of which is a scissors truss, a type Dakin was to use again for a church in New Orleans. The truss detail is quite exact, possibly indicating that these may have been working drawings, and that the church may have been built from Dakin's plans.

Dakin's authorship of the Mercer Street Presbyterian Church at 299 Mercer Street, is evidenced only by the existence of his original drawings, for the early records of the church are rather sparse. These drawings, fourteen in number, represent one of the largest sets of plans in the surviving Dakin drawings. Two plans date from July 1, 1834, and one from July 30, 1834.[31]

A completely new congregation, the Mercer Street group was well enough organized by October 8, 1835, by which time its church was probably completed, to request membership in the Presbytery of New York. As is the case with many of Dakin's buildings in New York, it is not known if he contracted for or supervised the construction of this church. But the lateness of the date, October, 1835, suggests

*Drawing of Mercer Street Presbyterian Church by James Dakin, 1834.*

that he could have supervised it between July, 1834, and October, 1835, which was about the time he left for Louisville.

The style is that of a typical English parish church, although its period fortunately made it too early to be influenced by the rigid guidelines later set down for this type of architecture by the Ecclesiologists. In all probability, however, it would have found some favor with them. Its exterior was of random stone, with diagonal buttresses set at each end and at the corners of a tower set in the center of the facade. The top of this tower, as well as the roof line, was crenellated. Label mouldings were placed over moderately long lancet-arched windows. The buttresses of the 102-foot tall tower were of the four-step variety. More square than rectangular, the church, as depicted in the drawings, was seventy feet in the front and ninety feet on the sides. The whole effect of the exterior was rather austere, which might be expected of a Gothic structure intended for a Protestant congregation at that time. The Gothic was still associated strongly in some quarters with Catholicism, and, in general, was not as popular as Greek Revival for that reason. Eventually, the pendulum was to swing the other way.

The interior was also rather austere. Dakin could have lavished all his expertise in Gothic only on a Catholic church where no restraints were necessary. The ceiling treatment consisted of only four vaults, the ribbing reduced to but a single rib. The main springer ribs end in a very simple corbel, which even Davis could not call ostentatious. Above the level of the galleries Dakin placed two small choir lofts which had a beautiful upward curving railing. In this graceful curved design, we can see Dakin's inventiveness trying to burst the bonds imposed by the overall severity of the plan.

The apse was a hemisphere containing eight semi-engaged columns. The latter were simple, clustered Gothic columns, tying into, rather than supporting, a series of very plain ribs forming a vaulting leading to a skylight over the podium. In this skylight was painted a dove, symbol of the Holy Spirit.

The Gothic detail was held to an absolute minimum throughout. The only concessions to ornament were a band of rather wide quatrefoil moulding on the tower, just below the crenellation. The windows were also very understated in their tracery, which was mostly of a plain Y-traceried type. The tower, it might be added, was supported by enormous spread footings some fifteen feet across.

As a measuring stick of Dakin's development, the Mercer Street Church (later renamed the Church of the Strangers) demonstrated that he was as at ease in Gothic as in Greek Revival. This church, plus his work on NYU, leave no doubt that Dakin's Gothic prowess developed parallel with his Greek.

The last identifiable building that Dakin prepared plans for in New York was the House of Detention, better known as "The Tombs." John Haviland won the competition with his famous Egyptian Revival building, one of the finest Egyptian buildings ever built in America. Several architects competed for the job, but Haviland's was surely much the better of the lot. Dakin's name has not turned up in any surviving list of competitors, but his drawings which are dated 1835, indicate that he entered the contest.[32]

His plan called for a monumental, two-story building, plus basement, with a huge Doric porch, slightly projecting. The whole was flat roofed, with the usual Doric details of triglyphs and guttae. A row of antefixae ran all around the roof line of the building. For the sides, Dakin set enormous square pilasters in a "pilastrade" effect, there being sev-

*New York House of Detention. Competition drawing by James Dakin,*
*1835. Exterior.*

*New York House of Detention. Competition drawing by James Dakin,*
*1835. Floor plan.*

enteen on a side and ten in the front. These front pilasters were set, five each, on either side of the porch's eight huge Doric columns.

But the most striking feature of the building was the massive round tower Dakin planned for it. It was designed with two tiers, the lower of which called for about twenty-two Doric semi-attached columns, and above this, a smaller drum with a colonnade of the Ionic order. Topping it off was a statue of Justice.

The cells were placed at the rear, arranged in a fan shape, amphitheater style. Directly behind the central portion of the building with the Doric porch was a court of sessions. In the middle of the whole structure, separating the courts and the cell area, was an open courtyard. Dakin always insisted on open space for light and ventilation in massive buildings throughout his career, and he provided for it here.

Not long after entering the House of Detention competition in 1835, Dakin decided to leave New York and try his luck in New Orleans, where his brother, Charles, and James Gallier had moved some two years previously. Before discussing this new, southern, phase of James Dakin's career, however, it is essential to examine the experience of Charles Dakin and James Gallier in New Orleans.

# 3
# GALLIER AND DAKIN
# IN MOBILE AND NEW ORLEANS

THE SOUTHERN PHASE OF JAMES DAKIN'S CAREER CAN BEST BE approached in the historical context of his brother Charles' arrival in New Orleans with James Gallier. There, these two engaged in a partnership called "Gallier and Dakin, Architects." (It should be remembered that it was always Charles Dakin and not James who was referred to in "Gallier and Dakin." Only a one-month period in late 1835 is open for speculation as to the makeup of the partnership, when James Dakin, who had then just arrived in New Orleans, may have been involved briefly with the other two men. The facts seem to weigh against even this.)

James Gallier, originally from Ireland, had studied and worked in architecture in England. In 1832, he decided to try his luck in America, arriving in New York on April 14, 1832. He states that there were many draftsmen there, but "properly speaking, only one architect's office, kept by Town & Davis. There was a Mr. Dakin, a young man of genius, who had been a carpenter and had studied architecture in Town's office . . . from him I obtained the first employment I had in America; and as he found me much better acquainted with business in general than any of the draftsmen at that time in New York, he proposed to employ me at four dollars per day; so I went into his office and remained there for several months."

(Gallier errs slightly in his recollection of his starting pay. An entry in the Town, Davis, and Dakin account records shows that Gallier was hired on May 15, 1832, at two dollars a day, not four, still a fairly good salary for the time.)

Not long after, Gallier sent for his wife and family from England, where they had been waiting for word from him that he would be able to make a good living in America. The two dollars per day must have seemed like a lot then to warrant sending for one's family![1]

During this same period, 1833, James Dakin also hired his younger brother, Charles, as a draftsman at about $1.65 per day. Nothing is known of Charles's previous experience or training, so we must presume that he learned his skills at the hands of his brother in the Town, Davis, and Dakin office.[2]

In 1833, the year that *The Modern Builder's Guide* was published, James Gallier left the firm of Town, Davis, and Dakin and entered into a partnership with Minard Lafever. Gallier relates, in his memoirs:

There was at that time in New York a draftsman called Lafever, who had been in the employment of a builder; he came to me and proposed to join me as a partner in opening an architect's office; he said he had an extensive connection of influential friends who would patronize us in business. After some consideration, I agreed to his proposal, and we opened an office in Clinton Hall, where we obtained from the builders orders for as many drawings as we could well make; but I found it very disagreeable work, and so badly rewarded, that I began to cast about and see if there was no other way by which I could improve my situation, and escape from the horse-in-a-mill routine of grinding out drawings for the builders.

It was then intimated to me by persons who had been to the South, that New Orleans would be a much better place for me to settle in than New York, if I could only bear the climate; for, though mercantile men went there during the winter months only, they returned northward in the summer to escape the yellow fever; this they continued to do until they in some degree became acclimatized; but an architect could not do this; he must remain all the summer from his first beginning, as that was the season when buildings were chiefly erected in New Orleans.

Lafever and I, having then dissolved our copartnership, I left with him the collection of various outstanding debts due to our firm, but of which I never received any part from him afterwards.

Shortly after this, Gallier and Charles Dakin set sail for the South.[3]

It is worth underlining the fact that Gallier here does not

refer to Lafever as an architect before their partnership in 1833, but rather as a "draftsman." Although Professor Landy fairly well established that Lafever was considered an "architect" by 1829 (although listed in the New York City Directory that year as a builder), it is nevertheless interesting to see how his partner, Gallier, felt about him.

Implied in Gallier's account of his and Charles Dakin's reasons for leaving New York is Gallier's wish to become both architect and contractor for the erection of their buildings. This was to be his way of breaking out of the "horse-in-a-mill routine." He knew where the profits were and wanted to share in them.

Gallier tells of the trip South with Charles Dakin in his autobiography:

Having determined to run the hazard of New Orleans, I prepared without delay to go there, and make a trial, leaving my family in the meantime at New York; so that, in October, 1834, I set off by sea, accompanied by a young man [Charles Dakin], a brother of Mr. [James] Dakin. . . . We landed at Mobile, where we remained a few weeks, until the yellow fever had for that season disappeared from New Orleans; we then went there, and hired an office on Canal St., hung its walls with plans and drawings, and began to look out for something to do.

The corporation of the city of Mobile having decided upon building a Town Hall, advertised for plans, and we made a design for it which obtained the first prize of three hundred dollars; though but a trifle [actually, this was a rather good fee], it served to place our names before the public, but in consequence of a fire, by which a large portion of Mobile was destroyed, the Hall was never built. We made plans for a church [the Government Street Presbyterian Church] and for a public school [Barton Academy], which were erected there [by Dakin and Dakin] and are still the most important looking buildings in Government Street.[4]

The firm of Gallier and Dakin did extremely well from the start. This was no doubt because of their own great ability (as well as the lack of professional architects of their caliber), but probably also because of the name Dakin having been known through the Town, Davis, and Dakin relationship. We have already seen how several merchants and builders obtained plans from Town, Davis, and Dakin in New York for their New Orleans buildings; having the name "Dakin" in their title meant that Gallier and Dakin were already "pre-sold" when they went to New Orleans.

The earliest example of their work seems to be the "Three Sisters," a row house on North Rampart Street, dating from December 20, 1834. It extended from the corner of Bienville toward Iberville Street, in the French Quarter. The "Sisters" were frame, two stories high, with four Corinthian columns, the capitals being of an embellished Tower of the Winds design. They were originally conceived as fine residences, but because of the commercialization of Rampart Street over the years and the growth of a small red-light district one block to the rear, they declined; by 1945, only one was left standing. It too was demolished about 1950.[5]

One of the finest buildings ever erected on Canal Street was Christ Church Episcopal, on the corner of Bourbon and Canal. The first church on the site, built about 1816, was designed by Henry Latrobe, the son of the great Benjamin Latrobe. We know little else about it, except that it was octagonal and had a cupola.[6]

The Episcopal congregation soon outgrew Latrobe's old church, and in 1835, it commissioned Gallier and Dakin to give them a plan for a larger edifice. *Norman's New Orleans* described it as "a fine Ionic building . . . designed by Gallier & Dakin, architects, and its erection begun in the autumn of 1835, under the direction of Mr. D.[aniel] H. Twogood [builder of the "Thirteen Sisters" by James Dakin, on Julia Street]. It was completed in the summer of 1837, and consecrated during the same year. The cost of the edifice was about $70,000. The form of the ceiling, being a flat dome, is much admired." [7]

The building was used by the Episcopal congregation for a number of years, but the location proved less and less felicitous. Bourbon Street, even then, was noisy and crowded on Sunday mornings. In 1846, the Jewish philanthropist, Judah Touro, accepted the church and land on the corner of Canal and Bourbon Streets in exchange for a piece of property he owned on Canal and Dauphine Streets. This Gallier and Dakin church thus survived as a synagogue until 1856 when it was demolished.

Other buildings by Gallier and Dakin in New Orleans include: some stores for Pritchard and Lanfear (Richard Owen Pritchard and Ambrose Lanfear), a warehouse, a bathing establishement for a "Mr. Morgan," and a house for J. R. Hyde, at Dauphine and Conti Streets. [8]

An early phenomenon of New Orleans was the public bath. Besides the one just mentioned, Gallier and Dakin built a very fine one called the Arcade Baths, so named because it was connected to the St. Charles Theater at its rear by a long arcade. Built adjacent to the American Theater on Camp Streets, it was part of a remarkable urban complex of shops, saloons, and theaters, which attests to the rather sophisticated degree of development that had taken place in parts of New Orleans by the 1830s.

The Arcade Baths is described as "a very pretty example of the Corinthian order, adjoining the Camp St. [American] Theatre on a front of 54 feet by a depth of 170. The edifice is four stories in height, the lowest being occupied in front by a coffee room, from which access is had to the bathrooms in the rear, twenty four in number, by a corridor supported by a double row of Corinthian columns, and also by a turning

*Arcade Baths, New Orleans, called here "Caldwell's Baths," by James Gallier and Charles Dakin, 1835. The lettering here is in Charles Dakin's handwriting. (Courtesy Tulane University Library, Archives Division)*

stair to the second stories. The second contains a ball room, 30 by 90 feet, and a large saloon for billiards; and the upper stories are divided into lodging rooms, 42 in number." [9]

The building contract was signed on July 30, 1835, by Gallier and James Caldwell, the owner, the cost to be $50,000. When the building was accepted on October 2, 1836, a portico which had been planned had been dispensed with. The original drawings for the portico show six Corinthian columns clustered at the base in groups of two, the lettering being in the handwriting of Charles Dakin. It was planned that the pediment contain a sculpture depicting sea goddesses, their chariots being pulled by two huge fish, and their leader holding a scepter, apparently a group of Oceanides and mermaids. The facade, minus the water creatures, is probably based loosely on the Temple of the Scisi, illustrated by Palladio in his Fourth Book of Architecture, Plate 76. It did not survive for long, for it burned on March 13, 1842, in the fire which destroyed the first St. Charles Theater. [10]

Finally, the last Gallier and Dakin buildings in New Orleans, the Merchants Exchange and the St. Charles Hotel, are so much involved in the split up of Charles Dakin and Gallier, that they will be dealt with in a later chapter. They will provide us then with an explanation as to how the split was accomplished. James Dakin, about to begin his journey to the South, was to figure in the split also.

# 4
# JAMES DAKIN GOES
# TO NEW ORLEANS

WHEN JAMES DAKIN DESCENDED THE MISSISSIPPI TO NEW Orleans in November, 1835, the mighty river and the virgin lands at its banks made a deep impression on him. Fortunately, he left us a vivid account of this trip in a letter to his wife in New York:[1]

You will learn by this that I am safely deposited in my destined haven at last. I left Louisville on the 10th., and arrived in N.O. on the evening of the 17th., so that we were just seven days in coming down the river, a very crooked distance of 1370 miles. My passage was very pleasant. We had an opportunity of going on shore every five or six hours. The boat would stop as often to take on————[letter damaged]. There were two boats in company. The————Louisville at the same time and arrived . . . within fifteen minutes of each other . . . victory was well contested on both sides. Our opposing boat was loaded with Theatrical ladies and gentlemen of rather low talent. We stopped at all the towns along the river and that was not many, for there are but very few settlements in the whole distance. We would go some hundred miles sometimes without seeing a dozen souls. The river winds its way in a sluggish and playful manner through an immense wilderness of low level land and vast swamps of fathomless mire and impenetrable darkness, caused by the density of vegetation of every description, from trees of 200 feet in height down to the slender cane and thick grass about knee high. We stopped at Natchez, and also at that notorious Vicksburgh, but we all got off without being hanged.

The width of the Mississippi is very wonderful. When we consider its length to be 4,490 miles, with the whole West and Northwestern world contributing to its waters, it is really astonishing to see this mighty stream running in about one parallel width of less than one half mile. However, the depth is very respectable, being about 240 feet in this place. The most trouble we encountered on our passage was an incessant quarreling among the women in the Ladies cabin. I found Charles and Gallier well and hearty and fu———. . . ————ishness, and also found the city much larg—— looking than I expected. I also f—— William Dakin at the same house. . . . The reason I have not written you before is because I have been waiting from day to day to hear from you, but nothing had come yet. The ship Nashville arrived yesterday, and I went on board today, but they have not commenced discharging her. I wrote you from Louisville last which I suppose you have received before this time. I shall make it a practice to write you once a week, and I wish you would write me as often and as much more so as you feel disposed.

I will send you $20 by this, although you may not be in much want of. You must always let me know in time when you want money and furthermore, please be careful and keep it from being stolen by servants. I will not ask you again to fix a pocket in your gown where you could keep it in safety and great convenience for I have so often asked that favour of you and have been denied. Only keep it safe and I will be satisfied, but do not keep it so close as not to use just as much as you want for your comfort and ease.

My best love to you and the children———— . . . and good night.

The ominous reference to Vicksburg concerns an incident there just four months before during which vigilantes lynched several suspected land pirates thought to be associated with the notorious Murrel Gang. Travel, at the time of Dakin's trip, could be hazardous! Dakin arrived in New Orleans on the steamer *Mountaineer* on November 17, 1835, and the passenger lists published in the New Orleans newspapers show him as "Mr. Deacon." [2]

But why, we may properly ask, did James Dakin choose to go to New Orleans? Why leave New York, where he was well known, to relocate in a city many miles away? First of all, we know for certain, from James Gallier's autobiography, that Charles Dakin, his younger brother, wrote him about the great quantity of business he and Gallier were doing.[3] Secondly, Dakin probably saw an opportunity to make a fortune speculating in land, which was plentiful in the lower Mississippi Valley, then the frontier of the United States. And thirdly, Dakin must have been driven by a desire to achieve great prominence in his profession, perhaps unconsciously realizing that he could better accomplish this outside of New York, where he would always be in the shadow of A. J. Davis, his former teacher.

Also, New Orleans was, at the time, the statistically logical place to go. It was then the second city of the United States measured in terms of its shipping, commerce, and rate of growth. It beckoned Dakin with its attractions, which a New Orleans newspaper summed up well:

The only rival New Orleans can have on the American continent is New York; and New York, although its commercial influences may be greater, will never have the same power over American civilization as New Orleans. . . . The Mississippi River is the great centre of the American confederacy . . . the band of steel that fastens together all the States of the Union. New Orleans . . . is the capital of the West. The influence of New Orleans over the western country is already perceptible, and is destined to be much greater. As Athens moulded Greece, and Greece Europe, so this city will influence the West, and through it, the whole American Continent.[4]

This was a bit overstated, in typical nineteenth-century newspaper style, but New Orleans was definitely the most vital city in the South. And the allusion to Athens is most fitting for this context. Straining this allegory further, we might note that if New Orleans was another Athens, James Dakin would be its greatest Greek architect for seventeen years.

Gallier also mentions the arrival of James Dakin and the ensuing breakup of the Gallier and Dakin partnership:

At the solicitation of my architectural partner, Mr. Charles Dakin, his brother came from New York in 1835, and they proposed that he should join us as a partner in the office; but I doubted whether three of us could agree together in such a business as ours. I therefore proposed to withdraw and leave the office to them, stipulating, however, that as the St. Charles Hotel and the Post Office [Merchants Exchange] were exclusively my own designs, I should continue to superintend them until completed. We separated upon these conditions. I paid over to Charles his proportion of what had been received by us from the commencement, and I left them with all the unfinished business in the office.[5]

Gallier's description of the split-up is in general borne out by the facts as we know them today, but the claim for the exclusive design of the St. Charles Hotel and superintendence of the Merchants Exchange is perhaps an exaggeration. There is solid evidence that the St. Charles was definitely a Gallier and Dakin building, although Gallier may have done the bulk of the work. This evidence includes the original drawings which are signed "Gallier and Dakin," contemporary engravings similarly captioned, and most importantly, a contemporary guide book, *Norman's New Orleans,* which says that the hotel boasts "a dome, of beautiful proportions, after a plan of Dakin, forty six feet in diameter. . . ."[6] Thus, Gallier's claim is at least suspect of being too extravagent.

His claim about the Merchants Exchange being erected under his superintendence is in doubt also, for the 1838 *New Orleans City Directory* states that it was "erected from the designs and under the superintendence of C. B. Dakin, Esq., Architect." But, in the errata section in the front of this book is the notation, "Substitute J. B. [*sic*] Dakin for C. B. Dakin." The latter would seem to be correct, for we have already seen how the officer of the Bank of Louisville missed seeing Dakin at the Exchange. And Dakin and Dakin had their offices in the building in 1837 and 1838, as it was nearing completion.[7]

The facts in the case seem to indicate that the designs were by both Gallier and Dakin, with the bulk of the work by Gallier, but with the dome of the St. Charles specifically by the Dakins, and the erection of the St. Charles under Gallier's supervision, and the Merchants Exchange under the personal superintendence of James Dakin. While the latter was going up, in the late 1830s, Charles was in Mobile, running a thriving business.

The Merchants Exchange, designed, as its name implies,

*Merchants' Exchange, New Orleans, designed by James Gallier and*
*Charles Dakin, erected by James H. Dakin, 1836-37. Exterior. (Draw-*
*ing by John Turner)*

to be an auction house and office building, was, on its exterior, one of Gallier and Dakin's most chaste creations. Its simplicity of line brings to mind much of today's architecture. It is almost devoid of embellishment, although the Dakins and Gallier were as capable of designing the most elaborate Greek detailing as any men then alive. Rather, they chose to let the manner of the fenestration provide the interest of the exterior. The openings were typical Town and Davis style, a modified Davisean, in that they extended two stories high. But unlike the true Davisean window, there was an obvious visible break defining the floor which separated the second and third levels.[8]

The ground floor was of the granite pier type, with a slightly projecting portico having the same granite pier treatment, and a small pediment. The roof line repeated this pediment, but simulated it in an attenuated way. The front of the building was ashlar granite, very smoothly fitted. Externally, the overall effect is one of massiveness and purity of detail. Internally, it is a different story.

The interior was one of exquisite detail. For the main business room, Gallier and Dakin used sumptuous Corinthian capitals, based on the Choragic Monument of Lysicrates, which sat atop huge square pilasters ringing the room. These pilasters were two stories high, extending from the floor of the second level to a moulding at the point from whence sprang a low dome.

In addition to the luxurious capitals, the mouldings in the business room were of varied and delicate detail. Four moulding courses, including two egg and dart types which ringed the room, were separated by dentils of refined proportions. A beautiful ink and wash drawing for the skylight in the circular oculus of the dome shows two concentric rings of bead and reel moulding surrounding a central leaflike motif of original design. Radiating toward

*Merchants' Exchange, New Orleans. Ceiling and column.*

the center are shafts of a motif containing anthemia and vines; and at the outer edge of the skylight, ringing the whole, is a panel of anthemia surrounded by two small bead-and-reel mouldings. All of this was painted on in "transparent colors." It was this skylight or a later version of it, perhaps modified by Dakin during construction, that so captured the fancy of the Bank of Louisville official. Thus, the interior of the Exchange was as lush as the exterior was stark.

The building contract was signed on March 18, 1835, by the president of the Exchange Company of New Orleans, Seaman Field, and by the builder, Daniel H. Twogood. Another contract was signed on March 30, 1835, by Charles Dakin and by Small and McGill, Builders, who were to provide the granite and marble. The total cost of the Exchange, as noted in the city guides, was $100,000, a formidable sum in 1835.[9]

About the turn of the century, when the entire French Quarter declined, a flophouse was improvised in the huge business room of the Exchange by the erection of a labyrinth of tiny rooms of lath and plaster. Fortunately, the integrity of the shell of the building was preserved, and in 1959, the Gallery Circle Theater leased the second floor and pulled down the chicken-coop affair, revealing the interior almost as Gallier and Dakin had left it 130 years before. The theater group gilded the capitals, repainted the walls, and had the building primed for many more years of usefulness when a pyromaniac put a match to the Merchants Exchange on December 3, 1960. It was reduced to rubble; thus went the last Gallier and Dakin building in New Orleans.[10]

The St. Charles Hotel deserves special attention in a discussion of the Dakins and Gallier. It was the largest and most imposing hotel in the United States at the time of its erection, and it never lost its grandeur during its entire existence. Only the Tremont House in Boston, by Isaiah Rogers, could be considered more important in an evaluation of hotels of the 1830s. The Astor House in New York, also by Rogers, was built a little later than the St. Charles, and neither it nor the Tremont could match the St. Charles in size or striking appearance.

It was the only hotel design Gallier was to be connected with; it and his New Orleans City Hall are probably his two best works. The conflict over what part of the design was Gallier's and what part was Dakin's has already been touched on. Descriptions of it are numerous, and it is hard to find any which do not speak of it in superlatives. Built in the second block of St. Charles Street, where the present St. Charles stands today, it probably did more to vitalize the American sector of New Orleans than any other factor. The city, which of necessity hugged the river bank for want of dry land, had generally developed in the old quarter below Canal Street, which Bienville had determined in the eighteenth century to be dry throughout the year. This area was naturally heavily settled by persons of French and Spanish descent. It was not until James Caldwell and others developed the old Jesuit plantation, at that time a virtual swamp, just above Canal Street near the river, that New Orleans really began to grow out of its old colonial boundaries. This section was known as the Faubourg St. Marie, where the Americans settled. The division of the city along geographical and ethnological lines was to lead to continuous trouble for almost seventy-five years, and it figures repeatedly in the story of Dakin's career in New Orleans.

In 1835, a handful of men from the American sector decided to bring New Orleans into the nineteenth century. They foresaw the necessity of a great hotel in a seaport the size of New Orleans, but more particularly, in their rapidly growing section. This need was obvious, if they were to keep up with the French Quarter which had just seen the beginnings of the erection of the St. Louis Hotel.

A group of twenty commissioners was formed and a charter was obtained from the state. Included were men like Maunsel White, John Hagan, Richard O. Pritchard, James Caldwell, Thomas Banks and James Freret. They ran an ad in the *Bee* on April 21, 1835, for "proposals to build the Exchange Hotel [its original name] ... according to the drawings of Messrs. Gallier & Dakin. ... " On May 1, 1835, John Hagan sold the required land (235 feet on St. Charles Street by 160 feet) to the hotel company, and by May 28, 1835, the building was under way. In October, the *Bee* noted that it should be finished in 1836, and on December 4, 1835, Gallier signed a contract for the granite work. Gallier signed alone, because the split with Charles Dakin was probably final by the date of the granite contract.[11]

The St. Charles has been described in the *Historical Epitome* as a "truly magnificent establishment, which for size and architectural beauty stands unrivalled. ... The building cost $600,000. The principal front on St. Charles St. consists of a projecting portico of six Corinthian columns, which stand upon a granite basement fourteen feet high, with a pediment on top."[12] Gallier says, "The basement story consisted of shops and offices which were rented to various occupants. The principal entrances were gained by a flight of granite steps at each end of a projecting platform, on which stood a Corinthian portico, having an inner range of columns, with a deep recess between them, where the entrance doors were placed."[13]

A colonnade of fluted Corinthian columns in the drum supported the dome, cited in *Norman's New Orleans* as "after a plan of Dakin, forty-six feet in diameter," which was topped off with a lantern patterned after the Choragic Monument of Lysicrates. "There is a large circular room under the dome, on the floor of which the spiral staircase terminates, and around the outside of which the circular colonnade forms a beautiful gallery eleven feet wide, from whence can be seen the whole city, and all the windings of the river for several miles in each direction. The effect of the dome upon the sight of the visitor, as he approaches the city, is similar to that of St. Paul's, London."[14]

"The dining room was 129 feet long by fifty feet wide, with twenty two feet high ceilings, in the Corinthian order, with two ranges of inside columns, so placed that there is space for four ranges of tables. A grand spiral stair case commences on the centre of the saloon floor [in an octagonal area beneath the dome] and is continued up to the dome. Around this staircase, on either side of the upper stories, a gallery is formed, which gives access to ... bedrooms."

The building, five stories high, and containing 350 bedrooms, was completed sufficiently in February, 1837, to accommodate patrons; it was entirely completed by May, 1838.[15] It was a real showplace of New Orleans and could boast of a statue of Washington imported from Italy which stood in the portico.

In 1846, the hotel had 502 boarders and 170 employees. Its daily consumption of food included "500 lbs. of beef, 30 pair of wild ducks, 30 dozen robins and other wild birds. ... "[16] This happy operation was not to go on forever, however. On January 18, 1851, the St. Charles caught fire and burned to the ground.[17] The fire which consumed the building was proportional in size to the hotel itself; all the efforts of the firemen could not save it.

This was the end of the Gallier and Dakin St. Charles, but not of their design, for the hotel was to rise again. A group was formed immediately to rebuild the hotel. The story of the second St. Charles Hotel and the part played in it by the architect Isaiah Rogers is best deferred until later.

# 5
# DAKIN AND DAKIN
# IN NEW ORLEANS

AFTER THE ARRIVAL OF JAMES DAKIN ON NOVEMBER 17, 1835, and the "agreement to disagree" that Gallier has told us about, only one slight connection between Gallier and the Dakins was left. On November 21, 1835, Gallier signed a contract to build a house for William Nott on Esplanade Avenue, with Michael Collins to be the builder and Charles Dakin to complete the house if Gallier became incapacitated.

Significantly, Charles Dakin signed the contract as an individual, and not as a member of the Gallier and Dakin partnership. Thus, it appears that the split of Gallier and Dakin took place almost immediately after James Dakin arrived on November 17. The abovementioned Nott house, incidentally, is still standing at 1020 Esplanade Avenue, concealed by a facade added in the 1920s in a pseudo-Italian style for the Unione Italiana. Charles Dakin probably had no further connection with it.[1]

With the split final, James and Charles Dakin were ready to embark on a new phase of their careers. On Christmas Eve, 1835, they signed a partnership agreement creating the firm of Dakin and Dakin, Architects. It was stipulated that it was to run for a period of five years.[2] The two brothers thus found themselves in a position to handle two offices, James in New Orleans and Charles in Mobile. Charles, of course, would benefit there from his previous exposure through the Gallier and Dakin partnership. He left for Mobile just before the new year and established an office there, calling the Mobile operation, "Charles Dakin & Brother, Architects." It appears that he must have been well known in that city, for the title selected for the new firm did not include the name of his more illustrious brother. Charles arrived in Mobile on December 31, 1835, New Years Eve, perhaps sensing a good omen that the new year would bring prosperity.[3] And it would do just that—it brought a boom comparable to that taking place simultaneously in New Orleans. In the next chapter, we will examine Charles's activities in Mobile during this boom.

James Dakin, meanwhile, set about establishing operations in New Orleans. He wasted no time in spreading the firm's name, for on January 25, 1836, he addressed a letter to the Louisiana state legislature: [4]

Sirs:—We have the honor of presenting herewith to the representatives of the people of Louisiana, a design of the Capitol of the State, planned for the ground of the present location, together with the interior plan and section; and also a drawing of the improved design of the Exchange [St. Charles] Hotel, now erecting on St. Charles St.

Should we be so fortunate as to excite a spirit of enterprise among our fellow citizens which might lead to the erection of this public improvement, we should feel ourselves fully compensated for the labor and anxiety it has cost.

Here, in the earliest known New Orleans project of Dakin and Dakin, James had put his name before the legislature, hoping to stimulate an interest in the erection of a new capitol, then badly needed. Eventually, he would succeed in this end.

An interesting aspect of this letter is the mention of an "improved design" for the St. Charles Hotel. It is unclear whether this refers to the dome Dakin did for the hotel, or to more extensive changes by the Dakins (possibly for the interior) in the area beneath the dome. But it does support the mention in *Norman's New Orleans* that the dome should be credited to Dakin. Neither the capitol nor the hotel has been identified in the collection of Dakin drawings, but there are several unidentified drawings which could be a state capitol, as well as many with domes quite similar to the hotel's.

In no time at all after his arrival, James Dakin was to get

an important commission which would place Dakin and Dakin as contenders for first position among architectural firms in New Orleans. The St. Charles Hotel had hardly begun, when it, in effect, begat another hotel to rival it in importance and beauty, if not size. The new hotel, designed by Dakin and Dakin, called the Verandah, was the direct result of a fight among the builders of the St. Charles.

The story of this quarrel was told many years later by a man who was present, W. H. Sparks, one of the promoters of the St. Charles Hotel. According to Sparks, the entrepreneurs held a celebration dinner shortly after the hotel began operations. Among those in attendance were Hagan, Barrett, and the Dicks, who were Irishmen; Caldwell and Pritchard, Englishmen; Peters, a Canadian; Henderson, a Scotchman; and Yorke, an American. Apparently the nationalism of the men was heightened by the libations consumed in the celebration, for a number of toasts were made to their native countries. Trouble began when Pritchard arose to offer his toast: "Gentlemen, I give you my native land. England, with all thy faults, I love thee still." "Damn if I do!" said Barrett, setting down his unemptied glass, and in a few moments the two were involved in expressions of old national hatred. The conclusion of the quarrel, Sparks said, came when "Pritchard turned from the table, took up his hat, and saying 'Damn your hotel! I will build one of my own,' left the room. This he did—the Verandah Hotel—at the corner of Common and St. Charles."[5]

This account could be dismissed as the reminiscences of an old man, colored by time, were it not for the fact that, not too many years previous to these events, an English cotton merchant, identified only as "Pritchard," who was in New Orleans during its annual celebration of the victory over the British at the Battle of New Orleans, made disparaging

*Richard Owen Pritchard, New Orleans entrepreneur. Co-founder of the St. Charles Hotel and builder of the Verandah Hotel. (Courtesy Mrs. Godfrey Parkerson)*

remarks about the "Yankees" and found himself in a duel in which he was badly wounded.[6] It is not known if this man was Richard O. Pritchard or a relative, but the source of the tiff between the hotelmen was the same: hot feelings between those of English ancestry and those of Irish forebears. New Orleans, heavily populated with Irish, was to be the scene of much nationalistic trouble in the 1800s.

Pritchard's Verandah Hotel was much more compact, compared to the block-long St. Charles — the Verandah being "only" half a block long — but it was considered to be just as beautiful. The 1842 *City Directory* describes it:

This edifice, called [the Verandah] from being covered on its front towards the streets to a certain height by a projecting roof and balcony, which protect not only the inmates of the building, but also the pedestrian from the sun and rain, is situated at the corner of St. Charles and Common Sts. diagonally opposite the Exchange Hotel.

The building is designed as a family hotel by its enterprising projector and builder, R. O. Pritchard, Esq. It was finished in May, 1839, and the splendid designs of its architects were fully accomplished in a manner that commands the intense admiration of every beholder.

The great dining room is probably one of the highest finished apartments in America. The ceiling especially is a model, being composed of three beautiful elliptic domes for chandeliers — dimensions of this room 85 feet, by 32 and 27 feet high. The chimney pieces of the parlors are fine pieces of sculpture, and the rooms are otherwise handsome. A statue of Venus adorns the ladies' private entrance. [Actually, it was Hebe, a copy of a sculpture by Canova.] The cost of the edifice, land, etc. was $300,000. [The site had been bought by Pritchard on May 4, 1835 for $39,100.00.] The whole was designed, and has been constructed by Messrs. Dakin & Dakin, Archts., well known in this city. It was begun October, 1836. The chasteness and simplicity of this edifice are generally admired.[7]

The *Courier* described it while it was still under construction:

The Verandah will be constructed on iron columns and have beautiful trellis work — the whole painted green. The hotel will contain about 200 rooms, independent of those in the basement story designed for fancy stores. The dining room for gentlemen . . . will be surmounted by three domes, ornamented by chandeliers lighted by gas in the evening — which will have a happy effect, particularly when it is considered that the whole of that dining room, as well as the principal parlours, will be glazed or lined with mirrors on every side.

The hotel consists of five stories, the whole being nearly 72 feet from the ground to the eaves. The front on St. Charles St. is 146 feet long and on Common St. 123 feet. . . .

The hotel will be finished in August next [1837] but is not expected to open before October in order that time may afford thoroughly drying the rooms.[8]

The Verandah was praised by other contemporaries, among them Eliza Ripley and A. Oakey Hall, the latter writing as the *Manhattaner in New Orleans.*[9]

The gallery of the Verandah holds special interest, for it appears to be a prototype of the iron balconies New Orleans is noted for, that is, those which cover the entire sidewalk and are roofed over to give protection from the elements. In Dakin's version, the balcony walkway is cantilevered, with the iron columns of its canopy not joined to the gallery itself. Of course, there had been iron balconies for years in the French Quarter, but at the present stage of research, there were none earlier than this one which covered the sidewalk completely and was supported from below by iron columns. The balcony of the Verandah survived into the 1850s, by which time iron balconies had become the rage. It may well have been the inspiration for the rash of iron gallery construction which began at mid-century.

The Verandah was later operated by the same people who ran the St. Charles, and it was then regarded as a kind of overflow hotel for the St. Charles during the busy seasons. Eventually, the Verandah went the way of many early

*Verandah Hotel, New Orleans, designed by James and Charles Dakin,
1836. (Courtesy Louisiana State Museum)*

buildings; it was destroyed by fire. On July 19, 1855, it caught fire early in the morning in a place near the roof; it was soon reduced to ashes. At the time of its demise, it was owned by an old associate of Richard O. Pritchard, businessman James W. Zacharie.

So, in a short period, New Orleans lost two great hotels by fire. First, the St. Charles on January 18, 1851, and then the Verandah in 1855. Together they, plus the St. Louis Hotel, had given New Orleans three of the finest hotels in the country.

The city was pulsating with a business boom, money was easily come by on credit, and speculation was rampant in the 1830s. Richard O. Pritchard was creating some of the boom atmosphere, and, riding its crest, he commissioned James Dakin to build for him a huge residence on Canal Street. It was actually to be four separate residences with a common facade, which could be partially rented by Pritchard as an investment.

Union Terrace is the name of the elegant block of buildings which has just sprung into existence among the numerous improvements of the last two years, and which is now raising its beautiful Ionic facade on the lower side of Canal St. [in the 900 block] opposite the State House. In its extent are comprised four private residences, whose interior arrangements and architectural taste are in perfect keeping with their exterior chastity of design. They were erected in the years 1836–37, from the designs and under the immediate direction of Messrs. Dakin & Dakin, Architects, at a cost of $100,000." [10]

In some ways Union Terrace recalls the row house, Lafayette Terrace in New York, for which Town, Davis, and Dakin had done some interior work. The two rows have in common a colonnade commencing at the second floor level. But at the Union Terrace, Dakin gave it a beautiful recessed, curved central bay. Oddly, although intended to be four

*Elevation of adjoining buildings*

*Union Terrace, New Orleans, designed by Charles and James Dakin, 1836. (Drawing by George T. Dunbar, 1843, courtesy New Orleans Notarial Archives)*

residences, Union Terrace breaks down visually into three parts. Dakin's creativity is displayed in his interesting handling of the columnation of the porticos of the two end pavilions. At their centers, stood two Ionic columns (of the Erechtheum variety, with necking bands), but at either side of these, forming the corners of the portico, are huge square columns which are made up of twin square pilasters, with a shallow recess between. These pairs of pilasters face on all four sides of the end columns. The entablature led up to the cornice in no less than ten courses of moulding of various widths and tasteful undercuts. All in all, the Union Terrace was a tour de force for James Dakin and, being so prominently located on Canal Street, must have gained him great reputation for his skills.

Besides Richard O. Pritchard, the other partners in the Union Terrace enterprise were Seaman Field, head of the Exchange Company which built the Merchants Exchange; William A. Gasquet, a merchant who frequently had Dakin do buildings for him; and Michel Douradou Bringier of New Orleans and St. James Parish, which lies below Baton Rouge, on the Mississippi River.[11] Bringier was the planter head of a family dynasty whose realm was on the banks of the Mississippi. The Bringiers, and the sons-in-law of Michel Bringier, owned much of the plantation land between Baton Rouge and New Orleans. One of Bringier's daughters, Nanine, was married to Duncan Kenner, himself a planter. It was he who was sent as a Confederate minister to England to try to persuade that country to align with the South, which in return promised to free the slaves. In a subsequent settlement of the Bringier estate, Kenner was to acquire part of Union Terrace.[12]

As Canal Street changed character, so too did the Terrace. In 1872, the *Picayune* told of its having been remodeled for business usage.[13]

The Varieties Club purchased one third of the building to rebuild the recently burned Varieties Theater. The other portions were used for sundry purposes, including, at one time, the studio of Canova, nephew of the famous sculptor, well known here mainly for his painting. In another part was located Victor's Restaurant, a favorite of New Orleanians for some time. It has been said that there was an air of elegance to pull up in a carriage on Canal Street, after attending an opera or the theater, and cap off the evening in the splendor of Victor's.[14]

Again, fire brought an end to this Dakin building, or we should say, to two thirds of it. On January 10, 1874, Union Terrace burned, taking Victor's Restaurant, plus a central portion owned by Duncan Kenner, leaving only the entrance of the Varieties Theater.[15] The club carried on in the remaining third, later calling their theater the Grand Opera House. One of the foremost theaters in the South, it was nationally known. Then, in 1906, a mercantile business offered to buy them out and they accepted.

In his *Golden Age of the New Orleans Theatre*, John Smith Kendall writes:

The last performance ever given in this historic theatre took place on April 30, 1906. The Times-Democrat contained a description: "At the ripe age of nearly 35 years, the Grand Opera House terminated its existence as a theatre. . . . There was a large and fashionable audience . . . and a brilliant presentation of Geo. Bernard Shaw's Candide. . . . Under the care of La Varietie . . . some of the greatest artists that have ever trod the American stage were introduced to the playgoing public of New Orleans." Within a few days, workmen were put in possession of the theatre, and its destruction proceeded apace.[16]

So, after fire had previously engulfed most of Union Terrace, the tide of business washed away what was left of Dakin's masterpiece.

*Varieties Theatre wing of Union Terrace, New Orleans. (From Jewell's* Crescent City)

Things were going well now for James Dakin in the mid-thirties. We find him in a good mood in a letter he wrote to his wife in 1836, then still in New York: [17]

The bearer of this is my friend, Mr. Endicott, who was in Orleans and roomed with me at my boarding house this last winter. He is a gentleman in every respect and any politeness or attention that you may render to him will much oblige one and your husband. Mr. Endicott will present you with the watch that I promised you. He will also inform you of the character of your husband in Orleans, etc. Show him the little ones and ask him if he can beat it. He will be some time in getting to New York and you will hear from me often before this reaches you.

Mrs. Dakin probably joined her husband in New Orleans about August of 1836, for there is a record of his buying a female slave named "Tishy" on August 23.[18] She was undoubtedly to be a house servant to help Mrs. Dakin with the twin girls, Mary Caroline and Julia. Some circumstances around this purchase of the slave tie in with a story told in the Dakin family and give us some insight into Dakin's personal life and, coincidentally, into a very important building he probably designed.

The family story is that when James Dakin arrived in New Orleans, he lived at the boardinghouse of a French lady in the Vieux Carre on Royal Street, and that when Mr. and Mrs. Dakin were away on a trip, this lady, without their prior approval, had their children baptized as Catholics. (Traditionally Dakin is considered to have been Episcopalian; however, I feel that since he designed so many Presbyterian churches, he must, at one time, have been of that faith. His brother Charles, as we shall see later, was most likely a member of the Presbyterian church.) [19] The story fits in well enough with the facts to show that Dakin lived at what is now 811 Conti Street, in what was the boardinghouse of Madame Emilie Armitage, widow of James

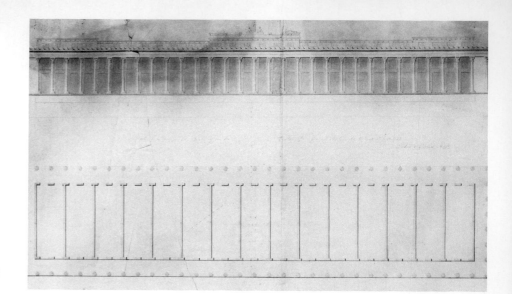

*Drawing of a proposed market for the Canal Street median, by James Dakin, 1837.*

Armitage. For it was she from whom Dakin bought the slave, "Tishy," and her boardinghouse was a block away from Royal Street. At the time, James Dakin was supervising the construction of the Merchant's Exchange on Royal Street, and he would have had but a short walk home to Conti Street.

In addition, baptismal records at St. Louis Cathedral also show that Madame Armitage was the godmother of Dakin's twin girls, and that she brought them to the church on the fourth of July, 1837, when they were baptized. The other godmother is listed as "Mrs. Jane Gallie," who may have been Mrs. James Gallier, although there is no way to be certain of this. One of the godfathers was a man who happened to be in the cathedral for the baptism of his niece which took place that same afternoon, indicating a rather informal preplanning of the ceremony.[20] The family story also checks out in that Mrs. Dakin was definitely in the New York area that summer and fall, where she gave birth to a son, Charles James Dakin, in Middletown Point (now Matawan), New Jersey, on December 14, 1837.

(The Armitage woman was actually Madame Emilie Passebon, having married a Pierre Passebon some years after the death of her first husband, James Armitage. For now, the name Armitage is incidental to our story, but it must be noted here that the marriage record of Emilie and James Armitage shows that he was a native of New York and that his mother's name was Abigail Loyal Armitage—a name which will recur later.)[21]

The residence at 811 Conti Street is still standing, although it has probably been much altered over the years. An 1859 view shows a three-story stuccoed building, with a very high first floor. Today, it is only two stories, but stuccoed, and with the tall first floor. Perhaps a fire in years past caused the pulling down of the upper floor. The house

was strategically located for Dakin, for it was at the rear of property owned by the Samuel Hermann family. The Hermann-Grima House is today one of the showplaces of the French Quarter, and it was the Hermann family for whom Dakin was to do several buildings. He may possibly have made their acquaintance as a neighbor and friend of Madame Armitage, who had lived on Conti Street for years.[22]

At first, it may seem incongruous that Dakin, a northerner (who probably had a Yankee accent when he arrived), would reside in the French Quarter. But at the time, the American section above Canal Street had hardly been developed, and the population of the city was mostly centered in the Quarter. In addition, his last name lent itself to "Frenchification." He was frequently referred to as "D'Aquin," the French pronunciation of his name. To this day, many natives of Baton Rouge still refer to Dakin as "D'Aquin." No letters written by Dakin in French have been found, but in this bilingual area, where the official languages of Louisiana were both English and French almost until the twentieth century, we must presume "Monsieur D'Aquin" became bilingual rather quickly.[23]

In 1837, James Dakin became involved in one of the most audacious ideas ever conceived for New Orleans, one which would surely shock the city planners of today. He himself describes it:

In January, 1837, I was employed to, and did, prepare design and estimates for building stores on the vacant space on the centre of Canal St. from New Levee [N. Peters] St. to Bourbon St., running back five squares from the river—and from the character of the gentlemen engaged in the enterprise, I have no doubt that the buildings would have commenced, had not the commercial crisis of that year appeared too early for the consummation of the enterprise.

The argument then in favor of occupying the vacant space in Canal St. was that the width of Canal St. and its vacant space was a great injury to commercial business, and therefore an incubus upon the city. These arguments were based upon facts and not upon imaginary or speculative foundations. These buildings were to have been 55 feet in depth, leaving seven feet, nine inches for each street.[24]

To achieve their end of erecting buildings in the "neutral ground" of Canal Street, the promoters, who included the noted financier Benjamin Story, requested approval by the Council of the Second Municipality, for an ordinance was passed on January 24, 1837, tabling indefinitely the proposal regarding the center of Canal Street.[25] The issue came up again, and the *Picayune* carried a facetious piece on the subject: "Among all the projects to turn the Neutral Ground or center of Canal St. into some profitable purpose, we do not recall seeing it suggested as a capital place for ten-pin alleys. Let the corporation 'block the game' on all the alleys now in the city, build up a row of them the whole length of Canal St. and then monopolize the income."[26]

Dakin's original drawing for the stores shows a long colonnade with much the same feeling of the French Market on Decatur Street, but in a more decidedly Greek Revival style. The capitals of the peripteral arcade were to be Corinthian, and a course of anthemia, like those ringing the Monument of Lysicrates, ran all around the cornice of the arcade above the entablature. Projecting a few feet above the level of the arcade was a flat roof with two low pedestals at either end and a larger one in the center, on which was to be placed a cluster of statuary. All along the upper edge of this low blocking course ran a row of small patera, accentuating the horizontal lines of the building.[27]

The thought of blocking Canal Street with a building in its median would be shocking to modern city planners, but at the time this was not the main business street of New Orleans. Chartres Street, which paralleled the river, had

that distinction, and it was not until much later that the great, wide Canal Street took over undisputed first place as the center of business. The plan for which Dakin made his drawing was an audacious one, but fortunately for later generations, it never materialized.

Dakin's first opportunity to design a church in New Orleans came with the contract for the Methodist Episcopal Church (now the First Methodist Church) on Poydras at Carondelet Streets, on the uptown-river corner. A building contract was signed by the church on April 21, 1837, with one Andrew H. Clayton for cementing and plastering "according to the plans of Dakin & Dakin, of the church now being erected on Poydras and Carondelet Sts." for $4,380.00. Signing as a witness was James H. Dakin.[28] The only surviving original drawing is marked on its reverse: "Drawing referred to in a contract made the proprietor of the Methodist Church at the corner of Poydras and Carondelet Sts., January 20, 1837." This January contract has not been found and may be presumed to have been a private, unrecorded contract.[29]

The April contract provides the only known description of the interior. There was to be a lecture room, an auditory or main room, with a Corinthian entablature. It was to have a coffered ceiling, with a "large center piece finished to form a vent." There was to be an arch over the pulpit with ornaments on the supporting *antae* and capitals. The cornices and ornamental panels of the breastwork of the galleries were to be of Natchez sand and Thomastown lime. The ceiling of the portico and the frieze of the architrave of the entablature were to be of cement; the basement of material to imitate granite. All other parts were of white marble. Dakin and Dakin were to supervise, and the church was to be finished in six months.

A contract of April 29, 1836 (recorded June 6, 1837) with

Washington Wools and Francis D. Gott was made for the furnishing of lumber for the seats in the auditory. And on June 21, 1837, Gott signed a contract for all the carpenters, joiners, carving and turning work for the church; the contract was for $5,475.00.[30]

The church was completed on time, for the 1838 *City Directory* describes it thus:

The new Methodist Episcopal church located at the corner of Poydras and Carondelet Streets is of the Grecian Doric order, the details of which are copied from the Temple of Theseus at Athens. The facade is in imitation of the first order of Greek Temples, being in the antae the most simple and beautiful arrangement. From the roof and over the pronaos of the temple, rises a large octangular obelisk, resting on a lofty pedestal, of the Egyptian order of architecture, combining a novel grandeur and beauty to be seen in no other similar structure in the Union.

The whole presents a bold and original taste in design. The height of the steeple is 170 feet from the sidewalk. This edifice was erected in the years 1836–37 by Messrs. Dakin & Dakin, architects, at an expense of $50,000.00.[31]

The description was true; the use of Egyptian details made the church unlike any "similar structure in the Union." James Dakin's Egyptian steeple was certainly unique in its marriage with a Greek building. The steeple rose from a low rectangular base, obelisk-like, with battered walls and arranged in two tiers. The lower tier had a small square opening, revealing two truncated Egyptian columns with lotus capitals. Above this tier was another one of slightly smaller circumference, with a square opening like the lower one, but with two full-size Egyptian columns set inside and a winged disc above. Capping off this tier was an Egyptian cavetto cornice. From this tier, an octagonal steeple reached to the sky. Dakin's original drawing of the steeple, in elevation and section, shows it to be of wood and standing 170 feet high.

*First Methodist Church, New Orleans, designed by James Dakin, 1836. Note the Egyptian steeple. (From* Norman's New Orleans)

*Drawing by James Dakin of detail of Egyptian steeple on First Methodist Church, New Orleans. This represents the first major use of Egyptian motifs in New Orleans architecture.*

Despite the glowing praise of the *City Directory*, not everyone liked it. In response to a statement in the Natchez *Free Trader* that the church was "of the pure Doric order of architecture, the only perfect specimen of that order in the United States," one newspaper critic commented: " 'The pure Doric order'! 'The only perfect specimen of that order in the United States.' Is this a fact? If so, we must confess that we know nothing of architecture—and we had the vanity to believe that we knew something about the orders, at least that we knew the difference between ORDER and CONFUSION. To the latter class, the above mentioned church seems to belong, in our estimation." [32]

Which critic was correct? Had Dakin this time gone too far? Earlier, at the Bank of Louisville, he had effectively adapted Egyptian battered walls to the facade. Now, he had grafted whole motifs, blatantly Egyptian, onto a Greek building. Dakin, again striving to avoid the archeological, had produced another creation which, on balance, seems a success. The steeple is rather interesting, and its wide base and the slope of the obelisk tower fit well atop the church. The solidity of its appearance and the restraint with which it was designed almost force one to accept it.

The description of the church as a copy of the Hephaisteion (Thesion) is not correct, for it is at best only based on this temple. Dakin designed it as an *in antis* Doric porch church, using the typical Town and Davis facade. This time, he gave it a double stairway leading up from either side to a wide platform in front of the portico.

Despite the criticism of the church, it made a spectacular addition to the New Orleans skyline. A view of the city, taken not much later, from the river, shows three outstanding objects: Dakin's pylonlike spire of the Methodist church, his dome for the St. Charles Hotel, and the steeple of St. Patrick's Church.[33] For St. Patrick's, Dakin was to

*Proposed Marine Hospital, New Orleans, by Dakin, Bell, and Dakin, 1837. Exterior.*

venture the use of a heavy masonry tower; but at the Methodist church, not yet wishing to chance the weight of brick on the soggy soil of New Orleans, he employed only wood for the steeple.

But the catastrophe which struck the St. Charles Hotel in 1851 was to strike the church as well. The night of the great St. Charles fire, red hot cinders were blown by the wind the three blocks distance to the church, and immediately, the roof was on fire. The newspapers reported: "We never saw a building burn so rapidly as the large Methodist Church at the corner of Poydras and Carondelet. The roof and lofty steeple were all wood, and not slated and old. In at least twelve minutes after the roof caught and a little smoke was first seen, the tall steeple was a burning pile. . . . Nothing now remains of it but the bare walls." [34]

Early in 1837, James Dakin was joined by an old friend from New York, Charles Lagarenne Bell. Like Dakin, Bell had contributed to one of the Lafever books, *The Beauties of Modern Architecture*. In fact, Bell had been a partner of Lafever in 1835, their office being in Clinton Hall, New York, where Dakin also had his office at the same time. Charles Bell succeeded Gallier as the partner of Lafever right after Gallier and Charles Dakin decided to try their luck in the South. Little else is known about Bell. He was a draftsman in New York as early as 1830 and was so listed in the New York directories until 1835, when cited as a partner of Lafever. After a one-year stint with Dakin in 1837, he completely disappears from the scene.

So, in 1837, James Dakin must have felt he had sufficient work for several associates, for Bell was taken in, and the name of the firm changed to Dakin, Bell, and Dakin, Architects.[35] Charles Dakin, then working in Mobile, received third place in the billing, although his Mobile branch was known as Charles Dakin and Brother. Dakin's next job, under the name, Dakin, Bell, and Dakin, was for the Marine Hospital at New Orleans.

The first plan submitted for the hospital was that of Dakin, Bell, and Dakin. Tracings of the original drawings (both originals and tracings are preserved) were forwarded by the local Collector of Customs, James W. Breedlove, to the Secretary of the Treasury, on June 1, 1837. He stated that he was sending "a plan for a suitable edifice," and that the "gentlemen [architects] have made no charge for their work, but rely on the Department for a suitable compensation." It is not known if Dakin was ever paid for this competition drawing. Its main drawback was that Congress had appropriated only $70,000, and the plan called for a much more costly building.[36]

In Dakin's transmittal letter with the plans, he tells Breedlove:

Permit us to observe that in the general arrangement of the plan and exterior of this building, we have followed your views as closely as possible, being convinced they were the best that could be given for this climate.

Strict economy has been studied in the arrangement, dimensions and ornament of the edifice, as was deemed compatible with the purpose, comfort and appearance.

We believe the design embraces every office or room that is required and will accommodate with ease and comfort from two to three hundred patients. The building should be constructed of bricks in such a manner as to render it durable and fire proof, the outbuildings not being shown on the plan.

The entire cost of the erection of this building will be from $125,000 to $150,000, according to the present prices of building in this city, which at all times are very fluctuating.[37]

Thus, Dakin's designs were for a building he knew would cost at least double the appropriation. He obviously had confidence that Congress would get around to appropriating more funds for this purpose.

It would have been a handsome building. Basically U-shaped, it appeared to be closed across the front of the U. However, the front consisted of a colonnaded breezeway, open through the colonnade, permitting light and air to enter into a rectangular garden forming a patio in the center. The hospital was Greek Revival, three stories high, with an Ionic colonnade across the front and two shallow projecting pavilions at each end of the facade. Set in these pavilions were two Ionic columns, arranged *in antis* and rising from the second floor level to the entablature. The building was flat roofed, and from its center rose a small dome supported by a colonnade resting on a wide drum. It was in the same vein as the St. Charles Hotel dome, but with more emphasis on the vertical rather than the horizontal lines. The original drawing of the front elevation is exquisitely detailed, with flowers and birds visible in the garden through the openings in the breezeway.

Despite Dakin's claim that it was designed for the climate, the inner walls facing the patio lacked sufficient galleries which would have enabled the sick to be wheeled outside for fresh air. The winning design, by Robert Mills, featured these galleries; Dakin's plan would have provided only the breezeway and the colonnade across the front for this purpose. Mills's plan, as executed, was in the castellated Gothic style, three stories high. The original Mills drawings have not been found, but a plan of his in 1837, following the same general shape of the building, is in the Greek Revival style, so that it is possible that other architects may have changed it to Gothic.

Congress, instead of funding the $70,000 appropriated, provided only $30,000 because of the Panic of 1837, and the building began to deteriorate in its incomplete state.[38] By the time it was finally finished in 1849, the total cost was $122,772.70, about as much as Dakin had projected. It is

unfortunate that Dakin's plan, modified with the addition of more galleries, was not accepted. Much anguish would have been saved and many more years of use would have resulted, for the building was constantly deteriorating. The first floor was frequently unusable because of dampness, and once a break in the Mississippi levee flooded the area. By the time of the Civil War, it had been abandoned entirely.[39]

Dakin continued designing one public building after another in the New Orleans area. His next project was the proposed new city hall. Today, of course, only "Gallier Hall" is remembered, the building erected by James Gallier in 1850. Few recall that James Dakin designed its predecessor thirteen years before, which was never built because of lack of funds following the 1837 panic.

On February 7, 1837, the Council of the Second Municipality (that is, the American section of New Orleans) passed an ordinance calling for the selection of a committee to choose a plan for a municipal hall at St. Charles and Hevia (now Lafayette) Streets.[40] On March 28, 1837, an ordinance accepting a plan by Dakin, Bell, and Dakin was passed, with the architects to supervise the construction.[41] It is not known if Gallier or anyone else competed for the job. On June 5, 1837, a building contract was signed.[42]

A contemporary guide book (1840), the *Historical Epitome*, described the plans:

The designs for this splendid edifice were made by Messrs. Dakin & Dakin [*sic*], approved by the Council of the Second Municipality ... and a contract made with the architects for its erection. ... It will·be of the Corinthian order, and the material of white marble. It is to have an 80 foot front, by 170 feet in depth, and will contain all the public offices of the Second Municipality, together with the Commercial Library, and two spacious armories for volunteer companies [of militia]. The roof is to be surmounted by an elegant cupola of circular form 150 feet in height, and when the whole is

*Drawing of City Hall, New Orleans, Dakin, Bell, and Dakin, 1837.*
*Longitudinal section.*

completed, it will rank in the first class of Municipal Architecture and will be surpassed by no other example extant. The entire cost is estimated at $200,000.[43]

Dakin's original drawings survive to bear out this description. The longitudinal section is one of the most highly detailed of all Dakin drawings, for it even includes paintings hanging on the walls of the third floor depicting various scenes in Louisiana history. The mayor's chamber is equally detailed, complete with desk and a flag above. This is a display of some of Dakin's finest art work and ranks with his plates for Fay's *Views in New York.*[44]

The cupola rises from a low drum, ascending in two colonnaded tiers, topped off with a small dome surmounted by a lantern. The interior of the dome, which is lacunar, is reached by a spiral staircase rising from the basement floor. The rotunda opening pierces the entire building and was designed to be supported on immense triangular spread footings, necessary because of its great height and weight. The opening for light in the rotunda through a small skylight under the lantern is quite small in diameter, about one fourth of the total rotunda circumference. Dakin was apparently not always consistent in his insistence on large quantities of natural lighting. It is also worth noting that the cupola and rotunda beneath are placed in a rather unusual position—not in dead center, which might be expected, but about three fourths of the distance back from the front portico.

Other plans exist which are apparently studies and variations on the same idea. A floor plan shows the whole building on a great plinth, with the rotunda in the center. Still another appears to be an optional cruciform plan if much more space were desired. Most are unsigned, and it is difficult to determine if they are actually for the New Orleans city hall, although they appear to be.

The project for the erection of this magnificent building went down the drain, however, in the Panic of 1837, for on May 26, 1841, the city of New Orleans, with its coffers empty, passed an ordinance releasing Dakin, Bell, and Dakin from their agreement to superintend the erection of the building. It also paid them the sum of five hundred dollars for their plans, copies of which the city retained, perhaps to be used again in the future.[45]

By 1845, the municipality felt able to proceed with the hall, and an ordinance of April 30, 1845, approved a plan by James Gallier.[46] It is not known if a competition was held this time, and it would be pure speculation to say that the earlier Dakin plan, bought and paid for by the city, influenced Gallier's design. Gallier's plan was Ionic, Dakin's Corinthian. Gallier utilized a projecting portico, Dakin a fully colonnaded porch. Gallier's plan did not have the luxury of a cupola or a rotunda space beneath, but it did have a central hall with much the same layout of offices. This plan, however, seems a natural one and not necessarily a copy of the Dakin design.

## JAMES DAKIN AND THE AMERICAN INSTITUTION OF ARCHITECTS

James Dakin, although now a great distance away from his old New York partner, Alexander Jackson Davis, maintained contact with him in the late 1830s. Dakin was to visit with Davis in New York on several trips he made to the East. Evidencing the cordiality that still existed between these two men and the personal esteem that Dakin had for Davis, is a letter from Dakin dated May 6, 1838. In it Dakin recommends a young student of architecture, Abram Vanamburgh, to Davis. Referring to Davis as "the most accomplished artist in the Union in your profession," Dakin asks that Davis do what he can to help young Vanamburgh.[47]

# 6
# CHARLES DAKIN
# IN MOBILE

IT WILL BE RECALLED THAT EARLY IN THE PARTNERSHIP OF Dakin and Dakin, Charles Dakin went to Mobile to open a branch office in that city. While James Dakin was establishing the firm in New Orleans with numerous public and private buildings, Charles was finding similar success in Mobile.

Thoughts of what the new year might bring, and hopes of success in a new venture must have filled the mind of Charles Dakin as he stood on the deck of the steam packet *South Alabama,* looking out on the moonlit waters of the Gulf of Mexico. It was the night of New Year's Eve, 1835, and he had just left his brother in New Orleans, bound for Mobile, where he was about to open the office of Charles Dakin and Brother, Architects.[1]

It was a big step for the twenty-four-year-old architect, and he surely must have felt excited on that bright, clear night. In his young life, he had already been a draftsman in the noted Town and Davis firm in New York and a partner of the well-known Gallier; and he was now to be a full partner of his illustrious brother James. To top it off, the branch was to bear his name: Charles Dakin and Brother, Architects.

Under the management of Charles, the Mobile branch of Dakin and Dakin was destined to be a thriving operation, rivaling the New Orleans branch in importance. It was to include among its achievements a bank, two hotels, a church—maybe two, with one in part by Gallier—a hospital, and many other buildings, public and private.

Up to now, the only source of information on the Dakins' operation in Mobile was James Gallier's autobiography. Charles Dakin's account book and further research now demonstrate that Gallier's version of their activities in Mobile was greatly deficient and, in part, entirely wrong. He incorrectly states that the two brothers practiced for a

year or so before Charles went to Mobile, and as we have seen, Charles left almost immediately after James's arrival in New Orleans. Of Charles's practice in Mobile, Gallier says that "among other business he [Charles] made a contract to build a range of brick stores and warehouses; but whether from the want of sufficient experience as a builder or proper care in the construction, the whole range of buildings tumbled down while the roofs were being put on; this misfortune so preyed upon the spirits of the poor fellow that, happening to take a severe cold, a rapid disease of the lungs followed, which carried him off in little more than a year."[2]

Gallier glosses over the Dakins' "other business" in Mobile, a business which included the long list of important works just mentioned. One of the Dakin-designed hotels was considered—mistakenly, but not by much—by a traveler to be the largest in the world. And Gallier's version of the collapse of a warehouse is extremely misleading. At best, it is a half-truth. As we shall see later, a collapse did occur while a minor commercial building was under construction, but it had no adverse effect on Charles Dakin's health or his reputation. The mishap occurred less than a year after Charles' arrival and before most of the best Dakin buildings were started or completed. Perhaps Gallier was badly misinformed or had forgotten the true story in the half-blind state he was in when he wrote his memoirs. Whatever the reason, his account has certainly not helped the Dakins' reputation.

Returning to the arrival of Charles Dakin in Mobile, the month which followed was one of preparation and making arrangements with the local craftsmen to erect the two buildings left over from the Gallier and Dakin partnership, Barton Academy and the Government Street Presbyterian Church. It is possible to assemble a very detailed picture of

Charles Dakin's activities because his account or receipt book, which has recently been found, serves as a kind of journal for the construction of the Dakin and Dakin buildings in Mobile.[3]

The first entry is dated February 13, 1836, and significantly, a receipt is signed by Thomas James for "work by me on the . . . Presbyterian Church." It has been common practice in Alabama reference books, up to a few years ago, to credit the church and Barton Academy to Thomas James of Mobile. How this myth got started is not known, but it appears that "tradition" has always credited James with the work. His name recurs many times in the Dakin account book, for he was the chief bricklayer and contractor for many of the Dakin buildings, but he was not the architect, as proclaimed by various histories and reference works on Alabama.

Besides starting the church in February, 1836, Charles also began construction on Barton Academy, located about three blocks west of the church on Government Street. The first entry in the account book for the school is also dated February 13, 1836, and Thomas James is again the recipient of the money.

Before the year was over, Charles Dakin had started at least fifteen other buildings. He must have spent much of each day just running about checking the progress of each and approving partial payments to the craftsmen as the work progressed. Charles did seem to have an assistant named Cary Butt for a time in 1837. Fifteen buildings would appear to be an extraordinary number for one architectural firm to begin in one year in a city the size of Mobile, but in 1846, this area was one of the most booming in the South.

Mobile was strategically located on the Gulf of Mexico from whence ships could ply between the other southern ports and sail on to the eastern seaboard. Lumber and naval stores made up a great proportion of its commerce, as did the ubiquitous product of the South, cotton. It is logical that Mobile was the financial center of Alabama, although not its political capital. The 1830s were boom years there, just as in the rest of the South.[4]

The 1830s boom spawned one of the great figures in Alabama history, its first millionaire, and one of the most dauntless entrepreneurs of his day, Henry Hitchcock. He was to call on the Dakins time and again for designs for his businesses. And he was a major contributor to the first two buildings which Charles undertook in Mobile, Barton Academy and the Government Street Presbyterian Church.

This church is an excellent example of the *distyle in antis* Greek Revival church as developed in the Town and Davis office. Two Ionic columns stand in a recessed portico, which is flanked on either side by three square pilasters on the facade. The windowless front creates a massive, yet elegant appearance.[5]

Because of the excellent state of preservation of the Government Street church, viewing its interior is an exhilarating experience; upon entering the church, one immediately finds himself surrounded by some of the finest detailing of the Greek Revival era in America. The church is the most intact example of the "Dakin finish" remaining, with the possible exception of the Bank of Louisville, which also has been relatively untampered with. Entering the church, one is greeted with the sight of the imposing reredos, shaped like the facade of a temple, having battered walls similar to the Bank of Louisville, and with a course of anthemia on its cornice like those of the Choragic Monument of Lysicrates. In a recess in the reredos stand four Corinthian columns supporting a large entablature with dentils and the course of anthemia on top.

*Government Street Presbyterian Church, Mobile, designed by Gallier and Charles Dakin, built by Charles Dakin, 1836-37. Interior. (Courtesy Library of Congress)*

The side balconies are decorated on their faces with motifs obviously derived from Plate 48 of Lafever's *Beauties of Modern Architecture*. That is, they are supported on columns with capitals based on the Tower of the Winds, having a small patera set on the abacus facing inward toward the congregation. A band of Greek key fretwork runs around the face of the galleries which are similar to, but not exactly copied from, the Lafever plate. A copy of the *Beauties of Modern Architecture* was recently located in New Orleans, signed "Charles B. Dakin, Mobile, Ala.," indicating that Charles probably used this book in preparing the final details for the galleries.[6]

The cornices of the interior walls are treated like an entablature. Three courses of moulding of increasing thickness are set beneath a course of dentils and small patera. In all, six courses of moulding lead the eye upward to the glorious unsupported ceiling, deeply coffered in a diagonal pattern, containing additional moulding within the coffers. The whole effect on the viewer is one of great detail, yet with a justness of scale and deployment which imparts a feeling of restraint. While this detail is not obtrusive, one cannot help but be conscious of the great inspiration of its design as well as the fine workmanship which executed it.

Advertisements for the material and workmen for the church were run in the Mobile papers starting on December 2, 1835, ending with the sentence: "The specifications and drawings can be seen at the office of the Mobile Steam Cotton Press & Building Co. Signed: H. Hitchcock, J. E. Collins, Building Committee." [7] The Mobile Steam Cotton Press Company was a Hitchcock enterprise, indicating that he was, in fact, the ramrod for the erection of the church, and it is to him that most of the credit belongs.

The date of the advertisement indicates that some plans were already available for the workmen to inspect by De-

cember 2, 1835. This date was during the interim period between the arrival of James Dakin in New Orleans on November 17 and the copartnership agreement between the Dakins on December 24, 1835, with the uncertain status in between. It is consequently impossible to determine what portion of the design was left over from the Gallier and Dakin partnership and what was by the Dakin brothers.

It may be significant to note here that Gallier is not known to have worked in the Egyptian style, while Dakin did so on several occasions during this period—the prison in Havana, the Bank of Louisville, and the First Methodist Church in New Orleans. Thus, the Egyptianesque reredos of the Government Street Presbyterian Church is most probably from Dakin's drawing board. It would appear, then, that credit for the interior of the church more than likely belongs to Dakin and Dakin, and for the exterior to Gallier and Dakin.

The Charles Dakin account book is extremely valuable to those seeking some knowledge of the craftsmen who were capable of erecting such a highly finished building in so remote a place as Mobile. The book, for example, shows that Thomas James received most of the funds expended on the building, having been paid $40,188 of a total cost said to be about $60,000. An "R. J. Barnes" also received a large sum. Granite for the church was receipted for on September 26, 1836, having arrived on the brig *Comet,* and on November 10, 1836, freight was paid for on "joiners work" brought in from New York on the ship *St. John.* Stone cutting work by Neal and Davis, who set the front steps, was paid for on December 26, 1836. The roof was tinned by Belknap and Eldridge in the same month. Martin and Tufsella were paid for "copeing the rear walls" on March 30, 1837; and the cost of the "arca[de] steps and portico flagging" was paid to Neal and Davis in March, 1837. Extra painting was done in

July, 1837, and the "replacing of crown moulding on the North end of the building displaced by wind [a hurricane?]" by Pomeroy and Shannon, on November 23, 1837.[8]

We can see from this account book that some parts of the building were imported by boat from New York and that some were made on the spot by local craftsmen. Even with the drafting skills of the Dakins, plus the graphic help of the Lafever book, it is amazing that artisans in an out of the way place like Mobile were sufficiently skilled to provide the high degree of finish necessary for this complicated building.

The church was completed in the summer of 1837. Church records show that on March 24, 1837, a committee was appointed "to secure the completion of the new church by April 9 for purposes of public worship."[9] And on June 1, a newspaper article said that the pews were being rented and that "it is a beautiful building. When the exterior is completed to correspond in neatness to the interior, it will be an ornament to the city."[10]

It must have been almost ready for use a little earlier than April 9, for on March 22, 1837, Charles Dakin was married there to Caroline Belcher. The church records spell his name "Daiken" and show Caroline's name as "Caroline Webb," but it is known that her last name was Belcher. Family tradition says that she was a widow (apparently of a man named Webb) and the younger sister of James Dakin's wife.[11] Unfortunately, no notices of the marriage have been found in the Mobile or New Orleans newspapers to clear up these inconsistencies. However, it must have given young Charles Dakin great satisfaction to be married in his own church, one of the great creations of the Greek Revival era.

One of the most important of the European travelers in this country, J. S. Buckingham, visited Mobile in March, 1839, and described the church this way:

Of churches, the Presbyterian is the largest and most beautiful. Its exterior is not in the best taste, but its interior is unsurpassed in chasteness of style and elegance of decoration in the United States. There is a singular, but at the same time, a very happy union of the Egyptian and Greek in the elevated platform, answering the purposes of the pulpit; and the semi-Theban and semi-Corinthian portico [reredos], which seems to rise behind the platform, with the rich diagonally-indented ceiling, and luxurious sofa-like pews, make this interior altogether the most strikingly beautiful I ever remember to have seen.[12]

Only one major change to the church has been made, and that, unintentional. A steeple which originally adorned the church was blown down in a hurricane in 1852. After some deliberation, the church decided not to re-erect it. The church, which is still in use, remains otherwise just as Charles Dakin left it in 1837, a monument to his and his brother's skill, and to the Mobile craftsmen who built it.

The other building left over from the Gallier and Dakin partnership was Barton Academy. Gallier, of course, had a hand in the design—how much is unknown—but Charles Dakin built it. It still stands on Government Street, located not far from the Presbyterian church. The account book of Charles Dakin and Brother is filled with entries regarding the school, again negating the reference books which attribute the school to Thomas James. As in the case of the church, James was merely one of the contractors.

The earliest reference to the building is an advertisement run on December 2, 1835, the same date as that of the Presbyterian church, asking for proposals from carpenters, bricklayers, and other workmen for "a public schoolhouse to be completed by October 1, 1836." The building committee included Henry Hitchcock, Willis Roberts, J. K. Collins, and G. Mordecai, the first three being officers of the Government Street Presbyterian Church.[13]

Thus, Henry Hitchcock was again in the forefront of a

movement to uplift the quality of community life in Mobile. The specifications for the building were available for inspection at the office of his Mobile Steam Cotton Press and Building Company. Hitchcock and Silas Dinsmore are said to have raised most of the funds for the erection of the school. The school derives its name from Willoughby Barton, the man who drafted the legislative bill creating the board of school commissioners for Mobile County.

The building is three stories high, with a portico supported by six Ionic columns, the columns rising from the level of the second floor. Two end pavilions project forward with four massive square pilasters reaching from the ground level to the entablature, which is decorated with mouldings of various widths. The Dakins seemed to revel in the use of mouldings, and the tastefulness of their application seems to have come naturally to them.

Perhaps the most outstanding feature of the building is its dome. It can best be described as a Dakin dome, for it is clearly patterned after the one James Dakin designed for the St. Charles Hotel in New Orleans. It is rather large in relation to the size of the school and reposes on a large, square drum. A ring of twenty-four Ionic columns supports the graceful dome topped by a lantern based on the Choragic Monument of Lysicrates. The dome still stands out on the skyline of Mobile, its beautiful appearance unmatched by any contemporary building there.

This building remained in use as a school until 1965, when it was converted to a school administration building. As happened with most large public buildings during and after the Civil War, Barton was taken over by federal troops after the fall of Mobile in 1865 and used as a hospital. Sometime before 1885, an iron balcony was added under the portico on the third floor level. That it was not in the original plans (which have never been found) is evidenced

*Barton Academy, Mobile, designed by Gallier and Charles Dakin, erected by Charles Dakin, 1835-38.*

by an illustration of the academy on the 1838 *La Tourette* map of Mobile which shows no balcony. By 1909, the dome supports had become unsafe, and a contract for $1,540 was signed to correct this. In 1914, the entire building was redone and enlarged. Projecting wings were added on the sides in the same style, so that they fit comfortably and make logical extensions for expansion. The architects for this work were Stevens and Nelson of New Orleans.[14]

In 1968, $1.8 million was appropriated to completely restore Barton's. The dome, sagging again, was to be lifted to its original level, the drum supporting it to be refinished from its stove-black color to conform to the rest of the structure, and the interior walls peeled to determine how the interior may have looked years ago. The architects for this restoration are Dillon March and Nicholas Holmes of Mobile.[15]

Henry Hitchcock was again to be responsible for the erection of a great Mobile building and he was again to ask the Dakins to build it. With the boom of the 1830s expected to continue indefinitely, it was clear that the busy port of Mobile was bringing in more travelers and businessmen than its small hotels could accomodate. James and Charles Dakin were to design for Hitchcock a great hotel known as the United States Hotel (Plate 6), or more popularly, the Government Street Hotel, because of its location on Government and Royal Streets.

In 1836, when it was begun, only the St. Charles Hotel in New Orleans, designed earlier by Gallier and Dakin, and the Tremont House in Boston, designed by Isaiah Rogers, were in the same league insofar as American hotels went. The United States Hotel, which occupied a half block at Government and Royal, was built on land acquired by the Mobile Steam Cotton Press and Building Company from Henry Hitchcock; the parcel of land measured 147 feet on

Government Street by 133 feet on Royal. Only the St. Charles Hotel in New Orleans was larger.[16]

The United States Hotel was Greek Revival, but again the Dakins created a new design from the Greek forms, basing it on the 1832 plan mentioned earlier from the Town, Davis, and Dakin era. The St. Charles seemed prosaic by comparison because of the St. Charles's use of the traditional central portico and pediment. For their Mobile hotel, James and Charles Dakin used no pediment, designing instead a flat-roofed building with an *in antis* porch extending from the second to the fifth (and top) floor. Four great Corinthian columns in the recess were flanked by three square pilasters with capitals suggesting the Doric order. The ground floor facade was smooth and stark, unornamented except by the interplay of openings for doors clustered in pairs, four on either side of a slightly larger door in the center, obviously the main entrance.[17]

The flat roof was crowned with a blocking course, but in a central area over the recessed porch was placed a sculpture group. There were three figures of unknown identity, two huddled low at either side of a central figure kneeling with his back to the facade of the building.

Above all this rose a magnificent dome, again based on Barton Academy and the St. Charles Hotel. This one was rather low and squat, colonnaded with about thirty-two slender columns and a row of anthemia. Atop the dome sat a small lantern.

The flanks of the hotel also utilized the same motifs of the front—three square pilasters, with the central section set back a few inches to repeat the feeling of the void of the *in antis* porch in front. A most unusual bit of decoration relieved the starkness of the sides. Dakin gave the central recessed section a huge two-story Greek "ear" entrance doorway. Because it was two stories high, it was pierced by

*Drawing of the United States Hotel, Mobile, by Charles and James Dakin, 1836.*

two windows on the second story, and a doorway opened to the first floor. It gave a pleasing touch, one which emphasized the great height of the building and increased the monumental effect of the whole.[18]

Charles Dakin's account book reveals that he began the hotel on July 30, 1836, just a month after the land was acquired. Again, his number one contractor was Thomas James. An entry shows that in January, 1837, casks of "hydraulic cement" were used in the construction, indicating the use of the latest types of materials. Cast iron was used in part, for an entry of May 16, 1837, shows payment for eight cast iron stairs weighing 1,280 pounds. The total in the account book for the hotel comes to $100,471.55 for materials and labor only, so that the whole building probably cost about $200,000 or more. But the hotel was destined never to be completed. The account book shows a steady flow of entries prior to May, 1837, then only a handful.[19]

It was nonetheless sufficiently complete to impress the English traveler J. S. Buckingham, who said, "One of the most splendid of all the public edifices is the Government-street hotel, which when finished, will be much larger, and certainly much handsomer than either the Astor House at New York, the Tremont House at Boston [both by Isaiah Rogers], or the American Hotel at Buffalo, the three largest and handsomest at present in the Union." Buckingham had not yet visited New Orleans and seen the St. Charles; when he did he corrected his judgment and called it the largest—which it was—but his comparison with the other great hotels leaves no doubt that the two biggest were the United States Hotel in Mobile by Dakin and Dakin and the St. Charles Hotel by Gallier and Dakin.[20]

Among the many other starts of new buildings by Charles Dakin in Mobile in 1836 were: a house for William Edwards on the northwest corner of Eslava and St. Emanuel Streets; a commercial building on the south side of the theater on St. Emanuel Street; a house on the north side of the theater; the Neptune Fire House; and six houses for the Gordon Land Company on Conception Street. (This may have been what was known as "Widow's Row.")

And the ubiquitous Henry Hitchcock kept Dakin busy with several more commissions—stores on Government, St. Francis, Water, and St. Michael Streets. The biggest of these smaller buildings was Hitchcock's cotton press buildings. These took six months to build and must have been rather substantial. Unfortunately, no views have survived.[21]

It was during this same period—1836—that the incident of the fallen building occurred. Charles Dakin began a structure containing six stores on the northwest corner of Water and St. Michael Streets in July, 1836. He probably should have gotten Thomas James to be his contractor, for on November 12, 1836, we find an entry in his journal for "clearing rubbish" and on December 15, for "hauling timber from the fallen buildings." On November 6, three of the stores collapsed and, according to the newspapers, "The destruction is complete; hardly one brick remains upon the other. The remainder of the row must, it is feared, be taken down."[22]

That Charles Dakin was not considered responsible for this incident is evidenced by the amount of business that he received for the next two or three years in Mobile—hotels, banks, residences. Nor was there any adverse personal reaction immediately after the event (this was certainly the time to feel the discouragement Gallier erroneously describes), for just five days later, we find his name in the newspaper among those Mobilians attending a meeting in support of Martin Van Buren as the Democratic candidate for president.[23] On December 17, 1836, a month afterward, his account book shows an entry for the purchase of season tickets to the theater. A little later, on December 29, 1836, his account book shows a purchase of military uniforms. Charles had apparently just joined the Mobile Guards, a local militia unit, because among the entries regarding Barton Academy, we find the notation of a draft "in full of all demand by the Mobile Guards on C. B. Dakin." None of these are actions of a man whose spirits were as dejected as Gallier's account suggested. Charles, in reality, married and prospered for three years more before his early death.

In 1836, Charles Dakin built a hospital for Dr. Henry S. LeVert, the foremost doctor in Mobile. Unfortunately, nothing more is known of his hospital except that it was on the corner of Government and Broad Streets, that it was begun October 24, 1836, and finished exactly a year later.[24]

Also late in 1836, Charles began another hotel, this one called the Royal and St. Michael Street Hotel. A drawing in the Dakin collection seems to be of this hotel. It is signed "C. B. Dakin & Bro," and is the only drawing in existence signed by Charles Dakin or, to be more accurate, by his office. This fact, plus several drawings by James Dakin of what appear to be Mobile buildings, indicate that the older brother did most of the plans for the Mobile office and sent them over for Charles to execute.[25]

The Royal and St. Michael Street Hotel was rather severe in its simplicity. Four stories high, it had a flat roof with dentils under the cornice and a first floor relieved in its starkness only by a small portico with two Doric columns. Much the same feeling is obtained from the Merchants Exchange on Royal Street in New Orleans. Another Dakin touch was the design of windows in the top floor shorter than those on the lower floors, creating an optical illusion of greater height. Dakin used this concept repeatedly.

The hotel was later given a less prosaic name, the Lafayette House. It was damaged considerably by fire in March of 1845; and it appears to have been extensively remodeled, for in later years the office of the Mobile *Press-Register* was on that corner, and old photographs show a much changed building.[26]

The Royal and St. Michael Street Hotel was not a great one, certainly not in the class with the United States Hotel, but it was a good, functional building. It demonstrates the fact that the Dakins could give a client an inexpensive, serviceable building as well as an elaborate and costly one.

The last major building in Mobile begun by the Dakins was the Planters and Merchants Bank on the northeast corner of Royal and Conti Streets. The site was acquired on May 31, 1836, and its location was selected to placate a group of businessmen who had fought in vain to have a branch of the Bank of the State of Alabama located in the lower part of Mobile, that is, below Dauphin Street. This area was rapidly being developed and one of the growing pains of the blossoming city was the location of the banking center in the upper part of Mobile. William Brantley says the businessmen "satisfied their desires by placing the glamorous Planters & Merchants Bank on Royal and south of Dauphin."[27]

Glamorous it was. We have a verbal description from a Mobile newspaper:

The new and splendid edifice of the Planters & Merchants Bank is just completed, and is open today [May 10, 1838] for the first time for the transaction of business. The building, though not faultless, is a superb one in finish and architectural arrangement. The massive front Portico, and the side view of Conti St. afford as fine and impressive a *tout ensemble* as we have ever seen. The Dome which is fortunately for the view not visible on these two sides, is awkward and ungainly, and the observatory on its apex, which is of itself very pretty, is disproportioned to the cumber-

*Probably a drawing of the Planters and Merchants Bank, Mobile, designed by Charles and James Dakin, 1837.*

some globe which supports it. The Banking room and the entrance to it are very beautiful, and the marble pavement, the fluted columns, supporting a concave ceiling, the massive panelling, mahogany counters and fretted ceiling, give it an air of solidity and substance which is very striking. The building is an ornament to the city.[28]

It appears that this commentator was not attuned to the new mode of placing low domes on Greek Revival structures. A. J. Davis had been criticized earlier for this deviation from "pure" Greek principles; but when done well, as he and others did, it could be effective.[29] The only known views of the bank show a very pleasing design. One view, taken from a portion of a Fire Department Association Membership Certificate done in 1860, may be suspect for its accuracy, for an entry in Charles Dakin's account book seems to contradict the picture. The entry records a payment for "building a pediment over the front columns," whereas the illustration indicates a flat roof. But the entry could have been written so hurriedly that Dakin meant entablature instead of pediment.[30]

Another possible view which follows closely the Firemen's Certificate illustration is a drawing by James Dakin. It shows an unpedimented building with a low dome topped by a small lantern. The facade however, consists of two square columns set *in antis*, rather than fully colonnaded as in the Certificate. The truth of what the bank really looked like probably lies somewhere in between these descriptions, with the 1860 view probably based on a hazy memory and the Dakin plan somewhat modified in their Mobile office.

Charles Dakin's account book shows the first entry for the bank on September 2, 1837, and the later ones include payment for such items as fifty-seven tons of granite, twenty-four tons of granite from another load, mahogany

*Planters and Merchants Bank, left, and United States Hotel, right, during the great fire of 1839 which destroyed both of these Dakin and Dakin buildings. Center structure is the Mansion House Hotel, also destroyed in the fire. (Courtesy Caldwell Delany, Curator, Mobile City Museum)*

*A photograph of Christ Church Episcopal, Mobile.*

mantles, and many other materials. The last entry is dated January 17, 1838, and it is known that the bank opened on May 10, 1838.[31]

Moving from those buildings known to be by the Dakins to a probable one, there is a massive Doric church in Mobile which evidence shows to be almost surely by them. The first non-Catholic church in Mobile, Christ Church Episcopal, at St. Emanuel and Church Streets, was built in 1838 and 1839 from plans originally drawn up in 1835 and revised later in the actual construction for reasons of size. On November 30, 1835, a committee charged with obtaining plans for a new church reported: "They have selected the design, from many which they have received, to present to the option of this general meeting, the first of which is that of a Gothic building. . . . The second design . . . is that of a Grecian Doric building 70 feet front by 196 feet deep, with a bell tower 109 feet from the doorsteps."[32]

No architect was mentioned; however, everything points to the Dakins. The committee obviously went to New Orleans, the only place from which they could have obtained "many" plans. It was in November that James Dakin had arrived in New Orleans and Charles had split with Gallier. Charles was well known in Mobile from his and Gallier's plans for the Mobile City Hall, Barton Academy, and the Government Street Presbyterian Church. And it is likely that Henry Hitchcock (who had been a member of this congregation prior to becoming Presbyterian) had influenced the thinking of the church committeemen in favor of the Dakins.

The style of the building points with certainty to a New York architect. The *in antis* portico, the "pilastrades" down the sides, and the Davisean windows are all out of Town, Davis and Dakin. It is highly unlikely that any but a New York-trained architect could have designed a church with all these new features. Significantly, Gallier does *not* claim the church in his autobiography.

A building contract for the church has been found, dated August 6, 1838, naming one Cary W. Butt as architect.[33] Butt's name appears in a cryptic entry in Charles Dakin's account book for October 4, 1837, in the form of a payment to Charles Dakin and Brother by a draft drawn in favor of Cary Butt. It reads:

| C. B. Dakin & Bro. | T. J. M. Sumwalt & Co. | |
|---|---|---|
| May 15,1837 | To paper | 1.00 |
| | To J. M. Sumwalt bill | 42.75 |
| | | 43.75 |

Mobile, Oct. 4—Rec'd payment
by draft, favor C. W. Butt [34]

The identity or significance of the Sumwalt firm is not known, but because Charles Dakin and Brother were paid by a draft in favor of Butt, and drawing paper was obviously involved, it would appear that Butt was employed in 1837 or earlier as a draftsman in the Charles Dakin office.

An entry in the Christ Church records shows that besides the $150 paid to Butt on April 20, 1840, as architect, one Frederick Bunnell was paid $160 the same day for "plans."[35] The latter may have been drawings required as the work progressed. It was necessary to re-draw the original plans, because the size of the church had been reduced from the 70- by 196-foot dimensions to only 62 by 90. But why Butt did not do all the revised drawings is not certain. Perhaps he was more a "clerk of the works" or supervising architect and Bunnell a draftsman.

Butt's credentials are hard to come by. The Mobile *City Directory* for 1837 (the earliest for the city) lists the Dakins in the body of the text as "C. B. Dakin & Bro., Architects, South side of Government St., fifth from Royal," and "Charles B. Dakin and James H. Dakin, composing the firm of Dakin & Bro." Butt is not listed in the front of the book, but is added in the Appendix as "Cary W. Butt, Architect and Builder, St. Emanuel St.," which would indicate that he may have left the Dakins late in the year.[36] Butt is listed in the 1839 directory, but not the Dakins, for they had closed their Mobile office by then; Charles was not even in the United States. Although Butt appears again in the 1842 directory (as does Bunnell), very little else is known about him except that he once owned a fine brick residence still standing at 256 State Street.[37] Thus it appears more than likely that Butt was not the architect for the original Christ Church plans of 1835, and the bulk of evidence suggests that Charles and James Dakin should be credited with Christ Church.

The church had an elliptical ceiling—another favorite Dakin device—which unfortunately was destroyed in a fierce hurricane on September 26, 1906.[38] The church voted not to replace the steeple which had fallen into the church and destroyed the ceiling. Certain other minor changes were made at this time, but Christ Church still stands, its exterior looking much the same as when it was built.

With growing prosperity all around him in Mobile and get-rich-quick schemes succeeding in the boom period of the 1830s, it is inconceivable that Charles Dakin, probably goaded by James, would not have tried to make his fortune too. The Mobile courthouse records are filled with transactions of speculation in land by Charles Dakin and Brother. Having so many business contacts from their enormous practice, they must have confidently charged ahead full speed. Charles lost no time after his arrival; his first purchase was made on June 7, 1836. Perhaps the biggest

speculation of the brothers was a title or, more properly, a "right" to land formerly submerged most of the time beneath the Mobile River, which was gradually changing its course. These were known as "water lots," and their titles were hotly contested in the courts for years by the federal government and the city of Mobile. It cost Dakin $50,000 for a one-third interest in this land, the title of which was clouded at best. Most of the other investments lost money for the Dakins, and they were not to capitalize on the boom atmosphere. The Panic of 1837 was to eliminate all hope of that.

The Panic was a cataclysm the like of which this country has seldom seen since, except perhaps in 1929. Business in Mobile literally ceased in April, 1837. The banks suspended payment in specie and everyone's notes were worthless, including the many that Charles Dakin had out on his land speculation. Notes given to him in turn, by his building customers which he used to pay his craftsmen or for building materials, were all suddenly just pieces of paper.

Henry Hitchcock, the Dakin's best client and the richest man in Alabama, went broke. He tried desperately to work out of his troubles—the story is told beautifully and in detail by his biographer, William Brantley—but despite some initial success, his fortune was to go down the drain. And he was to take the Dakins with him.[39]

By 1839, Mobile was a town just going through the motions of existence. The banks were all tied up, their specie—those that had any left—was suspended, and the worst was yet to come! That summer was to see the most terrible yellow fever epidemic yet to hit Mobile. Judge Hitchcock had been making progress in obtaining forebearance from his bankers on his obligations when, on August 5, 1839, he was stricken with the fever and died. His vast and complicated fortunes, on whom hundreds, perhaps thousands depended, were left ensnarled.[40] All work on the buildings the Dakins were doing for him had already stopped because of the Panic; Hitchcock's death meant they would never be resumed.

Yet the fever seemed nothing compared to what was to follow. In October, 1839, two great fires swept across Mobile, wiping out most of the business section of the city. On October 7, incendiaries set a fire which burned or ruined twelve square blocks. And finally, on October 9, another fire burned most of the principal buildings of Mobile; the unfinished United States Hotel, the Royal and St. Michael Street Hotel, the Planters and Merchants Bank—all by the Dakins—the Mansion House Hotel, a theater, and many stores in the Government Street area. These fires cut a swath across downtown Mobile, leaving the city prostrate from the three blows of financial collapse, yellow fever, and devastating fire.[41]

After the conflagration, the United States Hotel was described as having been "still incomplete." The fire left "only the walls and the lofty arches of the interior. All was now desolate, but presenting a certain grandeur, even in its ruins." What was left fell shortly after: "The remaining columns of the Government St. Hotel gave way under the sapping influence of heavy rain and fell to the ground blocking Royal St. They fell nearly perpendicularly and the roaring sound which they made startled the whole neighborhood and the shock made the solid earth shake sensible to a considerable distance." [42]

The Planters and Merchants Bank was a shell. The ruins were so precarious that they had to be demolished. A newspaper described the scene: "STAND FROM UNDER! The walls of the Merchants & Planters Bank are about to be pulled down. We are requested by the Architect to warn all side-walkers to stand from under." [43] It is not known who this "architect" was, but the new bank which was to go up in the old one's place looked suspiciously like the work of Dakin until it too was pulled down in the 1930s.

Had just these two buildings remained, the United States Hotel and the Planters and Merchants Bank, the reputation of the Dakins would have been substantially greater in the history of the Greek Revival movement. Certainly no one could have dared to say that the Dakins had just "a practice" in Mobile, or that Charles Dakin died of remorse over a small warehouse building.

All of these Mobile disasters—finance, yellow fever, and fire—put an end to the practice of the Dakins in Mobile. Entries in the account book of Charles dated in Mobile end with July 3, 1838; there is one final entry for granite supplied by Newton Richards for Barton Academy, dated August 1, 1838, but signed in New Orleans. Charles Dakin went back to New Orleans in 1838 and assisted his brother briefly.

Always the rover, Charles Dakin sailed for Europe some time in 1838. His purpose is unknown, although with the straitened circumstances following the Panic still prevailing, we can probably discount his making a "grand tour." It is more likely that Dakin and Dakin may have felt the economic pinch so badly that they wanted to look into conditions elsewhere.

It is even possible that some great competition was going on in Europe which attracted the Dakins. It would have been highly unusual for an American architect to compete for a European job, but not impossible, once residence had been established by the American in order to meet the usual requirement that the competing architects be "natives." There is no indication as to what countries Charles visited, or where such competitions might have been held. Whatever the attraction that drew Charles Dakin to Eu-

**Plate 1**  *One unit of the row house, the "Thirteen Sisters," designed by James Dakin, 1832. Designed in New York for a block-long development in New Orleans.*

**Plate 2**  *James Dakin's original ink and wash sketch for Plate 63 of Lafever's* Modern Builder's Guide.

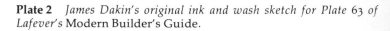

**Plate 3** *Drawing by James Dakin of his Washington Street Methodist Episcopal Church, Brooklyn, New York, 1832. A splendid example of the Town, Davis, and Dakin* distyle in antis, *featuring a pilastrade and Davisean windows.*

**Plate 4** *A study for the Duane Street Presbyterian Church, New York, by James Dakin, 1834. Alexander Jackson Davis found it "gay and ostentatious."*

**Plate 5** *Government Street Presbyterian Church, Mobile, designed by Gallier and Charles Dakin, erected by Charles Dakin, 1836–37.*

**Plate 7** *Bocage plantation, near Burnside, Louisiana,*
*remodeling of an older house, ca. 1830–40, probably by*
*James Dakin. Front elevation.*

**Plate 8** *Drawing of the Gayoso House Hotel,*
*Memphis, Tennessee, by James Dakin, 1842.*

**Plate 9** *Residence of Peter Conrey, Carondelet Street, near Melpomene Street, New Orleans, by James Dakin, ca. 1836–44(?)*

**Plate 10** *Old Louisiana State Capitol, Baton Rouge, by James Dakin, 1847. Front view. (Courtesy Louisiana Tourist Commission)*

**Plate 11**  *Old Louisiana State Capitol, Baton Rouge. Ironwork and stained glass of dome.*

rope, he did not stay long, for he returned to New Orleans on the American bark *Union,* arriving April 19, 1839. The *Union* had departed Marseilles, France, with three French passengers and "C. B. Dakin; 28 years of age; Residence: New Orleans; Intended Residence: New Orleans; Occupation: Architect." His baggage consisted of "3 trunks, 1 writing desk, 1 hat box, 1 valease [*sic*], 1 clothes bag, 1 bed, 1 bag." [44]

This trip is the last known activity of Charles Dakin. Two months later, he was dead. His gravestone was found recently in a country cemetery on the River Road, along the Mississippi, below Baton Rouge, Louisiana. It is in the St. Gabriel Catholic Church Cemetery, in St. Gabriel, Louisiana, located in what appears to be the former back area of the cemetery. The cemetery had to be moved for a levee setback; this area in the rear, which did not have to be moved, was commonly called "beyond the pale" and was where non-Catholics were buried. No entry appears in the cemetery records, for apparently only Catholic deaths were noted in the church records. At the base of the headstone, about an inch underground, is the inscription, "N. Richards, N.O." Newton Richards of New Orleans, whose craftsmanship had produced so much beauty in stone for many Dakin buildings, used his skill for Charles Dakin for the last time.

It has been impossible to determine why Charles is buried at St. Gabriel. Certain facts seem evident. He must have died of a dread disease—yellow fever and cholera were rampant that summer—or his body would have been brought to New Orleans for burial. Custom, and sometimes laws, prevented moving bodies of epidemic victims very far and insisted on rapid burial to avoid spread of the disease. No mention of the death was made in the Mobile or New Orleans newspapers, but Charles had not resided in those

*Gravestone of Charles Dakin, St. Gabriel Catholic Cemetery, St. Gabriel, Louisiana. This is the only documentation of the date of Charles Dakin's death.*

cities for some time. Unfortunately, no newspapers for the St. Gabriel area have survived; but in 1900, Charles James Dakin, James Dakin's only son, wrote in the "Letters to the Editor" of the *Daily Picayune* that his uncle Charles had "died in Iberville Parish in 1839, aged 28 years." [45] This is the parish (county) in which St. Gabriel is located.

It is quite probable that some construction of a Dakin and Dakin building was going on in that vicinity in early 1839 and required Charles's supervision. Significantly, St. Gabriel is just about ten miles or so from Duncan Kenner's Ashland plantation and just up the river from the Bringier family's string of large plantation houses. It is conceivable that Charles may have been doing work there.

The death of Charles Dakin was a tragic loss to his brother and his family, of course, but it snuffed out a young talent which surely would have made a much larger impact on his profession. His life and death reveal an interesting parallel with that of Henry Hitchcock of Mobile: both men died young, both were intimately associated with Mobile, both apparently died of a dread disease, both died in the summer of 1839. They both died at the height of their careers; and both, in their own ways, were visionaries — Hitchcock, the entrepreneur, and Charles, a creator.

Charles Dakin's tombstone inscription is worth quoting, not merely because it supplies us with facts previously lacking in reference works, but also because it demonstrates the feelings of his wife and family, mourning for one who died so young:

Sacred to the memory of Charles B. Dakin,
a native of New York, who died the 25th.
day of June, 1839, in the 28th. year of his age.
Husband
I needs must mourne for thee,
    that's best below,

Tis ever thus — tis ever thus, with all,
    always first to go,
The dearest, noblest, loveliest are.
He went amid these glorious things
    of earth,
Transient as glorious.

Charles Dakin has left us at least two impressive buildings in Mobile which stand as monuments to his talent. They speak for him far better than words.

# 7

# A SERIES OF DISASTERS:
# THE LATE THIRTIES AND EARLY FORTIES

THE LATE 1830S SAW AN OUTPOURING OF DRAWINGS FROM THE pen of James Dakin. In a great burst of activity, he designed ten major public buildings in New Orleans and several private ones. If one includes credit for the lion's share of the design work for the Mobile operation of Dakin and Dakin, which the evidence shows we must, his output during this period was prodigious.

In 1839, outside forces were to diminish this output. A series of crises struck James Dakin in rapid succession. Though he would overcome all of these disasters, their effect was to slow down his onrushing career.

The late 1830s started well for Dakin. In 1838, a physician who had become very popular in New Orleans for his heroism during a cholera epidemic, Dr. Warren Stone, called upon Dakin to build a large hospital for him.[1] Dr. Stone was the best-known doctor in New Orleans then and the first in New Orleans to use ether as an anesthetic.

Although Dr. Stone was a member of the faculty of the Medical College of Louisiana, which used the facilities of Charity Hospital, he and his partner Dr. William E. Kennedy decided to build their own hospital, and together they signed a contract with James Dakin for the firm of Dakin and Dakin to design and build it.[2]

They had obtained the land on December 26, 1838, from the heirs of the Marquis de Lafayette, who had been given property by the United States government in appreciation for his valuable help during the Revolutionary War. The lot was at the corner of Canal and Claiborne Streets. At this time, the area was considered the very edge of town, and remote enough for the quiet necessary around a hospital. The site is now virtually in the heart of the downtown business district.

By Dakin's standards, it was a rather plain building, the most archeological one he had done in years. Really but a simple box, it had a massive Doric portico in front, with four columns supporting the usual triangular pediment. Standard Doric detail was used: triglyph, dentil, and guttae. The building contract describes it as "three stories high, the first 12 feet six inches, the second 11 feet and the third 6 feet at the sides and 9 feet in the center in height in the clear, with a Grecian Doric Portico in front and two back galleries and a back building."[3] The attic story on the third level had those little square window openings so common in this period. In all, it was a very handsome building, although not as imaginative as Dakin's best work.

The Maison de Santé, its official title, was opened in August of 1839, and has been called one of the earliest private hospitals in America. It did quite well financially at first, then by 1852, the hospital had been taken over by the Sisters of Charity, and was operated by them in conjunction with Dr. Stone. In 1858, the sisters left the Maison de Santé and founded Hotel Dieu leaving Dr. Stone to continue alone.[4] Maison de Santé remained in use until 1875, three years after the death of Dr. Stone. By 1883 it had been destroyed.[5]

The next major building James Dakin was to design was the state arsenal on St. Peter Street, just behind the Cabildo at Jackson Square. It is now part of the Cabildo complex, openings having been made in the common wall to unite the two buildings.

The Cabildo area has long been the nerve center of Louisiana, even back to its earliest days. At the corner of St. Peter and Chartres Streets had been located the French Corps de Garde, which, after twice being almost totally destroyed by fire, was replaced with the Cabildo by the Spanish in 1795. This was the seat of government. Directly to the rear of the police headquarters, located in the Cabildo, was the prison. The site was still spoken of in the

*Maison de Sante, also known as Stone's Infirmary, New Orleans, designed by James Dakin, 1838. (Courtesy Historic New Orleans Collection)*

1830s as "the old Spanish prison." A state arsenal is also known to have been located in the prison area in 1830.[6]

In February, 1836, the state of Louisiana, probably feeling a shortage of room at the capitol buildings on Canal Street, decided that it needed a new arsenal building in the area near the Cabildo, to be located on the site of the prisons. An act of the legislature stated it would accept land for this purpose.[7]

It was not until almost two years later that the city got around to donating the land. On December 18, 1837, the council of the First Municipality, the Creole section—New Orleans had been divided into three parts—gave the state the site of "the old prisons," provided that the state built an arsenal there.[8]

The legislature responded with an act of March, 1839, authorizing the governor to "employ an engineer to draw plans and to advertise 30 days in three New Orleans newspapers for sealed bids" to construct an arsenal "on the site of the old prisons."[9] James Dakin, since coming to New Orleans, had established himself in the Louisiana militia, for which the arsenal was mainly intended. In 1838, he was listed as a second lieutenant in the Washington Guards, the parent of the famed Washington Artillery.[10]

Undoubtedly, Dakin's membership in the Legion was a factor in his selection as architect. However, his superb plan would surely have won any competition. The architectural historian, Samuel Wilson, Jr., has called the arsenal "a boldly designed Greek Revival structure."[11] The purpose of the building is powerfully asserted in its appearance of great strength.

Dakin achieved this strength by the use of four massive square pilasters with deep recesses leading to windows screened with heavy strap iron set in a diagonal pattern. The doorway in the center is of iron, with large rivets dotting its entire front. On either side are Davisean windows which run the full two stories with no readily visible break for the second story floor.[12]

Above the door is repeated the same theme of the square pilasters, only this time smaller in scale. These two pilasters are of wood and are set on an entablature above the massive doors. The iron screen is likewise placed behind these smaller pilasters.

The Greek Revival feeling was further expressed in the placement of guttae beneath a course of moulding above the entablature supported by the pilasters. A cornice with three courses of fine mouldings on the soffit extends above this.

The starkness of the flat roof line is softened somewhat by the extension of the four great pilasters up above the cornice, the center two being topped by another simple entablature. It too is relieved from plainness by a finely undercut moulding. It would be tempting to glibly describe this as a "blocking course with pedestals," but the cornice treatment is much more involved than this. Dakin's ingenious extension of the four main pilasters through the entablature to the roof, the placing of another smaller entablature over the center two pilasters, and the insertion of decoration in the recess thus created, all serve to remove the building from the ordinary.

The ornamentation of the upper part of the building is striking. In the openings above the entablature and just below the main cornice, the two openings to either side of the center one serve as frames for replicas of field artillery, with two crossed ramrods running diagonally behind the cannon. This repeats the criss-cross motif of the strap-iron grille across the Davisean windows below. The wider opening in the center contains two flags with tassels dangling, again criss-crossed left to right, with a shield of stars and bars circled by a wreath.

*State arsenal (behind the Cabildo), designed and built by James Dakin,*
*1839.*

Directly above this crossed flag motif is the opening in the "upper cornice" which balances the one below. In it stands the symbol of Louisiana: a pelican feeding her young, her wings spread, a score or more of her young at her breast. Rounding out the military feeling are four bomb-burst symbols — cannon balls with a tongue of flame emerging from each. These are placed at the very top of each square pilaster. Dakin's sure-handedness with detail is well demonstrated by this building. The decorations blend in with and repeat the motifs used in the building.

The search for a possible classical precedent or inspiration leads to the Choragic Monument of Thrasyllus. But the road to Athens goes by way of Philadelphia. In 1825, John Haviland designed the Franklin Institute there which was based, he said, on the Thrasyllus monument.[13] Like the arsenal, the Franklin Institute has four massive square pilasters on its facade, a flat roof, and a heavy entablature. What makes the arsenal different is its unique roof treatment just described, the Davisean windows, and an abundance of well-integrated decoration. Haviland, on the other hand, used for decorative purposes only a course of wreaths on the entablature like the Thrasyllus monument. It is possible that Dakin may have seen an illustration of the Choragic Monument of Thrasyllus in Stuart and Revett's *Antiquities of Athens* or that he saw the Franklin Institute in Philadelphia and adapted it for his arsenal, but there is no evidence of either.

The building contract with Dakin and Dakin for the arsenal was signed on July 1, 1839, by James H. Dakin, for himself and the "late Charles B. Dakin." His brother having just died a week before, James must have felt little elation over getting such an important and prestigious job as the arsenal. The contract was for $19,500, of which $500 was for drawings and preliminary work. A few details from the contract show the building to be erected on a lot approximately 30 by 107 feet, with foundations of flat boat planks.[14] Dakin's original drawings, however, show pyramidal brick footings. Probably the planking was set under the large footings.

Eight cast iron columns, six inches in diameter, on each of the two floors supported the upper floor and roof, with the lower set fixed on granite blocks. The front door on St. Peter Street was to be four inches thick, covered with iron or zinc, with iron screens in each window.

Specifications for the ornaments show that "the front of the openings will be filled with such ornaments as shown by the drawings. . . . In the center, above the cornice, will be placed the arms of the State of Louisiana made of cement or other durable material. All the other ornaments of the front and the entablature, and blocking the attic [windows] above the cornice, will be rough formed with bricks and stone work and finished with cement in imitation of marble."[15]

By October 3, 1839, Dakin almost had it finished. The newspaper said "The new arsenal at the rear of the First Municipality Hall [the Cabildo] was rapidly progressing to completion. If not impregnable, it was durable, and promised not only security for the city ordinance, but a common rendezvous for the Legion in an emergency."[16]

With some repairs made in the 1870s, the arsenal continued in use until about 1914, when it was converted into a "Battle Abbey," that is, a display hall for war relics and momentos.[17] Its final disposition came on February 18, 1914, when its displays and the building itself were given to the Louisiana State Museum, which was already operating in the Cabildo next door.[18]

The arsenal still stands, now rather run down, but awaiting restoration when funds become available. With the discovery of Dakin's original plans, the facade can be restored to its original beauty.

### 1839 — A FATEFUL YEAR

The winning of the arsenal job was to be the last bright spot in James Dakin's career for some time. The death of his brother was the first of a series of disasters in late 1839. Next in the series was the affair of the St. Patrick's Church. The problems associated with the construction of this church have long been misrepresented, because the only source of information has been James Gallier. His description has put Dakin in a bad light and left him there for years. Gallier's account of the St. Patrick's Church problem, like his account of the Dakins' Mobile operations, omits much. He wrote:

A plan having been made by [James] Dakin for a new Catholic church in Camp St., he was employed by the committee to superintend its erection; but, when the walls of the building had reached nearly to the roof, a disagreement between Dakin and the managers took place, and he withdrew from the undertaking. After much delay, the managers employed me to finish the structure; but before the walls of the tower had risen above the roof, they began to settle down toward one side, from a defective foundation; so that I had to take out the old foundation and put in a new one, without pulling down the walls; this caused much trouble and expense, but I finally succeeded in accomplishing it, so that it has stood firmly to the present day.

The whole of the interior arrangements, the groined ceilings, the altar, the organ, etc., were erected after my designs and under my superintendence.[19]

James Dakin did not, in fact, withdraw from the undertaking; he was forced out during a dispute by a group of arbitrators which included Gallier himself. Four weeks after this action took place, Gallier signed a contract with St. Patrick's trustees to finish the church. Dakin, meanwhile, appealed in the courts all the way to the Louisiana Supreme

*Drawing of St. Patrick's Church, New Orleans, designed by James Dakin, 1837. Front elevation.*

Court and won the case. However, by the time the decision was rendered, Gallier had finished the building.

This serves to make Gallier's statement about the settling tower and his propping it up without pulling down the walls seem somewhat exaggerated. The whole affair can now be re-examined—not just on the basis of Gallier's version of the story, but on the facts as documented in public records.

St. Patrick's Church was conceived in 1833 as the second Roman Catholic parish in New Orleans. The parish was very poor since most of its Irish congregation came from the working class. It began with only a small frame building; but through the efforts of Father James Mullon, it gradually gained economic strength.[20] By 1837, the parish felt it could go ahead with plans to replace the little wooden church with a larger, more permanent one. Representatives of St. Patrick's Church approached James Dakin in 1837 to design the new church for them, which *Norman's New Orleans* describes thus: "It surpasses every attempt at a similar order [Gothic] on this side of the Atlantic, and when completed, may proudly challenge comparison with any modern parochial edifice in Europe. The design is a triumph worthy of the genius of Gothic architecture, whether the dimensions or the splendor of the structure be considered." The book goes on to say that the church was to be built from "the designs of Messrs. Dakin & Dakin."[21] Why Gallier was not selected is not known.

In 1838, a building contract was signed with Dakin and Dakin by the then trustees, Charles Diamond and Martin Devereux.[22] Diamond was a well-known businessman in New Orleans, who had business dealings with Gallier in 1838, for a building contract, dated April 23, 1838, shows that Gallier built for Diamond two three-story houses on Tchoupitoulas Street.[23]

The St. Patrick's building contract, signed on June 6, 1838, was for $115,000. Attached to it are printed building specifications. Some nine pages long, these printed specifications were the first to be used in New Orleans.

The opening paragraphs set the style of the church as Decorated Gothic:

### SPECIFICATIONS.

Of the Materials and Mechanical Execution to be employed in the erection and completion of St. Patrick's Church, agreeable to a design by Messrs. Dakin & Dakin, Architects. . . .

The style of architecture exhibited in the composition of the design for the exterior is that of the Pointed Style of the Second Period of Ecclesiastical Architecture, and has been principally imitated from that unrivalled example of splendored majesty, York Minster Cathedral. The windows are in the florid Gothic style of the Third Period, which display more elegance in their tracery than earlier examples.

The ceiling of the interior is in imitation of the ceiling of Exeter Cathedral, which is also another gorgeous example of the Second Period. The slips and galleries are in the richest florid style of the Third Period, and display the most chastened elegance of the art.

The Altar and Tabernacle are composed in the style of the Second and Third Period, and in richness, elegance and variety, they possess all that the art is susceptible of.[24]

Some of the other specifications were rather spectacular for the New Orleans of 1838. First was a tower 185 feet high. This made it the tallest structure in New Orleans. It took a great deal of courage in 1838 to plan a masonry structure of such mammoth size on the treacherous and mucky subsurface of New Orleans. The longitudinal section shows huge pyramidal brick foundations under the tower and smaller ones to the rear (See Frontispiece).[25] The contract calls for them to be eighteen feet wide under the tower, and fourteen feet wide under the tower walls. Beneath all this there was to be planking from flatboat gunwales. Allowance was made by Dakin for settling of the huge tower at a rate

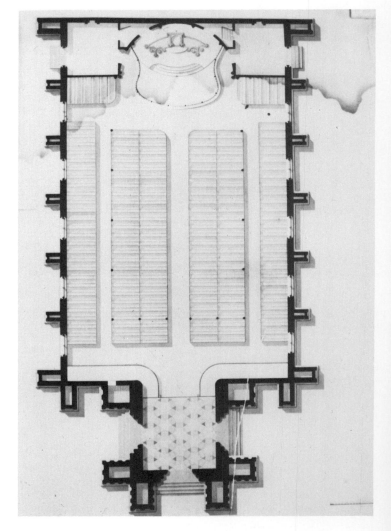

*Floor plan of St. Patrick's Church, New Orleans.*

*Drawing by James Dakin of transverse section of St. Patrick's Church, New Orleans.*

different from the rest of the building (note Dakin's plea for good workmanship here):

The foundations under the tower will be so built as to allow of the necessary settlement without forcing down the walls of the main part of the building more than their own weight would cause. The foundations must be joined together in such a manner as will permit the tower to settle down past the light parts without taking them with it, which must be done by grooving the small foundations into the larger ones, and in a similar manner for the superincumbent walls where they meet those of the tower; to obtain this object, great pains must be taken with these particular parts, and the subject must not be slurred over in the execution of the works, under any pretence whatsoever.[26]

The exterior cementing was to be in imitation of white marble, or any other material the building committee desired. "The ceilings of the auditory and vestibule will be arched, ribbed and finished precisely similar to the ceilings of the choir of Exeter Cathedral, and the intersection of the ribs at the crown of the main arch will be finished with flowers in a similar manner to those of the Cathedral referred to." The latter, of course, refers to the longitudinal ridge rib with bosses of flowers at the intersections.

For the roof, the "tie beams will be 8 x 14 inches," and instead of king and queen posts, as in ordinary cases made of wood, "iron bolts will be used 1¼ inches in diameter and the intersection of the tie beams will be secured with strong and efficient straps and bolts." Dakin's original drawing of the roof construction shows that he planned a scissors truss, with a king post of iron for strength and lightness. More importantly, the span covered by the truss was a mammoth seventy-three feet, with no interior columns in the church, resulting in an unobstructed view of the altar. This unsupported span was the widest attempted in New Orleans for years and is reminiscent of the same feature of the Government Street Presbyterian Church in Mobile.

The specifications further stated that "every necessary part of the works of this edifice will be secured efficiently with iron work if requisite." Even in the 1830s, Dakin was not hesitant in using iron, a relatively new material. His arsenal, it will be remembered, also employed eight cast-iron columns.

Again according to the specifications:

The entire building will be finished in every respect and particular in the true spirit and intention of the designs, and no advantage shall be taken of any omission to explain and describe minutely any and every minutia requisite to complete the work agreeable to the fullest intent and meaning of the drawings and specifications. The whole construction and completion of this edifice will be performed under the immediate superintendence and direction of the Architects, or their Clerk of the Works, whose decisions in all matters arising out of the works in question shall be binding on all parties concerned, in all such matters which properly belong to the department or duties of an Architect or Superintendent.[27]

Thus, we can see in these specifications that Dakin was attempting much with St. Patrick's Church. First, the exterior was to be done in the elaborate manner of the Decorated style. No other church in the New Orleans area had been built in such a grand manner and in such size as called for in the original plans of St. Patrick's.[28] In America, perhaps only Renwick's and Upjohn's Gothic churches in the East can compare with this great Gothic Revival design.

Secondly, Dakin was including several design innovations in the plan which were daring from the engineering standpoint. The 73-foot span of the interior without columns was a bold conception, and the great 184-foot tower was to be the tallest structure in New Orleans for twenty years, until Dakin's pupil, Henry Howard, built the First Presbyterian Church in 1857 with a 210-foot tower.

By 1838, then, the trustees had found sufficient money — or thought they had — to go ahead with the contract, even in the dark days of the Panic of 1837. The newspapers reported, on May 13, 1838, that they had seen "the plan exhibited some twelve or fifteen months previously at Banks' Arcade." It noted the public sale of pews four days later and congratulated Father Mullon for bringing the church "to its present state of advancement in the midst of many obstacles."[29] On July 1, 1838, the cornerstone was laid. This fact makes it the oldest existing church in New Orleans, St. Louis Cathedral having been completely rebuilt by de Pouilly in 1850.

It was in August, 1839, that Dakin began having problems over St. Patrick's Church. An attempt was made by the trustees that August to break the contract. From the files of the lawsuits that resulted, information is provided which is far superior to Gallier's autobiography. Most of the account which follows is based on these suits.[30]

In July of 1839, the third stage of the contract had been reached, that is, the walls of the church were up two thirds of the way. Under the contract, the first stage called for the laying of the foundations and the second for the "walls of the main body [of the church] up 1/3 of the height to the cornices." The church was inspected at the time of the third installment, and approval was given by the building committee on July 25 to make the third payment. Then began the difficulties.

One of the committee members, Thomas Fitzwilliams, was told by a Mr. Stone, the brick contractor, that bond timbers had not been placed in the walls. It had been expressly stated in the specifications that these timbers would be used. (According to Asher Benjamin's *The Builder's Guide,* a bond timber is "laid in walls to tie them together longitudinally while the work is setting." It should be noted that in New Orleans, the prevailing principle among builders at the time was that it was not so important that a building settled—they were expected to and did—but that it settle evenly.)

James Dakin and the building committee could not agree on the issues thus raised by the committee; therefore, in accordance with the contract, a panel of arbitrators was selected to settle the matter. Their decision was to be final and not subject to dispute in court. On August 23, 1839, Dakin and the trustees—that is, Father Mullon, Charles Diamond, and Martin Devereux—agreed to refer the matter to these arbitrators: James Gallier; Michael Collins, Gallier's ex-partner; Joseph Clohecy, Gallier's clerk of the works for the St. Charles Hotel; and Alexander Baggett, a local builder. A fifth member, an "umpire," was to be selected by these four arbitrators. They selected David Sidle, of Sidle and Stewart, builders of the earlier frame St. Patrick's Church. On August 27, they issued their award:

We, the undersigned Arbitrators, are unanimously of the opinion that Messrs. Dakin & Dakin have violated their contract by omitting to place bond timbers in the walls as was required by the Stipulations of the Contract, that the walls in consequence of said omissions are not, nor ever can be made so firm and secure as they would have been if bond timbers had been placed in the center at distances of four feet apart, in the height, and fixed all round the external walls, through or across the window openings at their ends, in the center of the Piers between the windows, and the bond timbers not cut out of the window openings until the roof had been finished, the mortar had become dry and the buildings had time to settle regularly down upon the foundations.

And further, that as the specifications require the inside of the walls to be furred for lathwork, we are of the opinion that wall strips should have been built in the brickwork as it went up, to which these battens could have been nailed and for want of which, the inside of the walls must now have wooden pegs or large spikes driven into the joints of the brickwork, which will tend to loosen the bond of the mortar and materially affect the strength of the walls.

This being the case, the only certain means of effectively correct-

ing these omissions would be to take down the walls surrounding the body of the Church to the height required for placing the first course of bond timbers and in rebuilding the walls, place the bond timbers and wall strips at the proper heights therein, and also secure the buttresses to the walls by means of iron anchors built therein, having the ends of the anchors hooked over the bond in the walls.

But, as taking down so large a portion of the brickwork would now incur much extra expense and considerable delay in the progress of the work, we are of the opinion that the walls may still be tolerably well secured by bonding them together in the space which will be between the tops of the windows and the roof.

As it appears that from some misunderstanding between the parties, feelings of a hostile nature have arisen between them which must inevitably prevent them from proceeding together with that degree of harmony which should exist between parties so connected, it is in our opinion much better for both parties that the contract between them be now annulled, but in doing this, a sufficient compensation should be made to Messrs. Dakin & Dakin for their plans and for the trouble they have had in conducting the progress of the building thus far, making due allowance, however, for the damages to which they have subjected themselves by the aforesaid omissions.

Therefore, we hereby award and unanimously decide the Contract hitherto existing between the Trustees of the Congregation of St. Patrick's Church and Messrs. Dakin & Dakin, Architects, and Builders, is hereby null and void.[31]

The arbitrators go on to make certain provisions. Dakin and Dakin were to get five thousand dollars for the plans but were to forfeit five thousand dollars for the "omissions." (This would mean they would turn over their plans to the builder completing the job, that is, to Gallier.) They were also to be allowed by the trustees 8 percent on amounts already spent on the building over the actual cost, "to be ascertained by vouchers or bills furnished therefor." "If, upon settlement of aforesaid accounts, Dakin & Dakin be indebted to the Trustees, the amount shall be deducted from the price of the drawings as above awarded."

The award document is signed by Gallier and the others, and witnessed by John Turpin (later Gallier's partner) and Henry Walters. It is dated August 27, 1839.

Before the church went to court to enforce the award, Gallier signed a contract with St. Patrick's on October 1, 1839, to finish the church. His contract called for a payment of one thousand dollars for making the drawings and 5 percent for supervising the construction. The one thousand dollars was payable half when the roof was put on, and the rest six months later.[32] Dakin, of course, had refused to turn over his drawings, and Gallier had to try to redo them. One thousand dollars seems a considerable sum for drawings in the light of the two hundred-dollar payments we have seen previously for Greek structures, although it must be said that a Gothic design involves much more detail.

Then, on October 11, the church filed suit against Dakin and Dakin to enforce the award of the arbitrators and get a settlement of the accounts. It was a hotly contested trial, and many things were brought out in the testimony which require close examination to arrive at a reasonable judgment as to what really happened.[33]

In this testimony, it was noted that the issue began when Mr. Stone, the brick mason, told the committee that bond timbers had not been used. It was then pointed out that the committee members were not aware that these timbers had not been placed in the walls and that they were not architects. Dakin's side countered with the fact of the approval by the committee and their acceptance of the work for the third payment under the contract, calling for a payment when the walls were two-thirds completed to the top.

The committee, it was said, had then looked harder at the walls and found "two or three" cracks in or around two windows. Some of the cracks had been plastered over and it was not stated how large the cracks were. On cross-exam-

ination by Dakin's side, the church's attorney said that one crack was in a wall area which was to be opened up for a door (an apparent modification in the plans), the implication of which is that it did not make much difference if a crack occurred in that area.

A witness for Dakin, who had served as his legal representative at the meeting of the arbitrators, said that the subject of furring (provision for attaching plastering) of the walls was not even brought up at the meeting. He said this was a matter on which the arbitrators ruled despite the issue not even being submitted to them. The witness also testified that the question of annulling the contract also was never considered for submission to the arbitrators. No signed copies of the submission can be found, but it is reasonable to presume that Dakin would not have agreed to raise the question of breaking the contract.

The personal conflict which arose at the arbitrators meeting was described by the same witness. He said that "the parties, Fr. Mullon on one side, and James Dakin on the other, were called upon to relate their difficulties between them and they did so. The explanation of the parties related entirely to personal difficulties between Mr. Diamond, one of the Trustees, and one of the defendants [obviously James Dakin]. The altercation was carried on until the arbitrators told them they had heard enough and did not wish to have anything to do with it." The witness did not "pay particular attention to it because he considered it entirely foreign to the matters in arbitration." He said that "Mr. Dakin stated that if he had given any offence to any of the Trustees or Building Committee members, he asked their pardon." The witness "understood him to disclaim all hostility to either the undertaking or Trustees or Building Committee."

It was added, by this same witness for Dakin, that he noted that the "Report of the Building Committee," apparently referring to the approval for the third payment under the contract, had not been introduced at the meeting. He then "asked Mr. Gallier, one of the arbitrators, if he wanted the Report of the Building Committee. He said he did not and that the arbitrators had all the papers they wanted."

After hearing all this testimony, the lower court judge ruled against Dakin and Dakin on November 30, 1839, and approved the arbitrators award breaking the contract. Dakin did not accept this and filed an appeal the same day in the Louisiana Supreme Court.

The appeal case finally came to trial on December 20, 1841 (why must all appeals take two years to come to trial?), with Dakin's side arguing that: (1) the award was null because the arbitrators exceeded their powers, passing on matters not submitted to them, particularly the cancelling of the contract; and (2) the award was void because of its uncertainty, for it did not enable the court to give a decree for any specific sum of money to either party.

The Supreme Court, headed by Chief Justice Francis Xavier Martin, made its decision on the case: "We have looked at it most attentively, and taken something more than the usual time for reflection upon it, but have to confess our inability of seeing what either party has gained, or ascertaining what advancement has been made towards the adjustment of the accounts between them. . . . Neither the award nor judgment has terminated their difficulties." The Supreme Court judgment continues:

We concur most fully in the opinion given by Judge Marshall [Chief Justice John Marshall of the U.S. Supreme Court] in the case of Carnachan et al vs Christie, 11 Wheaton 446 [rendered March 14, 1826] in which he says an award must decide the whole matter submitted and must not go beyond the matter comprehended in the submission; it must be certain, final and conclusive, and leave no matter of fact or of law undecided. . . . The courts are not to become mere auxilliaries to supply their [arbitrators' awards] defects and omissions.

In this case, we think that the arbitrators exceeded their authority in annulling the contract between the two parties. . . . The award is in itself so uncertain, that we do not see what judgment we could give on it that could be executed, and we must disregard it entirely, leaving the parties to exercise their rights under the contract.

This judgment of the [lower] court is therefore reversed, and ours is in favor of the defendants . . . the plaintiffs paying costs in both courts.[34]

Dakin had won in the Supreme Court by its ruling that the contract had been broken illegally. But it was a hollow victory, for Gallier had, in the meantime, finished the church. In addition, Dakin, while retaining his right of claim against the church, never got a chance to exercise it because the church soon went bankrupt.

A document has been found which sets forth Dakin's own feelings on the matter:

We claim of the Church of St. Patrick of the City of New Orleans damages in the sum of $30,000. The grounds upon which our claim is established are that, had we been permitted to have completed our contract for the erection of the Church which we commenced on Camp St. and erected to the height or nearly so of the roof, that we should have made a profit of $30,000 on the contract. The Building Committee of said Church commenced proceedings against us for the purpose of nullifying our contract and taking the matter into their own hands; thus far [1841], they have been successful. The suit is now pending in the Supreme Court where we expect within the course of the next term of the court to have the judgment of the Commercial Court set aside. Should such be the desired result, there will be no difficulty in proving, should the parties all live, that the conduct of the Building Committee in their measures against Dakin & Dakin as the contractors for the erection of said Church was the result of cold and premeditated aggression and a violation of every principle of equity and justice.[35]

Despite Dakin's inability to collect on his claim, the decision of the Supreme Court did serve to restore the confidence of the public in Dakin as a professional, if, indeed, he ever lost it. It has been only in comparatively recent years that the Supreme Court decision has been forgotten and only Gallier's memoirs remembered. And the only fairly contemporary newspaper reference to the events that this writer could find, which should be an indicator of the public's reaction, was written sixteen years after the incident and three years after Dakin's death. The paper asserted, *"We believe* that the weight of its [St. Patrick's] lofty and massive walls has had the same effect of somewhat impairing their solidity, by causing the foundations to sink—as is almost or quite universally the case with all the massive buildings in New Orleans—more than was expected or allowed for by the architects. It is nonetheless, a fine and substantial structure." [36]

Thus, the strongest wording in the newspapers was "we believe," and it refers to the usual sinking of New Orleans buildings, not an uneven sinking. I have found no mention in the newspapers or in the lawsuit of Gallier's claim about the tower leaning.

What conclusion can be drawn from what we know of the case? After sifting through the known facts, it is impossible to tell what really happened. Even the Supreme Court decision noted that "what the precise propositions submitted by the defendants [Dakin and Dakin] to the arbitrators were, does not distinctly appear." Thus, several major questions remain unanswered, such as: What were the points submitted for arbitration? A signed submission cannot be found. Did Dakin really omit bond timbers? Or did he omit them in part, perhaps with the tacit approval of the Building Committee who had approved the first three stage payments. Were bond timbers really that important? Experts who specialize today in restoration work in New Orleans cannot say that bond timbers were absolutely necessary, or that their omission was substantial enough to warrant the breaking of a building contract.

Also puzzling is the arbitrators' award which states that the walls did not have to be taken down; yet the contract had to be broken. If the award had been properly made, Dakin would have been required to take down the walls—if, indeed, bond timbers were held to be so important—and place timbers in at his own expense; the church would have lost nothing. Gallier did add interior columns where previously Dakin had planned none. But were they really necessary?

The matter raised by the arbitrators about the lack of furring can possibly be explained by the fact that some builders simply *prefer* to attach the furring after the walls are up. They feel the driving of a few pins in the walls may weaken them less than laying in strips of wood where brick and mortar should be. The final arbitrators' objection that the buttresses were not attached to the walls might be explained by comparing this phase of construction to the tower linkage with the nave walls, wherein there was and had to be, a sliding connection. When the tower sank lower than the walls because of its greater weight, it would not take the walls with it. Similarly, the buttresses, if not immediately attached, would not go down with the walls and could easily be tied in with iron bars after the initial settlement. The phrase in the contract stating that "decisions in all matters arising out of the works shall be binding on all parties concerned" should have been sufficient to cover this instance.

It is really impossible to choose sides in the case because

of all the factors involved and the lack of complete information about them. The church trustees had a right under the Louisiana Civil Code to dismiss the architects directly themselves, without relying on the arbitrators. Such a method, of course, would have enabled the architects to provide rebuttal witnesses in open court. Whatever we may glean from these facts, or their lack, one incontrovertible fact remains: the church has stood solidly for 134 years.

It is interesting to examine how the interior of the finished church differed from Dakin's original plan. Gallier, as noted, had added interior columns of clustered piers, with fan vaulting leading up to the ceiling.[37] The altar arrangement was quite similar to Dakin's; a half-dome was erected, but it lacked the intricate tracery that Dakin had intended. Gallier's altar itself is magnificent, a masterpiece of Gothic art. Yet so, too, would Dakin's have been, had it been executed. His was much different from Gallier's, incorporating two flying buttresses in the central portion, with the whole having a light, airy feeling. This would have been in keeping with the rest of the church. Gallier's, on the other hand, is massive and lush. It follows the Decorated style, the only part of the church completed in that style.

The exterior, unfortunately, was never finished in the Decorated style. It has a somewhat austere appearance today and tantalizes the viewer with what it might look like if ever finished according to Dakin's magnificent plans.

The year 1839 held more grief for Dakin. His friend, the entrepreneur Richard O. Pritchard, had been having financial difficulties as a result of the Panic of 1837. The statue of Hebe, with which Pritchard had had the good taste to decorate his Verandah Hotel, had to be auctioned off under court orders on April 13, 1839, to satisfy Pritchard's creditors. The auction must have brought home the gravity of the situation to Dakin, for it was held in the architectural office of Dakin and Dakin in the Verandah Hotel.[38]

When Pritchard was not any better off financially by the summer, he joined with others similarly distressed—James Caldwell, the actor-entrepreneur, and Samuel W. Oakey—and prepared a mammoth lottery. In it, the Verandah Hotel, the St. Charles Theater, and the Arcade Buildings on Camp Street were to be auctioned off in a lottery with a value advertised in the papers as $2,000,000.[39] Another awesome lottery advertisement ran concurrently offering Bank's Arcade and the City Hotel which were valued at $1,500,000. These were desperate measures for desperate times.

On October 16, 1839, while returning from a trip to north Louisiana, Pritchard accidentally fell overboard from a steamboat in the Mississippi in St. James Parish and drowned. Only forty-seven years old, he left a widow and three young children. With the death of still another associate, Dakin must have felt that fate was closing in on him.[40]

The fateful year of 1839 thus ended on a gloomy note with the death of Pritchard following those of Charles Dakin in June and Henry Hitchcock in August, and with the St. Patrick's Church matter pending in the courts. James Dakin's fortunes were to reach an even lower ebb with the start of the 1840s.

## BANKRUPTCY

The Panic of 1837 had cast its dark shadow over James Dakin as it had merchants and businessmen. Without the major job of St. Patrick's Church to provide a source of income and because of the disastrous fires in Mobile and the death of Hitchcock, who represented his last chance of salvaging anything from his practice in that city, Dakin threw in the sponge.

Bankruptcy, foreclosures, and insolvencies were the order of the day. In 1837, in New Orleans alone, 2,800 foreclosures were instituted.[41] In 1839, the worst year of Dakin's life, the New Orleans banks suspended payment in specie for the second time since the start of the Panic. By 1842, bank notes were worth as little as 50 percent of their face value; and on May 21, 1842, there were food riots in the French Market area of New Orleans when grocers refused to accept devalued bank notes in payment. The militia had to be called out to restore order there, and they occupied Jackson Square for some time.[42]

His own economic conditions in a shambles, James Dakin filed for bankruptcy in New Orleans on July 16, 1841. The petition to the court gives us a good summation of his problems: "That owing to heavy losses in his business and his speculating in real estate, he is unable to pay his debts or those of the late firms of Dakin & Dakin or that of C. B. Dakin & Bro., of which firms petitioner was a member." [43]

By 1842, the financial bones of Dakin's assets were ready to be picked, and a newspaper advertised, "Sale at Auction, on July 5, 1842, at Bank's Arcade, by order of Parish Court of January 28, 1842," of Dakin's assets. The paper listed only his real estate holdings, which made up the bulk of the assets, and the miscellaneous items were said to be "available at the auction." These consisted of very minor items of small value.[44]

Just as Charles Dakin's account book for Mobile revealed the nature of the materials and the names of the craftsmen employed in the construction of their buildings in that city, so the Dakin bankruptcy schedule of creditors lists many New Orleans artisans whose names have been obscured by time. Scores of stone workers, tinsmiths, slaters, carpenters and the like are named. It would be impossible to list all of them here, but a few of the creditor's names have special significance, particularly those who were suppliers or perhaps clients of Dakin's.[45]

A major creditor was given as "M. D. Bringier, of the Parish of St. James," due "cash advances to us for building Union Terrace—$3,002.50." Michel Douradou Bringier, as mentioned previously, was the head of a family whose impressive plantations ranged along the Mississippi for about twenty miles below Baton Rouge. Most still stand today.

In one set of Bringier's papers which have been preserved, the Dakin and Dakin name appears four times: in 1839–1840, "deux billets"; on January 1, 1839, "un billet" for $1,501.28. Another 1839 entry cites "dix billets," payable in 1840; and another notation, dated April 1, 1841, reads "Deux billets de Dakin & Dakin & Co. somme de $1,501.28, cheque protestés or deposé a la Banque de Cyté a la Nouvelle Orleans. $3,002.56." This matches the figure in the bankruptcy schedule.[46]

The strong connection between Bringier and Dakin appears to be the first tangible lead as to who designed the Bringier family plantations. Duncan Kenner's marriage to Nanine Bringier took place on May 31, 1839.[47] And it is quite possible that Bringier may have given his daughter a new house for a wedding present. A story persists in the family of the Bringier descendants that old Michel Douradou Bringier gave each daughter a new house upon her marriage. Perhaps Ashland, or Belle Helene as it is called today, was such a gift. It may also be significant that Charles Dakin, who is buried up the River Road about ten miles from Ashland, died just a month after the wedding of Nanine and Kenner. Could he have been supervising the commencement of the Kenner house?

*Bocage Plantation, near Burnside, Louisiana, probably designed by James Dakin, ca. 1839-40. In antis rear porch.*

Ashland is clearly New York Greek Revival. The square columns and the massive entablature look like they could have come from the drawing board of someone connected with Town and Davis. James Gallier has frequently been given credit for the design because of tradition in his family; and he may deserve the credit, because the house in his frontispiece for Lafever's *Modern Builder's Guide* is similar to Ashland. But Dakin also worked in this massive style, his arsenal building on St. Peter Street being an even more powerful statement of the same theme. The same huge square columns also appear in the form of a colonnade in the background of Dakin's drawing, "A Church in Brooklyn." Furthermore, not a shred of tangible evidence has ever been found to support an attribution to Gallier.

The other Bringier house which seems to be even more surely a Dakin design is Bocage (Plate 7), just a couple of miles from the site of Michel Bringier's own house, now destroyed. Bocage is actually a remodeling of an earlier eighteenth-century house into a Greek Revival plantation of great beauty. Bringier is said to have given this house and the land on which it stands as a wedding gift to another daughter, Françoise (Fanny) upon her marriage to Christophe Colomb.

The columnation is quite imaginative. Six square columns range across the front (these are slimmer than Ashland's massive columns) but with two slender columns in the center which are half the size of the others. The rear of Bocage is even more Dakinesque, for it is indented with an *in antis* porch, having two large square columns matching the ones in front. This is one of the few Louisiana plantations with an *in antis* porch in the rear. The house and all its details create the same feeling as Union Terrace on Canal Street which Dakin built for Bringier and others.

Inside Bocage, a huge Greek doorway, with the "ears" motif and sliding doors, separates the two main upper rooms. The door frame is decorated with patera and anthemia. The treatment is a good example of Dakin's monumentality. Leading onto the upper rear porch—in the *in antis* recess—from either side are two Greek "ear" doors, tall but slender and not as massive as their gargantuan fellow inside. The purity of detail at Bocage, obviously dating from the late 1830s or early 1840s, and the treatment of the *in antis* porch, the front colonnade and the connection to M. D. Bringier, all stamp this house as the handiwork of James Dakin.

Another entry in Dakin's bankruptcy schedule sheds some light on his peripheral activities: "Debt due Dakin & Dakin—From the State of Louisiana, for making the judges' seat and clerk's desk in the Supreme Court Room when located in the State House, as per bill—$275.00." [48] Dakin had apparently designed this furniture which was still not paid for at the time of his financial troubles. All efforts to locate this furniture or illustrations of it have been unsuccessful. It would be most rewarding to find it, for here was Dakin, the ex-carpenter, still involved in his old trade.

Gallier's name appears as the maker of a note for $8,206.66 which Dakin endorsed for him. It was in favor of Abijah Fisk, a local merchant. The date of the note is not given, but we may be assured that the endorsement predates the St. Patrick's Church matter. [49]

Much of the land advertised for the auction was in the Garden District or thereabouts, and it appears that it was then undeveloped property. No houses by Dakin are specifically mentioned. It was to be ten or more years before most of the great houses in the Garden District would be built, although any erected on his land before 1842 could be by Dakin. His choice of investment property here was excellent; he was just ten years too early.

For his Mobile activities, Dakin lists a claim against the Mobile Steam Cotton Press and Building Company for $1,700. This was probably some unrealized profit on his United States Hotel.

The sale price of some of Dakin's assets is a shock to the sensibilities: the claim against the state for furniture was sold for $14.00; the land in Texas, 1,280 acres, was sold for $115.20; an entire square in uptown New Orleans sold for $189.74; and another square went for $875.00. The claim against St. Patrick's Church was bought by Benedict Baggett and Joseph A. Beard on August 2, 1842. They paid $75.00 for it. It is probable that Benjamin Baggett, a builder, was the brother of Alexander Baggett who was a member of the arbitration board in the St. Patrick's Church case. Both Baggetts came from Alexandria, Virginia, and both were in the building business.[50] By May 25, 1846, the syndic for the creditors showed cash received from the sale of the assets of $412.44 and as paid out, $379.08, leaving a paltry $33.36!

This was surely rock bottom for Dakin. Caught in the whirlpool of the Panic, he was left with only the instruments of his profession, for he said in the July 16, 1841, statement of assets: "I, James Dakin, do solemnly swear that the above schedule contains a correct and faithful statement of all the property I possess . . . except however the clothes and linens . . . [paper damaged] use, and that of my family, my arms and militia accoutrements and the instruments indispensably necessary for the trade or profession which . . . the law authorizes me to keep." [51]

The schedule of Dakin's assets is in a badly deteriorated condition, so that it is difficult to determine how the assets compare to the liabilities, but it appears that there were about $70,000 in liabilities, excluding Gallier's note which Dakin had endorsed, and $55,225.85 in assets, excluding the $30,000 profit on St. Patrick's Church which would have been realized had the contract not been broken. So, it appears that Dakin ended up in bankruptcy court owing about $8,000 which circumstances had made it impossible for him to pay.

It was surely his land speculation more than his architectural transactions which led to Dakin's bankruptcy. He had probably come to New Orleans with great expectations of making a fortune as a speculator in land. Had it not been for the Panic he might have done so, for his Garden District property would have been an excellent investment in other times. Even his Mobile property (excluding the "water lots") was well situated in the bustling downtown section. At this point of his life, Dakin must have wondered whether he should not have remained in New York!

Dakin had not gone under without having made a fight of it. In 1840, he tried to pull out of his financial morass by designing a new state capitol for Louisiana. There had consistently been agitation for a new capitol, with the legislature still meeting in the decaying old Charity Hospital on Canal Street, opposite Dakin's new Union Terrace.

The site was known as State House Square, a commanding piece of property, comprising an entire city block. It had been acquired as part of the "commons" which ringed the city, from which Common Street derives its name. Fronting on Canal Street, the new capitol would have been a showplace for the state. Dakin's original drawings indicate what a grand and elegant building it would have been.[52]

His proposed state house was E-shaped, with the central wing detached from the outer "ring" and a courtyard between the buildings. The branches of the legislature and the court rooms were to be housed in semicircular rooms at each end of the outer ring. One large hemispherical room was to be located at the rear of the central building.

*Drawing of proposed Louisiana State Capitol, 1840, by James Dakin.*

*Drawing of proposed Louisiana State Library, 1839, by James Dakin.*

The capitol was in the Greek Revival style, but its floor plan—the E shape with its unconnected central wing—and its distribution of the orders sets it apart from the ordinary. The central building, with sculpture on its pediment, was of the Corinthian order, rising rather sharply above the outer ring, while the latter was of the Ionic order and flat roofed. The ends of these pavilions each had a group of statuary atop its roof, helping to offset the lower height of these buildings ringing their larger counterpart in the center.

No money was forthcoming from the legislature, for the state was in a depressed condition from the Panic as were her citizens. While Dakin's 1840 capitol was not executed, he eventually was to build Louisiana's capitol at Baton Rouge, its Gothic "castle on the Mississippi."

This had not been Dakin's first flirtation with State House Square (nor his last—he was to design the Medical College of Louisiana later), for in February, 1839, Dakin and Dakin had prepared plans for a state library. However, no funds were made available, and Dakin's plans were never executed.

Augmenting all of Dakin's financial problems in this period of his life were several family problems. He had taken into his home Charles's wife and daughter after Charles's death. Their presence was an additional economic burden.[53] Then, on June 20, 1842, his nine-year-old daughter, Julia, died of a "short, but severe illness." The burial took place from Dakin's home at Number 8 Erato Street, and the little girl was buried in the Girod Street Cemetery, the Protestant burial ground.[54] Julia's death left only two surviving children of a total of seven births, Mary Caroline (Julia's twin) and Charles James. In all, Dakin had five mouths to feed in the midst of the most trying depression that America had seen up to that time.

The early 1840s had a few bright rays of sunshine for Dakin, however. All of his buildings were not unaccepted proposals. On June 28, 1841, he did a plan for a building modest in function, but imaginative in design. This was a fire house and auditorium for the Louisiana Hose Company, a volunteer fire company located on the uptown river corner of Carondelet Street at Perdido.[55]

Two original drawings for this building still exist, one a study and the other a final plan. Their main value is to demonstrate how Dakin could take classical themes and recombine them in different ways to produce a new and effective building. The study shows a flat-roofed building (which was the way it was finally built) with the lower floor treatment in the vein of the Tappan store granite pier prototype. Far from being a dull, granite building, however, it was exquisitely decorated by Dakin. He could not let even a fire house be built without lavishing his skills on its design. Small patera graced the capitals of the four piers, and sunken panels in the doors were likewise tastefully decorated with rosettes. Two courses of dentils are set at the cornice, the lower being of an original design. In the executed version, the granite piers were changed to pilasters. A Palladian window on the second floor admitted light to the meeting hall.

What makes this drawing most interesting is the tower atop the roof. In this study, as well as in the final version, the tower is eye-catching in that it combines the form of the Tower of the Winds with the detail of the Choragic Monument of Lysicrates. The base of the tower is octagonal and, in the study, supports a round colonnade with Tower of the Winds capitals. Above this is another step of the tower, also round, and detailed with a row of anthemia patterned from the Choragic Monument.

However, the tower as built, and as in the final sketch, was done in an octagonal shape throughout its length,

*Drawing of Louisiana Hose Company, Carondelet at Perdido Street, New Orleans, 1841. Dakin combined several architectural motifs in this building.*

rather than partly round, retaining the Tower of the Winds form and the Choragic Monument's colonnade and capitals. The anthemia are omitted, and small square window openings pierce the upper level. Again, we find Dakin, as with the Bank of Louisville, avoiding a strictly archeological approach and using classical motifs in a striking and original way.

The station survived until about 1895, when the fire company sold it to the city on March 22. It was probably destroyed shortly thereafter, the city having taken over the fire-fighting duties from the volunteer crews in 1891.

The erection of this station, with its two highly imaginative plans, indicates that Dakin's creativity had not diminished in this period. Each plan demonstrates a higher degree of inventiveness in his work than in any other architect in New Orleans at the time. Dakin was still unmatched despite the turbulent events of the summer of 1839. His output was slowed by the Panic, but his imagination continued unimpaired. After his bankruptcy, his creativity was all he had left.

# 8
# A NEW START

BEGINNING AGAIN, WITH ONLY THE "INSTRUMENTS OF THE trade," James Dakin returned to the fray with a vengeance after the disheartening events of the bankruptcy. His first major commission came in 1842—for a great hotel in Memphis. The Gayoso House was to rival the St. Charles Hotel for its beauty and was fairly comparable in size. Memphis had its visionaries, just as New Orleans had its Caldwells and Pritchards and Mobile its Hitchcock. Robertson Topp, the entrepreneur of the hotel, was, like Hitchcock, a lawyer, land speculator, and legislator. Topp's Memphis real estate in the early 1840s was concentrated in the undeveloped southern part of the city. It was in this area that he, along with William L. Vance and Archibald Walker, two other investors, planned the construction of the Gayoso House.[1]

It is not known how Topp obtained the designs from Dakin. He may have come to New Orleans for that purpose, or Dakin may have heard of the project and submitted plans for it. The only surviving original drawing (Plate 8), a front elevation, is signed simply "James H. Dakin, Architect, New Orleans, 1842."[2] Shedding a little more light on this is a yellowed, fragile piece of paper found in 1899, following a fire, in a hollow space inside the hotel's cornerstone. It reads:

GAYOSO HOUSE

Founded July 4, 1842
by
Archibald Walker
Wm. L. Vance
R. Topp

Jas. H. Dakin & M. Quigly, Archt.
G. O. Ragland, Brick Mason
J. A. Toon, Stone Mason

Deposited this 4th. day of July, AD 1842

W. L. Vance[3]

This indicates that Dakin provided the plans for the Gayoso House and that "M. Quigly, Archt." probably supervised the construction, paralleling the situation with the Bank of Louisville. Dakin has definitely been placed in New Orleans in 1842 and the years following; so it is probable that he did not move to Memphis for this job, although he could easily have made several short trips there during construction.

In the Greek Revival style, the Gayoso House had an imposing portico of the Corinthian order. It stood four stories high, the portico commencing at the second-floor level and flanked on either side by four square pilasters, rather sharply set off from the facade, creating a sense of great strength. Steps placed within the portico, leading from the ground floor to the second, came up both sides and were invisible from the front. A great doorway met the steps under the portico. Each pilaster was topped with a wreath on the entablature and on the cornice was placed a row of anthemia. The top of the pediment was decorated with a large anthemia at the center and antefixa at the sides.

Perhaps not as original as the United States Hotel in Mobile, it was nevertheless a building which, for beauty of detail and tasteful handling of the elements of the facade, could have been built only by a handful of architects of its day. It would have been worthy of Isaiah Rogers, the "father" of the American hotel.

The Gayoso was the showplace of Memphis. No interior plans have been found, but it was said to be most elegant. The Semmes family, well-traveled and sometimes ballgoers at the White House in Washington, wrote: "The Gayoso House here is positively superior to any house in New York, that is, on the inside . . . and is crowded daily (in June) by planters and their wives and daughters en route to the Springs."[4] Not only planters, but luminaries such as

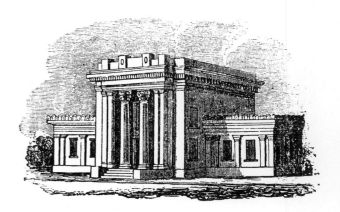

*Medical College of Louisiana, New Orleans, designed and built by James Dakin, 1843. (From Norman's New Orleans)*

Generals Sam Houston and Zachary Taylor, Presidents James K. Polk and Andrew Johnson stayed at the Gayoso in the years before the Civil War.

During the war and the Federal occupation of Memphis, the Gayoso was the scene of much excitement, including a raid into the rotunda on horseback by General Nathan Bedford Forrest's forces. After the war the hotel fell into disrepair, enduring a period of neglect until 1885, when, refurbished, it returned to its former glory. In a ceremony symbolizing the end of animosity between the North and South, President Grover Cleveland visited Memphis and attended a lavish reception at the hotel. The Gayoso continued to serve as the city's foremost hotel until July 4, 1899, when it caught fire and burned to the ground, fifty-seven years to the day after its cornerstone was dedicated. It was rebuilt a year later, but in a style much changed from Dakin's plans. Even its replacement is gone now, but in the annals of Memphis history, the name will always figure prominently. James Dakin had provided the community with a great Greek Revival hotel, a focal point for the events of its time. It must surely rank with its contemporaries as one of the more important hotels of the period.

Dakin followed his design of the great hotel at Memphis with one for another major public building in New Orleans—the Medical College of Louisiana. It was his second medical structure in New Orleans, for, as we have seen, he had designed the Maison de Santé for Dr. Stone.

The Medical College of Louisiana is the institution to which Tulane University traces its beginnings. Other departments were added later and the school came to be called the University of Louisiana, but the founding of the medical school in 1834 gives Tulane University the reason for the date in its coat of arms.

In the autumn of 1834, a group of seven doctors saw the need for more physicians in the New Orleans area. Virulent plagues of various kinds in the years just preceding had made this pointedly clear. Their first official act was to run an advertisement in the *Bee* on September 29, 1834, announcing the formation of the Medical College of Louisiana.[5]

Much controversy ensued initially, though all seven men were highly respected in their profession. Their youth had probably been a factor in the discussions, for each man was only about twenty-six or twenty-seven years old. But they encountered little difficulty after the first furor, and on April 2, 1835, the college got official recognition from the legislature, receiving a charter on that date.[6] It soon became obvious that such a school, performing invaluable community services and especially ministering to the needs of Charity Hospital (where the faculty gave most of their lectures), was entitled to financial support by the state. Numerous attempts were made in the legislature in the late 1830s for appropriations for a building, but, probably because of the Panic of 1837, all such moves were thwarted.[7]

By 1842 the faculty, tired of waiting for the legislature to act, decided to go ahead with a building, the cost to come out of their own pockets. On February 27 of that year a committee was assigned the job of "maturing a plan" for a building.[8] Hope was then raised that the legislature would at least provide the land; surprisingly, it did, on March 22, 1843. In exchange for the services of the school's faculty at Charity Hospital for ten years without compensation, the state leased the corner of State House Square at Common and Philippa Streets (now University Place), the lot measuring 120 feet square. The building, just two blocks away from Charity Hospital, was to revert to the state after ten years.[9]

James Dakin had earlier prepared a plan for a state library on State House Square; now he was going to be able to erect a building there at last. Although it was a new plan, it did seem to retain one element of the library—two low wings projecting from either side. A view in *Norman's New Orleans* shows a three-story Greek Revival building, flat roofed, with an *in antis* portico in which stand two Corinthian columns. The two low wings featured a pilastrade across the front and a row of antefixes on the cornice, creating a rhythmic feeling similar to that of the Choragic Monument of Lysicrates.[10] The floor plan and proportions of the central building to the wings were similar to the Perry house Dakin had done in Brooklyn some years before. It is not clear, however, whether the wings at the college were ever built. If they were, they were removed not long after. Dakin lost no time in erecting the building, for it was begun in May, 1843, and finished by November.[11]

The Medical College was probably conceived by Dakin as part of a master plan for the development of State House Square. He had already provided the legislature with designs for a new capitol building twice, once in 1836 and again in 1840. When it appeared that appropriations might be forthcoming, he had designed a state library, and now the Medical College. Dakin was eventually to fill the back of State House Square, and build a capitol, but not there.

The architectural scene in New Orleans was slowly improving as the city came out of the doldrums caused by the financial crisis of 1837–1842. A large number of contracts involving James Dakin have been found in this time of rebirth in the early 1840s. Many of them were for small commercial buildings and residences and are too inconsequential to mention here in detail. But the stores were usually of the granite pier type, and the residences, alas, have apparently all been destroyed, making a further study of Dakin's residential style almost impossible.

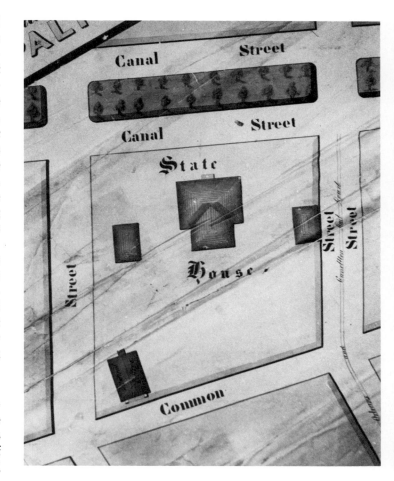

*Ground plan of State House Square, Canal, Common, Baronne Streets and University Place, New Orleans. Building at lower left is Medical College of Louisiana. The University of Louisiana later filled open area at lower right.*

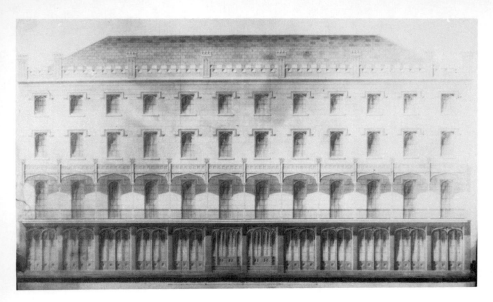

*Drawing of an unidentified Gothic commercial building by James Dakin.*

That business was picking up again was apparent from an advertisement that Dakin ran in the New Orleans newspapers starting on November 12, 1842, and continuing through most of 1843. It read:

ARCHITECTURE. I have again commenced the practice of my profession and will gratefully serve my friends and the public upon terms that shall be satisfactory. Every gentleman will find it much to his interest to have plans and specifications of the intended buildings made by a disinterested person before any attempt is made to procure proposals for the execution of the works; because, when the contractors or builders are required, as they very often are, to estimate and make their calculations from verbal explanations and rude sketches, many difficulties and misunderstandings arise, involving hundreds of dollars in the differences, and much that is troublesome and disagreeable to all parties. A few dollars paid in the commencement to some architect, who understands his business, will save hundreds in the end.

JAMES H. DAKIN, Architect
#48 Canal St., between Chartres St. and Exchange Pl.[12]

This is, in some ways, a rather cryptic ad. "I have again commenced the practice of my profession" would perhaps indicate that Dakin had been out of town for a while, maybe in Memphis or New York. Or it could mean that he had been ill. A similarly cryptic statement had, in fact, appeared in the bankruptcy proceedings regarding St. Patrick's Church, when he used the words "should all the parties live." This may have been an allusion to himself, for we know that he was quite ill at various times in his life.

It seems likely that in the 1840s Dakin did a row house (for investment purposes), not as elegant as his Thirteen Sisters on Julia Street, but in many ways very fine. The row was popularly known as "Gasquet Row," a series of some nine brick houses, in two sets, on the east side of Camp Street, between St. Joseph and Julia Streets.[13] From their balconies one could see the Thirteen Sisters at the opposite end of the block across Camp Street.

Amazingly, parts of the row still stand, despite the commercialization of most of the neighborhood. The corner building sets the character of the end set of four; it had the typical gabled ends of the period, culminating in double chimneys, with both of the upper two stories having finely scaled wrought iron balconies. The entrance doorways are in a massive Greek Revival style, but not of the "ear" variety. Within rectangular enframements, two square columns with fine mouldings in the capitals support a handsome entablature with dentils beneath its cornice.

These first four at the corner of St. Joseph Street seem ordinary in comparison to what remains of the other set of five houses. These were in a different style and probably done at another time. Only two remain, and one has been seriously altered into a Victorian style. But its neighbor remains intact, including the entrance doorway. Dakin lavished on this door the finesse with which he designed the Lafever doorway plates for the *Modern Builder's Guide*.

The enframement consists of two large square columns with deeply undercut Doric capitals, and set between these stand two columns, identical in shape to the outer two, but half the size. In the space between the pairs of columns, Dakin set a perpendicular row of octagonal panes almost the length of the columns. Above each of the large columns is a wreath, framing, as it were, the area of most interest. On the entablature over the door was placed a beautiful acroterion similar to the crest of the Bank of Louisville. Honeysuckle swirls curl their way about under the crest, winding in leisurely fashion to the tops of the smaller columns. Now almost obscured by additions to the front of the row, the doorway is a pleasant surprise when one comes upon it suddenly, hidden away like a small but valuable treasure.

The little buildings (only twenty-five front feet each) were probably erected in 1842, or perhaps a little earlier, at

Gasquet Row, Camp and St. Joseph Streets, New Orleans, designed by James Dakin, ca. 1843.

Gasquet Row, view of center doorway.

the request of William and James Gasquet and their business associate, Henry Parish.[14]

Dakin's next major building—another public structure—was the Canal Bank, designed in December, 1843.[15] This oddly named bank was in reality the New Orleans Canal and Banking Company; included among its founders or early directors were such prominent New Orleanians as Maunsel White, Glendy Burke, and Beverly Chew.[16] It was a typical New Orleans "improvement bank," organized to finance a specific enterprise—in this case, the digging of the New Basin Canal from the American section above Canal Street out through some of the worst yellow-fever mosquito-infested swamps in the city to Lake Pontchartrain. The lives of hundreds of workers—mostly Irish—were lost in the digging of the canal.

Dakin's design was the bank's second building, the first having been located on the same site. The original bank had been designed by the man who designed the canal, Captain Richard Delafield, who was later to make a name for himself at West Point. Delafield's bank was not a particularly distinguished Greek Revival building of 1829. Its chief Greek characteristic was an exquisite little Doric portico projecting from the front.[17] The building was outgrown by 1843, and Dakin was then asked to commence the new, larger building.[18] The block between Gravier and Natchez streets, on Magazine, contained three banks. Dakin built an impressive granite building which still stands, though it is in need of sandblasting and grouting.[19]

Attached to the building contract for the bank is the second set of printed specifications known to be used by Dakin in New Orleans. Concerning the brickwork, he says: "The loose and careless manner of laying bricks as generally practiced in New Orleans shall not be taken as the guide or standard of laying the bricks in the works of these building under any pretense whatsoever." This unusual comment might make it appear that he was alluding to the St. Patrick's Church matter and was still smarting from the consequences.

The specifications call for the incorporation into the new bank parts of Delafield's old building. The old bank must have been a distinctive sight on Magazine Street, and its management probably wanted to retain an essence of it in some fashion as a "trade mark." Dakin was obliged to fit the two Doric columns and the entablature of the old portico into his first-floor facade. It was incorporated fairly well, creating an imposing entrance. Dakin cleverly repeats the double columns and entablature motif on each floor above the entrance, each time reducing it in scale and detail. The second-story treatment employs two square pilasters and a simple unadorned entablature; the third (and top) floor omits the pilasters and contains only a suggestion of an entablature. A blocking course above the cornice and three pedestals centered above the entrance top off the building.

The central section, defined by the old entablature on the first floor, is slightly recessed, except for the cornice of the entablature which projects slightly. The whole arrangement results in a nice interplay of shadows.

Perhaps more interesting than the transmutation of the portico up the front is the effect of starkness created by the use of the Town and Davis pilastrades down the side and across the front. The side, above the entablature over the granite piers, is absolutely bare. The fenestration serves to accentuate this, for it consists of extremely simple rectangular holes punched in the smooth surface of the wall. There

*Canal Bank, New Orleans, designed and built by James Dakin, 1843-44.*

are no lintels, and only a small sill below the third-story windows relieves the stark quality of the facade. The granite piers on the first floor, with their flowing regularity, increase the total effect.

The windows were also designed to give the building an illusion of greater height. The windows of the second floor were tall and slender, with the ones on the third floor being shorter by about one third. Viewed from the sidewalk, the bank seems taller than it really is.

This building, though Greek Revival, is modular and has in common with many modern buildings a boxlike regularity. Its geometrical order and the virtual monotony of its fenestration are characteristic of many contemporary buildings. If Dakin had lived to work in the period of the skyscraper, he would surely have used the Canal Bank as his prototype. Built in 1845, the bank seems to be looking in both directions in architectural history.

Today, the building is much altered internally. Originally, Dakin had used an elliptical skylight (measuring twelve by seven feet) over the banking room; this room had a gallery around it, supported in cantilever style.[20] This has all disappeared with time and the lowering of ceilings. Dakin's building was sold to an investor in 1847 for $105,000 and rented from him until 1850 when the bank moved again. Since that time, the building has been generally used as a place of business for dry-goods merchants. Now, it needs only a good sandblasting to renew its original exterior appearance.

In 1844 we find an example of Dakin's increasing activity, an ad in Kimball and James' *Business Directory for the Mississippi Valley*, published in Cincinnati. It covered such cities as Pittsburgh, Cincinnati, Louisville, St. Louis, Memphis, Natchez, and New Orleans. In the New Orleans section, on page 434, we find an advertisement reading, "James H. Dakin, Architect."[21]

The book was published only that one year, but it is significant because of the geographical area it covered, both in total area and the manner in which the cities were related. The Mississippi River was the highway for commercial activities in mid-America at the time. Dakin placed his advertisement in this directory, exposing his name to potential customers along the Mississippi from Pittsburgh to New Orleans. He had already done work at Louisville, Memphis, and New Orleans, and apparently he stood ready to go anywhere on the river for future jobs. Tradition in the Dakin family has it that he did work in Cincinnati and St. Louis, but so far nothing by him has been found in those cities.

Another manifestation of Dakin's inclination to look beyond New Orleans for work was his being considered for the job of constructing the Tennessee state capitol. On June 4, 1844, he was asked by Samuel D. Morgan, of the Tennessee Board of Capitol Commissioners, to submit plans for the new capitol. Dakin wrote his reply on June 15, 1844.[22]

The following day, as Dakin was mailing his reply, the committee discussed the possibility of getting William Strickland of Philadelphia, who was available, to do the job. He seems to have been their favorite immediately.

It is not known if Dakin ever presented plans for consideration, although it is recorded that Gideon Shryock did so, making two trips to Nashville in the process. But Strickland was their man, and he was signed on June 18, 1845, to supply the plans and superintend. It was to take fourteen years to finish his capitol—so long, in fact, that Strickland died before finishing it. (Upon his death on April 6, 1854, he was honored by being buried in his own building.)[23]

Fate decreed that the careers of James Dakin and James

Gallier would come together again with the erection of a commercial building for the New Orleans Gas Light and Banking Company. The building contract, dated January 24, 1844, said it was to be erected on "the lot now covered with the ruins of the Arcade Baths and adjoining the Camp St. Auction Mart." This would place it in the 300 block of Camp Street, opposite the intersection with Natchez Street:

Its builder was to be James Gallier and Company, Builders; but its plan was by James H. Dakin, Architect, and Dakin was to supervise its construction! No reason can be found to show why Gallier was not chosen as architect and supervisor as well as builder, nor is it known how the two got along during construction, with it coming so soon after the friction over St. Patrick's Church.[24]

The building was intended as a combination meeting hall and stores. The meeting hall was on the second floor and was reached by two doors in the center of the ground level. Flanking these doors at either side was a store, having a large warehouse area in the rear.[25] Stylistically, the design was not really typical of Dakin, although it showed that he could work with a variety of motifs, including the Palladian, which is not usually identified with him. The feature of this building was its great Venetian window for the meeting hall. The large rounded arch in its center and the two flanking columns with smaller windows at the sides followed the Palladian form (Dakin had used a smaller and simpler one for his Louisiana Hose Company shortly before). But encompassing the whole was a relieving arch concentric with the inner one. This is said to have been developed and popularized by the great English advocate of Palladio, Lord Burlington. The two columns in the Venetian window were Corinthian, and radiating out from the relieving arch was medium-heavy rustication (not very common in Dakin's work).

*Drawing of a building erected for New Orleans Gaslight and Banking Company, Camp Street, by James Dakin.*

The Venetian window was flanked by two other windows with Palladian round arches, and above these were set two square panels (of the same width as the side windows), decorated, honeycomb-like, with octagonal lights, a favorite Dakin device. Above these was set an entablature, not extending to the outer edge of the building, and a rather large overhanging cornice with dentils. Atop the building stood a blocking course of the same width as the Venetian window, decorated by a wreath at either end.

The ground-floor openings gave the effect of a granite pier building, although the piers were flush with the facade and had no capitals. In his composition for the building, then, Dakin had combined several styles—Palladian, Greek Revival, and the granite pier style of his Town, Davis, and Dakin days. The building probably survived no longer than 1849, by which time several fires on Camp Street had erased most of the structures there.[26]

The granite ashlar for the building came from St. Genevieve, Missouri, and was provided by the firm of A(ntoine) LaGrave and Company, stone cutters. A year later, this same company also supplied the stone for a large tomb in Donaldsonville, Louisiana, which, in all likelihood, was the product of James Dakin's creativity.[27]

In the Catholic Cemetery in Donaldsonville stands the tomb of Joseph Landry, who was named the first commandant of this area under the American regime in 1804. Although he died in 1814, his tomb was not erected until 1845. The monument is basically octagonal, with huge X-shaped projections, giving somewhat the feeling of the Tower of the Winds. Its four massive piers projecting outward are battered in the Egyptian style, and in between them, on the facade of the central core of the tomb, are twin Doric square pilasters set *in antis* in blind porticos. The front portico has an iron gate opening to the vaults within.

*Tomb of Joseph Landry, Donaldsonville, Louisiana, probably designed by James Dakin, 1845.*

*Design for a prison, by James Dakin. Note the striking resemblance the tower of the Landry tomb bears to this design. Both contain the same combination of Greek and Egyptian Revival elements.*

Above the massive battered wings, and running all around the structure, is a plain entablature and cornice. Rising above the central core is a Grecian templelike tower; its four sides all have triangular pediments and entablatures supported by two Doric square pilasters set *in antis* in blind porticos, like their larger counterparts below.

The walls of this tower are also battered, giving an effect not unlike that of the reredos of the Government Street Presbyterian Church in Mobile. All of this strongly hints of Dakin; yet an even stronger bit of evidence that this tomb is probably his design is a drawing in his collection of a building which almost matches the facade of the tower of the Landry tomb.[28] The drawing depicts a Greek Doric temple, with triangular pediment and square Doric columns, but with a striking departure from the ordinary — its outer walls are battered in the Egyptian style, much like the Bank of Louisville and the reredos at Mobile. In the background of the drawing can be seen an obelisk and a pyramid. This undated drawing is labeled simply, "Design for a Prison." The building bears some resemblance to the facade of Claude-Nicolas Ledoux's Barriere de St. Martin, a tollhouse outside Paris. In both instances, the lower half of the inside wall behind the porticos is solid for half of its height, with window openings only in the upper portion. However, while Ledoux's structure is low and squat, Dakin's is taller to emphasize and take advantage of the Egyptian batter of the walls.

Many important architects have designed tombs — Strickland, Latrobe, Lafever, and de Pouilly immediately come to mind. It is therefore not surprising that Dakin might try his hand in such a design. He may have been asked to design it by one of Landry's sons, Joseph A. Landry or Trasimond Landry, both active in politics. The latter was lieutenant governor when Dakin built the capitol

at Baton Rouge, and he had been in the legislature in the 1840s where he may have come into contact with Dakin over the many state projects Dakin was involved in.

James Dakin seems to have reveled in the combination of Greek and Egyptian motifs. The obelisk tower of his First Methodist Church, the Bank of Louisville, the church reredos, and this prison drawing all evidence this predilection. The Landry tomb therefore appears to be his work, primarily because of its Greco-Egyptianesque characteristics which were almost a Dakin trademark.

In the Dakin family, there survives a story that James Dakin designed a house, later known as the Sylvester Larned Institute after its conversion into a school. The evidence is considerable that, like most of the other Dakin family stories, this one is true.[29]

The owner of this massive Greek Revival house was Peter Conrey, a partner in the firm Gasquet, Parish, and Company. No building contract has been found to prove that Dakin designed it, but we have a statement by Conrey which, together with the family tradition, provides convincing evidence. In 1847 Conrey's statement to a notary public in Dakin's behalf said: "I have known Mr. Dakin about 14 years. Dakin was employed by me as an architect and supervisor for about 20 buildings and I was well satisfied."[30]

Conrey's house stood on the east side of Carondelet Street between Euterpe and Terpsichore Streets. It was two stories high, set on a tall basement. Dakin gave it a heavy looking portico, with a pediment and four Ionic columns. The windows of the first floor were huge, while those above were rather insignificant by comparison. Where the portico met the roof line, there was set a massive blocking course, deeply paneled, as were four pedestals set in this parapet.

Entrance was gained to the portico from a graceful double

*Henry Howard, Architect,* ca. 1849, *pupil of James Dakin, shortly after he left Dakin's office. (Courtesy Victor McGee)*

curved walkway leading to a straight flight of steps. Inside, on the first floor ran a central hallway, flanked on either side by double parlors. Across the back of the house ran a loggia with six slender columns. This description is possible only because Pilié and de Pouilly made a handsome water-color view of the house in the 1850s [31] (Plate 9).

Conrey had to give up the house in 1851 because of financial difficulties, and by the 1870s it was in the hands of the Presbyterian church, which used it as a school called the Sylvester Larned Institute.[32] With its ponderous dimensions and impressive portico, it lent itself more to a public institution than a residence. But a little later, it became the home of the mayor of New Orleans, Joseph Shakspeare. In 1905, it was sold to Beth Israel Synagogue and converted into a temple, again demonstrating its suitability for something other than a residence. It so remained until about 1924 when it was demolished to make way for a new church.

The size of the house indicates that Dakin seemed to work consistently in larger scales, whether for public or private buildings. In the case of the Conrey house, it may be that the client, knowing of Dakin's monumental work, asked for something in the same vein. While the Conrey house is not terribly distinguished in itself, it does serve to demonstrate what kind of residence Dakin was designing at the time.

By 1845, Dakin had so much business that he was able to hire as an apprentice draftsman a young man destined to succeed him as perhaps Louisiana's best architect of the next generation. Henry Howard had arrived in New Orleans a few years before and, like Dakin, learned the rudiments of building by entering the carpentry trade. Howard said that in 1845 he "studied Architecture for a short time with the late Col. James H. Dakin, an able Architect of the city." [33]

In recent years, Henry Howard has finally received some recognition for his work. He was acclaimed, for example, by Samuel M. Green in his book, *American Art,* for having designed "three of the most distinctive plantations in the South." These are Woodlawn, Madewood, and Belle Grove, all in Louisiana.[34]

Woodlawn, built about 1849, had a predecessor in New Orleans, an exact twin except for the wings, from which it may have been copied. Dakin was the probable architect of this house. It is likely that Howard was at least influenced by Dakin in his design.

We have already seen that the godmother of Dakin's two daughters, Madame Emelie Armitage, had been married to a man named James Armitage, whose mother's name was Abigail Loyal Armitage. The house which was the prototype of Woodlawn was recently found to have existed on Annunciation Street, between Thalia and Melpomene, and was built for a Mrs. Abigail Loyal Armitage Slark. The younger woman, Mrs. Slark, was undoubtedly the niece of Madame Armitage.

Mrs. Slark, wife of Robert Slark, a wealthy merchant of New Orleans, had come from Baltimore upon the death of her first husband. She and her infant daughter probably lived with Mr. and Mrs. Armitage at their place on Conti Street, the rooming house where Dakin lived when he arrived in New Orleans. Not the least interesting fact is that the young daughter later married Colonel John Walton, who served with Dakin during the Mexican War.[35]

It is not known who built the Slark mansion, but there are two links to Dakin. First, he probably knew Mrs. Slark through the Armitage family; and secondly, he apparently knew Robert Slark, for the latter supplied Dakin with hardware for the Louisiana state capitol about two years after the mansion was built.[36] In addition, the house is very

*Residence of Mrs. Abigail Loyal Armitage Slark, New Orleans, probably designed by James Dakin, ca. 1844. (Courtesy Morgan Whitney Collection, Tulane University)*

*Woodlawn Plantation, near Napoleonville, Louisiana, designed by Henry Howard, ca. 1849. (Courtesy Library of Congress)*

much in Dakin's style. Greek Revival, it has square piers at either end of a flat-roofed portico, with four Ionic columns between. The architrave is in correct form (three courses of mouldings) and has a course of dentils beneath the cornice. The two square piers feature sunken panels, and the walls on the sides culminate in huge gable ends with two chimneys. The overall effect is quite similar to that of Union Terrace or the arsenal on St. Peter Street.

The interior had a central hall opening to two large double parlors at either side.[37] The front door was enframed in a Greek "ears" motif, with a well-scaled course of dentils under its cornice. The house was a showplace, many notable families of New Orleans having been associated with it. In 1896, it was sold to Urban Koen, a well-known tobacco merchant. It was supposedly dismantled and moved to St. Louis about 1914, but it has not been located.[38] In that year, the Texas-Pacific Railroad Terminal was built on the entire square on which the house stood.

Dating the house is somewhat problematical. The land and assessment records indicate a date of 1844 or early 1845.[39] Mrs. Slark bought the land in November, 1842, and in the 1846 *City Directory* (there was no 1845 directory) she was listed at that address.[40] The date is crucial, for Henry Howard tells us that he studied with Dakin in 1845. If this house was begun in 1843 or 1844, and completed by 1845, it was built before Howard went out on his own as an architect, because he cites as his first job a "house for Mr. Thomas Pugh in 1846."[41] This is Madewood plantation, near Donaldsonville. Most important of all, however, Howard does not list the Slark mansion in the long list of works he appends to his autobiography.

The main difference between Woodlawn and the Slark house is the addition by Howard of low, one-story wings on either side of the plantation, attached by small exten-

sions from the side of the house. He also followed this plan at Madewood, for which another antecedent can be found in Town, Davis, and Dakin sources. Madewood, with its two wings at either side, produces a total effect similar to the Ithiel Town plan for the Bowers house. Here is the old Town design being repeated in the cane fields of Louisiana some twenty-five years after its development. Howard, of course, deserves credit for adding the low wings at the ends of the projections, making a pleasing variation on the original idea. He undoubtedly saw plans in Dakin's office for the Perry house in Brooklyn by Dakin and the Bowers house by Town. This writer also believes Howard saw and adapted for his use at Woodlawn the Slark house as designed by James Dakin.

## A MILITARY INTERLUDE

In 1846, Dakin's again-thriving career was interrupted briefly by the outbreak of the Mexican War. Dakin's military exploits were not of an epochal character, but, as a part-time soldier in the Louisiana militia, he was much admired as a leader and instructor of his troops. His military career culminated in his organizing and leading a regiment of his volunteers to Mexico.

It is possible that James Dakin had been a member of the New York militia before coming to New Orleans. However, because all pre-Civil War records of the New York militia have been destroyed in a fire, this is impossible to trace. What is significant is the fact that Dakin began his career in the New Orleans militia as an officer. He joined in 1837, and he first appears in the 1838 *City Directory* as Second Lieutenant James H. Dakin of the Washington Guards.[42]

The following year, when the state decided to erect the arsenal on St. Peter Street, Lieutenant Dakin was tapped for the assignment. Dakin remained in the militia, reaching the rank of captain by 1843.

On February 24, 1843, Dakin chaired a meeting held at Bank's Arcade for the purpose of organizing a new group of four companies of men to be called the Louisiana Volunteers.[43] Such volunteer units fulfilled the military service requirements of the day.

The Minute Book of this unit has survived, written in Dakin's own hand. The unit seems to have begun officially on April 22, 1843, with Dakin having the title of major. He was a stern officer, for, on more than one occasion, he ordered charges to be drawn up against those officers who failed to call out their companies for various functions.[44] On October, 5, 1843, Dakin's men unanimously elected him Colonel, a title by which he was to be known to most persons for the rest of his life.[45]

In the spring of 1845, Dakin was to have an experience denied to most men: the opportunity to see one's own obituary in print. Like Mark Twain was to do years later, Dakin could have announced that the reports of his death "were greatly exaggerated." The *Picayune* mournfully announced on April 10, 1845:

Col. James H. Dakin. Our citizens, more particularly those residing in this Municipality [the Second], to whom Col. James H. Dakin was generally known, will be pained to hear of his sudden demise. The fact of his having been chosen Colonel of so large and influential a body of Citizen Soldiery as the Louisiana Volunteers is proof of his popularity; his worth can only be appreciated by his family and intimate friends. The Second Municipality bears many testimonials of his professional ability as an architect, in which vocation he had assumed a distinguished position.[46]

That evening, Dakin walked into the *Picayune* office. The paper, faced with the subject of the obituary, made a retraction the next day:

Not Dead. We cannot recall a visit that was more gratifying to us than the one we received from Col. James H. Dakin yesterday. We had announced his death upon the authority of a rumor, which obtained such general credence that several officers of the Louisiana Volunteers who were in our office the night before last, were speaking of his demise in such terms as so melancholy an event was calculated to suggest. He had been recently so much indisposed that the report of his relapse and sudden end was less startling from its improbability than an account of the pain the loss of such a citizen occasioned. We are happy, however, to state upon the authority of Col. Dakin, whose word is good upon any subject, and conclusive in the present case, that he is not dead!—and we may add, from our own observation, that he looks as little like a corpse as any man we have seen for many a day. The Col., we would fain believe, will make no effort to have us indicted for killing him off before his time as he knows that there was no malice in the act to make it criminal in the eye of the law. Now that he has survived a newspaper paragraph of so fatal an import, he should promise himself a long life of happiness as we are sure it will be one of usefulness.[47]

Dakin's health was soon to be endangered by more than the *Picayune* article. The United States and Mexico were on the threshold of war over Texas. Within the year, thousands of Louisiana militiamen would find themselves in the chapparal of the Mexican desert.

General Zachary Taylor had been ordered to take up a position at the Nueces River, the border which was in hot dispute between Mexico and the United States. A rumor was spread in New Orleans that a large Mexican force under General Arista was marching down on Taylor's little army. The New Orleans newspapers were filled with calls of "To Arms! To Arms!" Although this first call to arms was canceled because the attack did not materialize, it was only a postponement of the inevitable. On April 25, 1846, the

Mexicans attacked, and Taylor sent a letter to the governors of Louisiana and Texas for reinforcements.[48] He requested that four regiments of infantry be sent to Point Isabel, the staging area on the Rio Grande at the Gulf of Mexico.

Meanwhile, in Mexico, two major battles were being fought, Palo Alto on May 8, and Resaca de la Palma on May 11. Taylor, although outnumbered, defeated the Mexican forces in these initial encounters. He was nevertheless in bad shape numerically at this moment and in danger of being driven into the sea. His strength was only 4,000 men compared to Arista's 8,000. America was in danger of having a preview of Dunkirk. But the volunteers from Louisiana soon arrived, swelling the count to a much safer total of 11,000 men. The volunteers from Louisiana numbered some 4,500 men, all raised in two weeks time. They, in fact, outnumbered the regular army and doubled the total volunteers from Texas, Alabama, Kentucky, and Missouri who also came forward immediately with help.[49]

Dakin, with five companies of men, sailed for Point Isabel on May 19, 1846, on the ship *Ondiaka*. His regiment was split up on the Point and on a nearby island, Brazos Santiago.[50] Albert G. Blanchard, one of Colonel Dakin's subordinates, a West Point graduate who had been working in a civilian job in New Orleans until the crisis, kept a diary; and it is through this diary that we know much of the difficulties, physical and political, of the volunteers from Louisiana.[51] Blanchard records that the trip was made in "fine weather, calm sea — men well, but crowded, the heat of the sun is intense and no shelter." Of Point Isabel, where headquarters was, he wrote: "The place is surrounded by an entrenchment with cannon, Mexican prisoners and booty." On May 29, Blanchard noted, "Col. Dakin sick. Col. Davis in command. Regt. getting organized by degrees."[52]

Dakin must have recovered immediately, for the New Orleans *Daily Delta* reported, "Col. Dakin appears to be in admirable health and his command is about 750 strong . . . making the force now collected on the end of the sand bank [Brazos Santiago] nearly 1,500, no trifling reinforcement for the war."[53]

On June 24, an interesting event involving Dakin took place. Blanchard records simply: "Dakin was drilling the men on defensive positions when he charged a square [of men] and his horse received a severe bayonet wound in the neck." But the story was reported more fully in two newspapers after Dakin's death years later, as an example of his leadership and dedication to his job of training the volunteers. It gives us a good look at this tenacious man and the determination with which he went about his business, whether it be architectural or military. The *Picayune* tells it:

In speaking with a friend about . . . Col. Dakin, he related a little anecdote which is so characteristic of the man that we cannot refrain from repeating it. . . .

The Col. commanded one of the six regiments raised in the state after Palo Alto and Resaca de la Palma. . . . he was an old disciplinarian, very strict and capable, and in a short time, his regiment excited the admiration of even veteran regular officers by the ease and precision with which it drilled and manoeuvered.

One evening, the regiment was standing at ease after a variety of charges and evolutions when the Col. took it into his head to put their discipline to a strong test. The regiment was thrown into a square to receive cavalry. The commander rode off a few hundred yards, and then wheeling his horse, came down, sword in hand, at a fierce gallop, straight at his men. He and his steed formed an imposing looking object, for he was a big man [his exact height is not known, but he was probably over six feet, for his son was six feet four inches tall] and his steed was a big horse and neither appeared to fear the glittering and bristling array of bayonets against which they were rushing. The men stood the charge very well until the horse and rider were within a few feet; then they broke right and left in confusion and opened a broad passage for the "Cavalry" into their ranks.

Of course, the Colonel was wroth, and the way the men and officers caught it for a few moments was by no means agreeable to the feeling. "You form a square! You repel cavalry! Why, what would you have done if a thousand dragoons had charged you as I did?"

"Well, just try us again, Col., and see if we don't hurt your feelings," cried a number of discomforted volunteers. The square was again formed; off rode the Colonel; round he wheeled and again he came at full speed, rushing straight at the bayonets, and looking as if he would crush them to powder under his charger's heels. The bayonets wavered not, though; the horse came faster and faster, and finally, with a terrible sound, sprang at the square. The square stood the shock, and the next moment, the horse was stretched on the ground with a broken bayonet in his side, and his limbs quivering in the death agony, whilst the stout rider lay with his foot and knee caught, and himself unable to rise. Not a man moved—the square was silent, steady and unbroken. In another instant, the Colonel was on his feet. He replaced his sword in the scabbard, looked gravely and cooly at the dead horse and at the firm array of soldiers and then said in his usual quiet way, "Very well done boys—both the horse and the square did their duty. Now you're ready for the lancers." [54]

The men cheered—not a little. [54]

A reader of this piece in Baton Rouge a few days later took exception to a few points and clarified some of the details. Identifying himself as one of the soldiers who had formed the square, this man corrected the *Picayune* on the death of the horse. He said that the horse "was severely wounded, but the wound was entirely owing to the unmanageable manner of the horse." The man went on to praise Colonel Dakin as a soldier and as a man, referring to him as one who "can look upon the dangers of the battlefield with a perfect composure, but who is perfectly unnerved at the sight of the suffering of his gallant steed." [55]

This incident gives us some insight into the kind of soldier Dakin was, but he and his men were not to meet the enemy in Mexico. After they had spent three months there,

drilling rigorously and suffering exposure to the weather, an order came from the secretary of war in Washington disbanding all six-month volunteer units. The basis for this order was an act of Congress—which had been passed just a few days before the men had volunteered—stating that volunteers must enlist either for twelve months or for the duration of the war. With much resentment and displeasure, the Louisiana volunteers returned to New Orleans in the late summer of 1846. New Orleans newspapers vented their rage for weeks over the mishandling of the enlistment of the volunteers.

## THE UNIVERSITY OF LOUISIANA

After returning from Mexico in 1846, Dakin, now forty years old, gave up his interest in militia activities and once again devoted his full energies to his chosen profession. It was at this point that Dakin embarked on a period of achievement which would match his best previous years, the mid-1830s. In the next five years he was to build Louisiana's new capitol, design its first major university, and superintend the construction of the largest building in the United States, excluding the national Capitol.

The Medical College of Louisiana had been trying in the state legislature for years to obtain funds for a new building; failing that, as we saw, the faculty had come up with the money themselves; the state provided only a lot in State House Square. By 1847, the school had achieved such success and become so widely known that the legislature finally relented and appropriated some cash for a change, this time for a complete university.

It was felt the medical students were lacking in preparation before entering college because there was simply no adequate university at which they could learn the humani-

*Drawing of the University of Louisiana (later Tulane University), New Orleans, designed by James Dakin, 1847. Two-thirds view; the other third of the complex, the old Medical College, stood at left of this view.*

*Old print of University of Louisiana.
(Courtesy Tulane University
Medical School Library)*

ties.[56] The legislature decided to create a school to be called the University of Louisiana which would absorb the Medical College and offer academic courses as well. It was to be built next to the existing building in the rear of State House Square.

Authority to erect the building was granted by an act of April 22, 1847. It provided $25,000 in funds and stated that "the plan of buildings for the University of Louisiana drawn by James Dakin and presented to the Legislature for their consideration be . . . approved and adopted."[57] A contract was signed on June 25, 1847, with John Mitchell, Joseph M. Howell, and Moses M. Coates, builders, to execute Dakin's plan.[58]

The new university complex (in the Greek Revival style) formed an E shape, including a central building with a portico supported by six Corinthian columns with a triangular pediment, very deeply recessed. The old Medical College building, at the left of the new central wing, had a twin, placed to the right of the main building. Only the two newer buildings were connected, there being a low wing at the rear of each for this purpose.[59] The new wing at the right duplicated the characteristics of the Medical School: a flat roof, with two Corinthian columns set *in antis* in a recessed porch.

The overall plan of the university bears a striking resemblance to the design by the English architect, George Hadfield, for the City Hall at Washington, D.C., 1820–1823.[60] We find the same E shape and the pedimented central building, flanked by two flat-roofed wings with columns *in antis*. There are a few readily discernible differences. Hadfield used Ionic columns and not Corinthian; he set them in a double row in the central building, whereas Dakin used only one row; and he employed steps for the front entrances to the side wings which led to the second floor from either

side (at right angles), whereas Dakin used steps leading directly to the entrance which was on the first floor. It is not known if Dakin visited Washington before making his design (he probably did), but the resemblance is intriguing. In 1832, Alexander Jackson Davis brought back to his New York office a copy of Hadfield's plan which Dakin may have seen and remembered in making an adaptation for the college.[61]

The new parts of the university complex—the central building and the right wing—were built in two stages, the central wing being completed in 1848 and the other wing in September, 1855. The 1855 appropriation of the legislature also included funds for a beautiful cast iron fence around the entire school.[62]

When the central portion was finished in 1848, the newspaper said:

With much good taste, the architect has selected the Corinthian order of architecture and planned the different rooms with an eye both to their utility and beauty. The central college is 100 feet in front by 109 feet deep, fronted by a very beautiful facade, which is supported by six Corinthian pillars. There are three lecture rooms, each capable of containing 600 pupils, two dissecting rooms, 100 feet long, a splendid room intended for the museum, 60 x 45 feet, seven private rooms for the professors and a large library room.[63]

The interior of the Medical School was said to be patterned after the University of Virginia Medical School, one of the finest in the country. A detailed description is not possible here, but one can be found in *Hazard's Review*, November 6, 1830.[64]

In 1857, some improvements and alterations were performed by the firm of Gallier and Turpin. Comparison of views before and after indicate that they must all have been to the interior.[65]

In 1858, the school ranked fifth in the nation in the

number of medical students graduating.[66] With the coming of the Civil War, however, the school was closed entirely. It fell into disrepair, but funds were obtained from the legislature again for restoration, and it reopened with part of the building being used as a freedmen's school for a time during Radical Reconstruction.[67]

The school thrived again, and on July 5, 1884, the legislature converted the University of Louisiana into Tulane University to utilize the gift of Paul Tulane to the institution. Tulane University gradually outgrew its little campus, and in 1895 erected a new one uptown on St. Charles Avenue. The class of 1895 was the last one to be graduated from Dakin's school.

In March, 1898, the school felt a need to use the property in a profitable way (the city had grown up all around it and the land was very valuable). The old school was demolished, and almost immediately, a theatre was erected on the site.[68] The Exxon building now stands there, on land still owned by Tulane, successor to the University of Louisiana.

Had these buildings not been demolished, perhaps Gallier Hall would not have a monopoly on being the epitome of the Greek Revival in New Orleans. Dakin's name might have been as much a household word in New Orleans as Gallier's. Expressing the restless nature of Dakin as a Greek Revivalist who went beyond the purely archeological, the complex of buildings on State House Square was certainly at least the equal of Gallier Hall.

# 9

# A GOTHIC MASTERPIECE:
# THE CAPITOL AT BATON ROUGE

THE ERECTION OF THE LOUISIANA STATE CAPITOL BY JAMES Dakin was to be the fulfillment of the promise inherent in his abilities (Plate 10). Of the many great buildings Dakin designed in his lifetime, the capitol of Louisiana is the one for which he will probably be best remembered.

Its Gothic style poses a problem for modern viewers trying to decide for themselves the importance of this building. The building is perplexing to those observers who have forgotten that the Gothic Revival once had its heyday in this country. To those contemporary with it, the capitol was, for the most part, easily accepted; many people considered it one of the finest buildings in the South.

The Gothic style had been used for a state capitol once before, in the old capitol of Georgia at Milledgeville (1807–1837).[1] This building has virtually been forgotten, unlike the Louisiana State Capitol which has remained eye-catching—even spectacular—into the twentieth century. Its imposing location on the banks of the Mississippi River at Baton Rouge has, no doubt, helped make the Louisiana capitol more memorable. But more importantly, it is one of the finest examples of secular Gothic designed in America during the Revival period. Dakin has frequently been remembered in reference books as a "Gothicist";[2] his Louisiana State Capitol justifies that reputation.

Louisiana needed a new capitol building in 1845—there is no doubt of that. The then-existing capitol, the converted Charity Hospital on Canal Street, was referred to as "that miserable, old and dilapidated structure known as our State House."[3] Even more vehemently, the *Daily Delta* commented that "it was a crying disgrace to the State to compel the highest officers to occupy such hovels as have been allocated to them . . . and to compel our executive officers to visit such rat traps."[4]

An article in the new constitution of 1845 moved the seat of government to Baton Rouge; thus, in 1846, the legislature provided for three commissioners (appointed by the governor) to accept a site from the city of Baton Rouge and to supervise the construction of a new capitol.[5] The move to Baton Rouge was not so startling, even though Baton Rouge was then but a hamlet, for New Orleans had long been considered too strong a distraction for legislators attracted to the variety of pleasures the city offered.[6] The "country" parishes also felt that a more centrally located capitol would be preferable.

To supervise the erection of the new capitol, the governor chose Maunsel White, a Democrat, representing Plaquemines Parish in the state senate; Dr. Walter Brashear, a Whig of Brashear City (now Morgan City), representing St. Mary Parish in the senate; and Daniel D. Avery (later a judge), a Whig representing East Baton Rouge Parish in the house. Avery replaced George Cook of West Feliciana Parish, who resigned the commission in 1847. All were men of character, who got along well together in their duties as commissioners, despite the fact that they received no compensation from the state.

While it is not an essential part of the story of the capitol, it is interesting to note that two of the three commissioners were the founders of the hot sauce industry in Louisiana. Daniel Avery, for whose family Avery Island is named, began cultivating pepper plants in his kitchen garden before the Civil War. Afterwards, his son-in-law, Edmund McIlhenny developed the growing of these plants into the flourishing industry we know today as the Tabasco sauce operation. Maunsel White, who owned the sugar plantation, Deer Range, in Plaquemines Parish, also grew hot peppers there, and his concoction bore his name: Maunsel White Sauce. It was made until at least the 1890s and is still

*Maunsel White,* ca. 1853, *commissioner for the erection of the Louisiana State Capitol at Baton Rouge. (From* De Bow's Review, *January, 1853)*

remembered by some Louisianians. It is still unclear which man was the first to grow those distinctive hot peppers which are the necessary ingredients of this gourmet sauce. It is probably no coincidence that both were on the same commission for the state capitol.[7]

The leader of the commissioners by tacit understanding was Maunsel White, an excellent example of the American success story. Born in Protestant Ireland in 1783, he soon immigrated to America. As a boy in Louisville, he grew up with and became a close friend of Zachary Taylor. He arrived in New Orleans, penniless, in 1801, when the Spanish still owned Louisiana. Maunsel White fought in the Battle of New Orleans, there meeting Andrew Jackson, who became a lifelong friend. By 1850, Maunsel White's wealth approached a million dollars. White's son gives us a good perspective on his father's character, saying: "He first made a name and his name made the money—none stood higher for integrity—his word was inviolate as an oath." [8]

Maunsel White took an almost fatherly interest in Dakin and perceptively recognized the great talent this man had for architecture. It was mainly through White that Dakin received the commission for the Louisiana State Capitol. Through White's letterbook we can see his esteem for Dakin both as a man and as an architect.[9]

By an act of January 21, 1847, the commissioners were empowered to advertise for plans and propositions to build the capitol.[10] Dakin, wasting no time, submitted his design on January 26, 1847. It must have startled the members of the commission when they saw it, for it was in the new style of the times, Gothic. Dakin's proposal is contained in the diary he kept on the capitol:

In making the Design, I have endeavored, first, to give the necessary apartments and accommodations for the State Legislature and the different officers of the State. Second, to adopt such a taste and style of architecture as would give the Edifice a decided, distinctive, classic and commanding character and be appropriate to its purpose. Third, to accomplish these objects with proper economy in the erection of the building.

I have used the Castellated Gothic style of Architecture in the Design because it is quite as appropriate as any other Style or Mode of building and because no style or order of Architecture can be employed which would give suitable character to a Building with so little cost as the Castellated Gothic.

Should a Design be adopted on the Grecian or Roman Order of Architecture, we should accomplish only what would unavoidably appear to be a mere copy of some other Edifice already erected and often repeated in every city and town of our country. Those orders have been so much employed for many years past that it is almost impossible to start an original conception with them.

My Design is represented by plain geometrical drawings which is the usual mode adopted for important Public Buildings, as perspective drawings give the Artist the power to introduce fancy scenery and high coloring, and various ficticious accessories, which often blind and deceive the spectator and divert his attention from the real merits of the Design.

A Building could be erected according to the Design for $100,000 using bricks and cement for the walls and cast iron for the window frames and ornamental details. If built of Marble, it would cost $200,000.

The utmost economy or liberality may be employed in erecting a building in the Castellated Gothic Style with propriety either way, all of which will depend upon the judgment or pleasure of the Commissioners.

> Very respectfully,
> Your obdt. servant,
> James H. Dakin, Architect[11]

His rough estimate included "one large skylight in the roof over the court [rotunda]," "372 circular stair steps," and the notation that "the rooms are not encumbered with columns and are free of all obstructions."

In this submission, we find in the words of one of the finest Greek Revival architects in America a disavowal of the Greek and Roman styles as having been overworked.

Even Dakin—who helped develop the *in antis* plan, the pilastrade, the Davisean window, and was the creator of the imaginative Bank of Louisville and the Louisiana State Arsenal—had to admit that it was "almost impossible to start an original conception" in the Greek style. Here we can see a symptom of the voracious appetite for styles of the mid-century architect in America who, in but ten years, was to go down the road of eclecticism, lose his way in the Victorian era, and re-emerge with the creations of Sullivan, Richardson, and Wright.

Despite the obvious need for an architect for the construction of the capitol, strong opposition arose in the legislature over whether an architect should be hired at all, or whether the task should be put entirely in the hands of a contractor or the commission. This obstructionism extended further to a fight over the addition of two more commissioners to the panel for the capitol. The chief antagonist was Duncan Kenner, a Whig of Ascension Parish. But Maunsel White was a match for him.

Addressing the senate on April 9, 1847, White presented the report of the commissioners on the necessity of employing an architect to supervise construction of the capitol. The statement, obviously prepared with the help of an architect (probably Dakin), outlined in some detail the complexities of designing and erecting a building. In an effort to demonstrate the futility of nonprofessionals attempting such an undertaking, White made reference to the need for mathematical accuracy in the design, for specialized skill in remedying possible foundation defects, and for careful calculation of such detail work as windows, mouldings, and pilasters. White concluded his address as follows:

We venture to say that in the design now in the hands of the Commissioners [Dakin's], there are not more than two men in this city that could carry out its details to completion. [The men were obviously Gallier and Dakin.] It is original, grand and unique in its design, partaking of the boldness and simplicity of the middle ages, softened down by modern improvement and invention.

Its conception does infinite credit to the inventive genius of the man whose towering mind produced it. . . . Mr. James H. Dakin is the architect of this splendid drawing and capable in every respect to conduct its erection. There is not a more honest, faithful or trustworthy man, and he is the choice of at least two of the Commissioners, and probably may be of the other also.[12]

The next day, White arose in the senate to explain the problems in acquiring a suitable site for the capitol in Baton Rouge. Two groups in that city were divided, with one recommending a site on the United States military base near the present Pentagon Barracks.[13] White objected to the price asked by the federal government and pointed out that the other group suggested a site which was cheaper and more desirable because it overlooked the Mississippi River. White had the foresight to know that placing the capitol on the high bluffs of the Mississippi would ensure a dramatic view of both the building and the river and make a superb setting for the new capitol. He also suggested the possibility of purchasing the adjacent lots. Dr. Brashear pointed out that the open area thus obtained in front would provide space for a botanical garden which could be added later. The extra lots would cost only three thousand dollars more, and he did not consider this a sum significant enough to quibble about.

At this point, the commissioners' antagonist, Duncan Kenner, barged in with various charges, the first being that he had heard that the comissioners "were disposed to erect marble facades and balustrades" which would run the cost above the $100,000 total expected cost. He added fuel to the fire by stating that he "heard of botanical gardens—they may add mineralogical and perhaps zoological gardens." Brashear countered by stating that if they should erect a

cheap building, costing $30,000 or $40,000, those persons opposed to locating in Baton Rouge would be pleased, for it would give them a pretext for moving the state house. This, he said, was why objective commissioners were selected to serve and without pay.

Kenner also brought up the question of additional commissioners and suggested that they be required to reside at Baton Rouge and to serve without pay.[14] A howl of disagreement followed this proposal. Kenner's suggestion that the commission supervise the construction was answered by Senator Moore, who pointed out that no matter how great the energy of the commissioners, no one could be found to superintend a work of this kind "unless he were a professional architect and knew his business."

Maunsel White objected to Kenner's idea because the two new commissioners, who would have to be from Baton Rouge if they were to supervise, would come from a city already torn into two factions over the site. He said he "considered this proceeding a mere introductory scene in a ludicrous farce." But when a vote was taken, White, a statesman and not a politician, voted to *add* the commissioners to demonstrate that he had no desire to dominate the building commission. A ten-to-ten tie resulted, and after an executive session, the original membership of three men emerged.

In a few days, when the house sent over its resolution fixing the supervising architect's annual salary at five thousand dollars and a payment of five hundred for the best model of the capitol, Kenner began another attack—this time on the profession of architecture. He moved to reduce the figure to three thousand dollars and was supported by Dr. Brashear.[15] White arose to say that the model they had selected was "in truly elegant style, something of the Gothic grandeur of former years, blended with the simplicity of

plans and superintendence except the word of the writer, who, of course, remains anonymous.

What the TIP writer overlooked completely was the fact that White voted with Senator Hereford to economize on the capitol. On April 21, Hereford moved, in senate debate, to reduce the appropriation for the capitol from $150,000 to $100,000, and Maunsel White voted in favor of the motion.[20] This anonymous letter must have been one of the most scurrilous abuses the commissioners had to endure.

Shortly after Cook's departure from the commission membership, Dakin commented very ungenerously in his diary that because his plan was chosen, Cook had been "defeated in his project to make the building cost much more than was contemplated and in getting a larger slice of the funds to stick to his avaricious fingers upon the principle: 'To the victor belongs the spoils.' " [21]

The fees paid to Dakin actually compared favorably with those paid to William Strickland for the Tennessee State Capitol, which was then just under construction. Strickland was paid $500 for his plans and $2,500 per year.[22]

The legislation which resulted from all the debate on the capitol was passed on May 3, 1847, and provided $100,000 for its construction, with a maximum of $150,000, which would include the architect's salary and contingent expenses. The $500 for the plans and model were paid separately. An earlier act, in 1846, had set the date of completion of the building as January 18, 1849, which allowed an extremely short period of time for the size and complex detail of such a Gothic building.[23]

With the legislative and other wrangling out of the way, the construction of the capitol could now begin. The site was accepted by the commissioners on June 19, 1847, from Mayor John R. Dufrocq of Baton Rouge, transferring the square bounded by North Boulevard, St. Philippe Street,

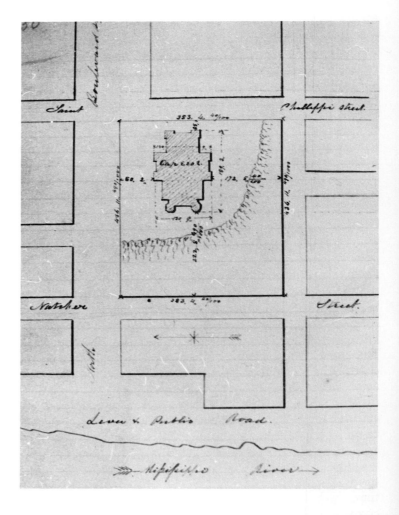

*Sketch of the ground plan for Louisiana State Capitol, Baton Rouge, by James Dakin. (From Dakin's capitol diary. Courtesy Louisiana State University Library Archives)*

America Street, and Natchez Street. Five thousand dollars was appropriated by the commission to help defray the cost, the balance coming from public subscription in Baton Rouge.[24] Title was actually transferred to the state on September 11, 1847. The square, which belonged to Judge T. G. Morgan, was located on the high bluffs overlooking the Mississippi, the first high land to come into view when ascending the river. It was an ideal site.[25]

The story of the erection of the capitol has been made much more vivid for us by the existence of James Dakin's diary for the period of construction. It is both technical and general and gives us an insight into his character and temperament. The diary is unique in that it is the only document of such length in Dakin's own hand. It begins with the parts previously quoted concerning the competition, and ends on January 10, 1850, shortly before Dakin resigned to take over the New Orleans Custom House job.

From the diary, we learn that on the morning of June 27, 1847, Dakin sailed for Baton Rouge to lay out the site. Arriving the next morning at seven he fixed the location, noting that "it clears Judge Morgan's house by about 3 feet. The purpose of the fixing of the building was to show the contractors where they could deposit their bricks, sand, etc, as they were anxious to do so. McHatton, Pratt & Co. say they cannot commence to lay brick until the first of October; consequently, it will be best for me to start to Pittsburgh at once for the iron work." [26]

The arrangement with McHatton, Pratt, and Company was based primarily on the fact that they were the lessees of the Louisiana State Penitentiary at Baton Rouge. At that time, the penitentiary was leased out by the state to private companies who were empowered to use convict labor to make brick, weave fabric and other material. This arrangement lasted until 1902.[27] Though it served to keep the

prisoners busy, it nevertheless reduced the likelihood of getting good quality products from this unskilled prison labor. The state, it was thought, would save money on the capitol by utilizing the cheap convict labor, but the commissioners, as we shall see, became concerned over the poor quality of the bricks before the building was even begun; throughout its erection, Dakin was to have no end of troubles over the bricks.

At the same time all the activity over the capitol was going on, Dakin had applied for the job of supervising architect of the new custom house at New Orleans. Although he had been accepted as architect for the Louisiana capitol, he expected to fare better financially with the federal government. This job would have lasted longer also, for the custom house was to be the largest building in the United States, excluding the national Capitol.

So, the trip to Pittsburgh Dakin referred to had a twofold purpose. First, he had to go to the office of Knap and Totten to make arrangements for the cast iron their foundry was to supply for the capitol. But the trip also allowed Dakin to make a side excursion to New York and Washington to see the secretary of the treasury concerning the custom house job, which he was seeking with Maunsel White's approval.

On July 14, 1847, Dakin left for Pittsburgh, taking with him his wife and children on the riverboat SS *Glencoe*, bound for Louisville and Cincinnati. After a ten-day journey from New Orleans, Dakin dropped his family off at Higginsport, Ohio, forty miles above Cincinnati (where they apparently had relatives). An incident which occurred in Cincinnati was recorded by Dakin. Upon arriving in that city, his nine-year-old son, Charles James Dakin, saw one of the steamboat passengers steal his father's roll of drawings for the iron work of the capitol. The man had already gotten the roll of valuable detailed drawings into his cart before

*Side view of Louisiana State Capitol. (Drawing made for 1966 restoration. Courtesy George M. Leake, architect)*

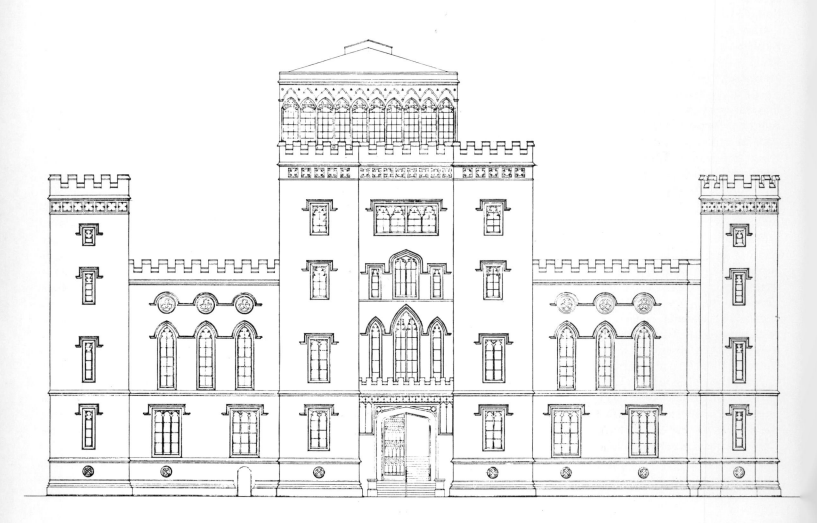

being discovered. Dakin noted, "My little son told me about the theft, or I should have lost the drawings." He did not record how he dealt with the thief, but we may presume that it was not gently.[28]

Changing boats twice because of low water, Dakin arrived in Pittsburgh on July 28, 1847. At the meeting with Knap and Totten, he recorded seeing a friendly face, F. S. Hermann, who happened to be having a steamboat built for the Lake Pontchartrain to Mobile trade.[29] This was probably Florian Hermann, son of Samuel Hermann, Dakin's old neighbor from his days on Conti Street with Madame Armitage. After dropping off the iron work drawings at Knap and Totten, Dakin was on his way to Washington on custom house business. His meetings there will be touched on briefly in the next chapter.

Meanwhile, Maunsel White was busy getting ready to make the myriad purchases necessary for the capitol. He wrote Daniel Avery at Baton Rouge: "I notice your remarks relative to the bricks. Our contract is for *good hard burnt* bricks, and no others can be admitted. Mr. Dakin told me when we parted that he would be in Baton Rouge in October." [30]

White mentioned the bricks to Dakin, writing him on September 8, 1847, in Pittsburgh:

Mr. Avery says there are a million bricks and 5,000 bbls. of sand now deposited on the site and your presence will positively be required by October 1. Also, there are a great many bricks . . . on the ground not half burnt . . . and may provide disagreeable consequences. I cannot allow the least deviation from the contract. . . . We want a cornerstone. Can't you get one somewhere as you come along, with proper inscriptions thereon. This is Mr. Avery's idea. I, for my own part, care nothing about burying my name under the State House to be found out some thousand years hence. Perhaps we can have the names put in some more conspicuous place, but do as you please about it.[31]

On October 3, Dakin left Pittsburgh on the SS *Isaac Newton* and arrived in Cincinnati on October 7, where he drew a draft for three hundred dollars and gave it to Mrs. Charles B. Dakin, his late brother's wife.[32] This is virtually the last shred of evidence to show what happened to her and her little girl, then about nine years of age. Dakin picked up his wife and children there and returned to New Orleans on the SS *Henry Hudson,* arriving October 22, 1847.

While in New Orleans, Dakin ordered the cornerstone and a copper box to be shipped immediately to Baton Rouge, for which he departed the next day, October 25. On November 1, the contractors began laying the foundations in the trenches. Dakin said of it: "Finding the soil to be of clay instead of sand and gravel as I first supposed, I thought it necessary to increase the width of the footing the length of one to two bricks more in all the foundations."

With the foundations thus under way, the ceremony of laying the cornerstone could now take place and was scheduled for November 1, 1848. It seemed as if all of Baton Rouge turned out for this gala occasion. In those days, the town had a population of only about 3,900 persons, of whom about 2,500 were white.[33]

The Masons were in charge of the ceremonies, as they always seemed to be, and a large contingent from the Grand Lodge came up from New Orleans. The commissioners were represented by Maunsel White and Daniel Avery, with the latter delivering a short speech. The principal speaker was Judge Canonge of New Orleans. After he spoke, dinner was held at the Warf Boat, and at 9 P.M. a candlelight procession moved toward the St. James Masonic Lodge. Dakin was himself a member of the lodge and a Royal Arch Mason. The following morning, the New Orleans delegation visited the pentagon barracks at the United States military base and departed for home. Dakin was

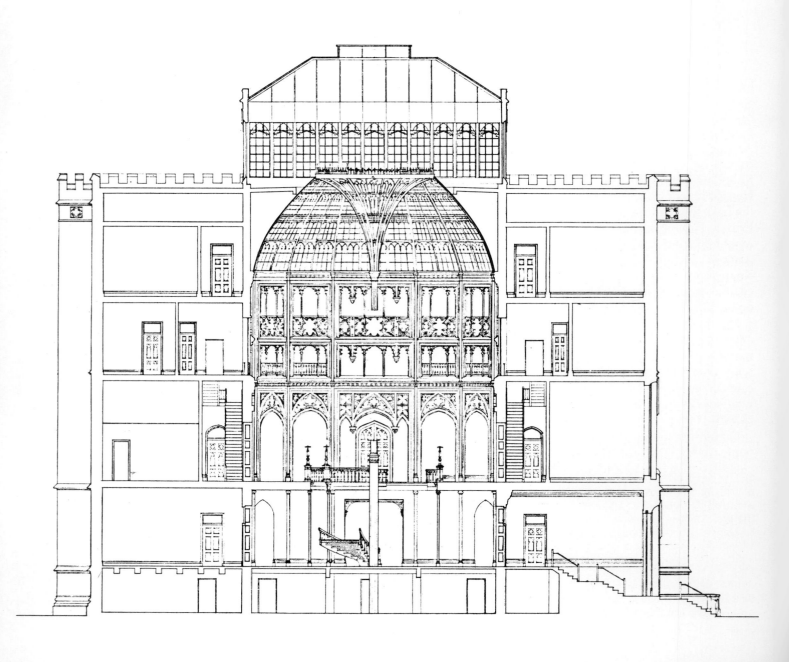

*Transverse section of Louisiana State Capitol. (Courtesy George M. Leake)*

afterwards congratulated by the newspapers for his part in the ceremonies: "We want words to express ourselves in a manner commensurate with the modest and efficient activity of the excellent architect, Col. Dakin, through the whole proceedings of this auspicious day, a day to be remembered by its present generation as among the proudest and happiest in the short and simple annals of the little town of Baton Rouge." [34]

Dakin now really began to rush the work. Newton Richards of New Orleans, a supplier of marble and granite, complained to him in December, 1847: "I fear you are getting along too fast for me. I do not expect any of the granite until about January." The other marble supplier, Pierre Monsseaux of New Orleans, also had to get an extension from White for a delay, but Dakin suggested that he be warned that it might be necessary to substitute cast iron for stone if he failed to live up to the contract. Already, we see Dakin about ready to abandon the old building methods and move more and more toward the new technology just becoming available.

In February, 1848, a group of legislators from the Public Buildings Committee, Messrs. Duncan, Hubert, Patterson, and Lanier, inspected the work and pronounced that it was proceeding satisfactorily.[35] This approval by the legislature had been expected by Dakin, for he had confidently written Knap and Totten in December, "I warned them not to proceed [with the old drawings] as the Commissioners want another appropriation to finish the interior 'more splendidly' than planned."

The legislature indeed responded in the spring session of 1848 with another $100,000 for the capitol, $50,000 being allocated for 1848 and a like amount for 1849. The section of the act for 1849 stated that the money was "for the purpose of embellishing the interior of the State House agreeably to the plan and estimate of the architect employed by the Commissioners." [36]

This was a remarkable appropriation when one considers the haggling in the senate before the capitol was begun. It, in effect, doubled the original appropriation. In the senate, the prime mover was Senator Hereford. Ironically, this was the same Senator Hereford whom A. T. Wood had praised for holding down the cost of the new capitol. Hereford was now the champion of White and Dakin. It is also interesting to note that this senate included Duncan Kenner, who had previously objected so vociferously to the original appropriation. He apparently did not raise his voice this time, for the newspapers, in describing the day's work in the legislature when the bill was passed, said only: "The Senate did nothing of particular importance today." It appears that the acceptance of the new, large appropriation was concurred in by both the press and the public.

A further advantage gained in the legislature that session was an act extending the time for completion of the capitol. The act changed the target date to December 1, 1849, instead of 1848. This gave Dakin and the builders more breathing room and was a much more realistic goal than the previous date.

Delays in obtaining iron from Pittsburgh hampered progress, and in the spring of 1848, White replied to what must have been a pointed letter from Dakin:

I plainly perceive from the tone of your letter that you were not in the most happy of humor, and I do not escape some of your shafts. . . . I always thought and still do that you were imbued with the most sincere desire to keep within the limits [of the appropriations], but there are others who are not. And truly, I don't know why I should give myself such anxiety about it, when, if I can't do well, it is so easy for me to retire and let the Governor appoint someone else in my place. . . . You know full well that I am for going ahead and that delays and disappointments must be accounted for by someone, and if I don't apply to you, you must be well aware that the whole burden of the business will be placed upon my shoulders, and in case of failure, who do you think the Legislature and the Public would look to but Maunsel White in this drama. . . . I'll come up again when I can and when I get out of those scrapes of public duty, I promise you that I shall never be caught again meddling with them.[37]

The iron continued to be late and bad. Dakin wrote Knap and Totten that the window heads were breaking and the string course of moulding was too thick and not according to specifications. On May 27, 1848, work had to be stopped altogether, because the iron had not come in.

All the frustrations and difficulties with the suppliers and contractors must have made Dakin feel, at this point, that his responsibilities far exceeded the salary he was receiving. He apparently wrote White to ask for the contract for the whole job so that he could deal directly with the contractors and suppliers himself. White replied:

After weighing carefully, coolly and dispassionately the claims, the reasons and everything else that could be brought into the scale to favor your wishes and desires to obtain the whole and sole contract of the building and finishing of the State House, I found myself so perplexed between a desire to serve you and my duty as a commissioner that I could not come to the conclusion to tell you abruptly that the law, as passed by the Legislature, would not authorize us to enter into the contract you desire. Without consulting the Governor, to whom I handed your letter of May 30 to read and requesting his opinion and advice, I explained to him all the vast labors you had to undergo and urged it as a reason that you were not paid for your services, but often considering the law and reminding me of my remarks made in the Senate chamber relative to the duties of an architect, and that upon my recommendation, an *architect* was appointed with the salary of $3,000 a year, it could not be altered and that if any accident should occur putting you in possession of the contract by our consent, we would be charged with collusion, and that the State looked at the Commissioners as men morally bound to carry out the law and to more practicality than anyone else. . . . [These problems] threw so much new light

on the duties I had assumed and expected of me, that I could not help regretting that I ever had anything to do with the matter. Nor indeed would I, were it not more particularly on your account. And if I had to pay you a thousand dollars a year out of my pocket, would I, rather than see you desert a post, which to leave now would injure you and me too. . . .

You will now see how I am pleased with every desire and wish to render you all and every service in my power, consistent with honor. I know you would disclaim any other motive; I cannot in the present case comply with your wishes. . . .

You are aware of the general dislike there is throughout the State to the present location, and there are hundreds who would lay hold on any pretext to defeat the erection of the building even at the risk of destroying your, mine or anyone else's character, no matter could they attain their ends.

Hold on, then, my friend, and carry out your noble design; it will ultimately remand to your honor, and if I can help it, be assured you shall not be the loser.[38]

White's prediction was far more prophetic than he could have imagined. The state capitol is indeed the only major building in Louisiana by James Dakin which is consistently remembered as being by him. Thus, it was through Maunsel White's good judgment and not his own that Dakin stayed on to complete the building he is best remembered for in Louisiana.

Despite White's letter, Dakin must have continued to want out as architect of the capitol, but the creation of the post of assistant architect seems to have resolved the issue.[39] This assistant was Alex Mather, a member of the state house of representatives from St. James Parish who served that year, 1848, on the Committee of Commerce. His role with regard to the capitol is not clear. He probably was not a builder or, even less likely, an architect, in the real sense of the word. Mather must instead have served as a kind of clerk of the works with limited supervisory powers on the site, but with authority to handle details concerning materials. At the very least, he probably served as a liason man between Dakin and the suppliers and contractors. His membership in the legislature also assured good relations with that body.

Dakin must now have been more satisfied that the work could go on with a minimum of trouble, for a letter from White indicates that Dakin was planning to go to New York. It is not known why Dakin wanted to go there. Perhaps he had designed a building in New York and sent drawings up which now required his presence for revision. Trips to New York from New Orleans were surprisingly easy in those times; steamships were capable of reaching New York in ten days, even with a stop in Havana and Savannah, Georgia. However, we know that Dakin did not leave as planned on the steamship *Crescent City* which departed August 15, for his diary contains entries dated just after this period. Although no evidence exists that James Dakin designed buildings in New York or the East in the 1840s or 1850s, with such easy access to New York, it is conceivable that he may have done work there. Only future discoveries and research will establish this.

Dakin was not destined to take that boat for New York, for, on August 3, he became embroiled in fisticuffs with William Pratt of McHatton, Pratt, and Company, over their bad bricks. While the story of this fight has generally been looked upon with amusement for its romantic, almost swashbuckling aspects and, not the least, as a reaffirmation of Dakin's determination to see the job done right, the encounter also had a not-so-humorous side to it.[40] The aftermath was to prove costly to Dakin. He won the "first round," but was not to be the winner in the end.

The story is indeed a colorful one, and Dakin's diary entry for August 3, 1848, begins it:

In consequence of the very bad quality of bricks furnished by Messrs. McHatton, Pratt & Co. for the State Capitol this day, and daily for the last month, Mr. Pratt and myself came to a personal conflict on the stagings of the building. I had, during the morning, been employed in throwing from the stagings a large quantity of soft and very bad bricks and thrown over some portion of walls which had been built with said bad bricks, in the midst of which occupation Mr. Pratt came suddenly up to me in a hostile attitude at which I became enraged and struck at Pratt. A general contest then commenced and blows were passed without much damage, however, to either party. [It was a fairly even match, for Dakin was then forty-two years of age, and Pratt forty-six].

On the morning of the 4th., the Mayor of Baton Rouge had us both arrested for disorderly conduct and tried. He fined me $10 and $3 costs because I struck the first blow. He fined Pratt $3 cost and discharged us without comment. This terminated the affair for the present at least.

Mr. Pratt had for some time showed the most abandoned spirit of villainy in furnishing bricks for the Capitol, which would all have been avoided had any of the partners [in McHatton, Pratt, and Company] been present, but unfortunately they were all off in Kentucky or elsewhere and Pratt alone managed the contract. He manifested such a faithless and dishonest disposition in the matter and appeared to be determined to persist, notwithstanding all our complaints or protests, that Mr. Avery found it requisite to serve me with . . . [a] letter of instructions . . . [insisting on suitable bricks].[41]

Armed with this letter, Dakin was then instructed to select and furnish McHatton, Pratt, and Company specemins of good brick, to number them, and deposit them in the office of the commissioners, so that they could then be used for further reference if the matter had to be taken to the legislature. He was also empowered to remove or have removed, at the contractor's expense, all defective bricks deposited on the site. An extra compensation was to be paid to Dakin for this additional trouble. Alex Mather personally delivered a copy of the instructions to the brick contractors on August 8.

One would suppose that all this involved procedure, not to mention the altercation, would have been enough to bring about an improvement in the bricks, but a week later, Dakin was again notifying the contractor that "you have been depositing at the Capitol a great quantity of arch and eye and other bricks which are far below the samples or standards. . . . You will cause all these defective and rubbish bricks to be removed forthwith."

They removed the bad bricks, but the next day deposited more of the same. Another warning letter from Dakin followed, then the notation in his diary: "Brick masons obliged to stop work this morning [August 16, 1848] for want of good bricks." It was not until August 21, upon the return of James McHatton from Kentucky, that Dakin records receipt of suitable material.

Maunsel White was taken aback by the fight over the capitol walls. He expressed his dismay to Daniel Avery, but acknowledged "from the quality of bricks that that gentleman [Pratt] was furnishing at the time I last visited Baton Rouge, I foresaw that if persisted in, it must come to an issue of some kind, but I did not contemplate any personal contest between the parties." [42] White then wrote Dakin and expressed his regret for this added difficulty. "If you find that we cannot get along without a lawsuit," he said, "make up a statement of facts and I will present them to the Senate. Mr. Mather will be a good and sufficient witness and can lay them before the House." [43]

Had the matter stopped at this point, it is probable that Dakin would have dropped the whole thing. But Pratt continued the fight verbally. He began to slander Dakin and went about Baton Rouge stating that Dakin had "accepted a bribe from James McHatton to swindle the State." Pratt said that McHatton was to give Dakin an interest in the brick contract, while Dakin, in return, was to pass over bad bricks in his capacity as supervising architect.

Dakin, of course, could not tolerate this smear campaign; he filed suit against Pratt on October 23, 1848, for slander, asking $10,000 damages. At first glance, this seems an appropriate rebuttal to such a malicious act, but, as most astute attorneys will advise, bringing a slander suit opens a Pandora's box for the revelation of every objectionable act one has done in his lifetime. Pratt, in his defense, paraded out a list of witnesses whom Dakin would have been better off not hearing from. Some obviously had personal grievances and were probably eager to vent their feelings against Dakin in an open court.

The slander by Pratt was, in the first place, patently absurd, for he was, in effect, accusing his own partner of the same thing he now publicly slandered Dakin for—a deal to defraud the state. And was not Pratt himself as liable as his partner if it were so? How could one partner keep such a secret from the other, especially when, under partnership law, each partner is responsible for the business actions of the other? But Dakin persisted in this suit, and the record of it does at least provide us with a little closer look at the altercation.[44] (The source cited in note 44 contains all of the material summarized or quoted below from the trial.)

One of the brickmasons at the capitol, Henry Tomlinson, testified that he had separated the two men after the fight had begun. Tomlinson said, "I believe I saw the commencement of the difficulty. . . . I thought at the time that Dakin had struck the first blow. . . . It was at the request of Mr. Mather that I separated them. Col. Dakin did not request me or any other person to part them, but requested Mr. Pratt to quit." This witness went on to say that after the fight, Dakin had gone into his room (probably Judge Morgan's old house was retained as an office) and returned with a sword. Tomlinson added that he had heard Mr. Pratt say that Colonel Dakin "was bribed or that he believed he was." Another bricklayer, Oliver Potts, testified that Pratt was very excited after the fight and had "sent home for his gun, and before his gun came, he stated that Col. Dakin was bribed by James McHatton . . . and that he could prove it." F. M. Kent, penitentiary manager for McHatton, Pratt, and Company then testified that he had sent the gun down to Mr. Pratt, upon his request and had gone to the capitol site himself. Kent continued, "Mr. Pratt was a good deal excited at the time, and my object was to get him home as quick as I could. . . . At the time myself and Mr. Pratt were passing Bonnecaze's Corner [a combination grocery and bar], Mr. Pratt was pretty bloody, and it is possible that Bonnecaze called to him and asked him what was the matter. Pratt . . . reiterated the charge against Dakin, that Dakin had been bribed by James McHatton."

Daniel D. Avery, the commissioner for the state house who resided in Baton Rouge, gave his testimony:

A large quantity of brick which had been deemed and considered objectionable had been brought on the ground from time to time, and about the time of the difficulty, were being used in being placed in the walls. I called Col. Dakin's attention to the fact repeatedly and directed his assistant, Mr. Mather, not to allow them to be placed in the walls.

Col. Dakin was employed in his office at the time, most of the time in drafting plans. I was informed by Mr. Mather of the difficulty that had taken place on the walls of the building between Mr. Pratt and Mr. Dakin, that my presence was required at the State House.

On reaching the Building, I found Mr. Pratt surrounded by the workmen and the laborers of the Building and that the work had been suspended by their withdrawal. I inquired into the reason of the suspension of the work. Then Mr. Pratt replied that he had

whipped or chastised Mr. Dakin for pulling down the walls and for breaking off his bricks. . . . [Pratt] used a great many opprobrious epithets in reference to Col. Dakin, calling him a damned swindler and corrupt scoundrel and that he had been bribed by James McHatton in the contract to cheat the State.

Mr. Pratt replied to a remark that I made that it was a grave charge, saying that he could prove it, and Mr. Pratt wished at the time to enter into an explanation about the difficulty . . . which I declined to receive at the time; Mr. Pratt was very much excited at the time. Three days after, he called on me at my office to make the explanation I had declined to receive at the time of the difficulty. He then reiterated the charge of Mr. Dakin's having been improperly influenced by Mr. McHatton in reference to the contract in building the State House.

I am aware that Col. Dakin is an architect and depends on his profession as a means of his livelihood. My opportunities of judging Col. Dakin's ability and character as an architect have been very ample for the last four years; in every situation, he has proved himself capable as an officer and as a man of strictest probity, enjoying the confidence of the Commissioners to the fullest extent. He is a man of family; he has a wife and two children.

On cross-examination, Avery added that both men had been extremely agitated. He said that Pratt "had some marks of blood on his clothes. I did not notice where the blood came from, for my attention was more particularly directed to the fact of his having a gun in his hand with which he threatened to shoot Col. Dakin, as he said Col. Dakin had drawn a sword upon him."

On re-examination by Dakin's side, Avery was asked if he had investigated the charges for the commissioners:

I informed Pratt that the charges were of so grave a character that if they were substantiated, the Commissioners would dismiss Col. Dakin, but that Pratt was not in a frame of mind to prefer charges at that time, and that I would defer hearing from either of the parties until Saturday; as the charges were not reiterated by him on that day and the parties having acquiesced in the written regulations made by me on behalf of the Commissioners for the future conduct of the work and the furnishing of materials, no further action was taken by the Commission.

Having such a poor defensive stance to work with, Pratt's attorneys were forced to pull out all the stops to impeach Dakin's character. They uncovered several men who were thought to be his enemies and subpoenaed statements from them. Some, however, backfired, their statements being straightforward and undamaging assessments of Dakin as a man and as an architect.

One of the more interesting testimonies, and not among those which backfired, was that of Francis D. Gott, the man who had done the interior of the Methodist Episcopal Church on Poydras Street and had worked on the skylight for the Bank of Louisville in the 1830s. Something must have happened between the two men in the interim, for Gott's testimony was not very kind to Dakin:

By the builders of New Orleans, he is considered a botch. The reputation of James H. Dakin as regards his deportment towards those who undertake his contracts for buildings under his supervision is bad. He is brutal in the extreme—his language is rough, and he frequently threatens to cane persons who come into contact with him. I have refused and I know several others who have refused to estimate or make contracts under his superintendance. I frequently heard him say that his builders were thieves, liars and rascals and the painters were the same.

This testimony seems much overstated. What, one wonders, were the circumstances which brought about Dakin's alleged hostility to the contractors? Could the St. Patrick's Church incident have made Dakin extremely cautious and critical of his contractors following the dispute? And why didn't Gott mention his successful collaboration with Dakin on the Methodist Church and the Bank of Louisville instead of discussing only derogatory things? In fairness to Gott, if

we remove much of the personal vituperation, his statement is still valuable as a source of knowing how at least some of the New Orleans workmen (or was it only Gott?) felt about serving under Dakin. He may not have been as tyrannical as Gott made him out to be, but Dakin surely had a reputation for being stern and demanding, at least from 1839 forward.

Pratt's lawyers attempted to continue the pressure. They obtained a statement from George Cook, the legislator who had resigned as a commissioner for the capitol because of the selection of Dakin's plans. Cook testified that he had opposed Dakin's plan and Dakin's employment as architect for the state house:

My reasons for opposing the employment of Mr. Dakin were that, in my opinion, much better plans were laid before the Commissioners than his, showing superior architectural skill in their mode of construction, for durability, beauty and cheapness. And furthermore, judging from the plan of Mr. Dakin, as well as from the opinion of some of the best practical builders in the city of New Orleans, I did not believe him to have the capacity requisite to design and superintend the erection of such a building.

James Gallier was also called upon to give a statement for the trial and did so, but it appears to be missing from the court file. The only trace of it is in the record of notarial fees incurred in the taking of the deposition in New Orleans. It would have been most interesting, to say the least. Perhaps new light would have been shed on the St. Patrick's Church issue, especially since Gallier would have been commenting in his prime, rather than in the near-blindness and old age of his autobiography.

Dakin's attorney asked for depositions from several persons for whom Dakin had done work. William Gasquet, who was mentioned by Gott, was one of these: "I have known Mr. Dakin since, I think, 1832 or 1833. I have been well satisfied with his efforts. He has supervised for me and my partners at least 25 buildings. I have great confidence in his capacity and I know of no one I would sooner have to superintend a building for me." Newton Richards also spoke on Dakin's behalf, saying that he did not believe Dakin would reject material without cause. Richards said, "I know him as an architect and have furnished materials for buildings he was connected with. From the knowledge I have of him, I believe him to be capable and upright." Others who spoke in praise of Dakin's integrity, personal and professional, included Peter Conrey, James Bogert, Samuel L. Hermann, and Glendy Burke. Maunsel White of course testified in Dakin's behalf: "Yes, I have known Mr. Dakin for several years. . . . I employed him for four houses in New Orleans, and I was perfectly satisfied. I know him well, and he would not likely reject any material that was fit. He is perfectly acquainted with the profession." In crossexamination, White was asked if, at the time Dakin was selected by the commissioners, he (Dakin) had previously been asked by the keeper of the penitentiary to assist them in the making of an estimate for the brick work and if Dakin was to get a profit from this. White replied: "No. If I had known of such a shape of things, I would not have employed him [Dakin]. I do not believe Mr. Dakin capable of such improper conduct."

The whole question of this estimate for the brick work was cleared up by the testimony of Pratt's partner, James McHatton. He was asked whether any offer had been made to Dakin to take an interest in the contracts for the brick work and, if such an offer was made, whether it was proposed before or after Dakin was appointed architect for the capitol. McHatton explained that he had gone to Dakin for assistance in calculating his bid for the brick work. However, at this time Dakin had not yet been appointed architect and Commissioner Cook assured McHatton that Dakin would not be appointed. With this information, McHatton then returned to Dakin and asked if he would consider taking one-fifth interest in the contract and superintending the brick work. Dakin "replied that he thought he would yet be appointed architect, and if not, he would probably see me." Several days later Dakin was appointed architect and McHatton testified that Dakin had not made the calculation and he did not then see Dakin again for nearly a year. McHatton concluded by saying, "The proposition made to Col. Dakin to take an interest was made upon the contingency of his not being appointed architect. . . . I never told Mr. Pratt that Col. Dakin had been bribed, or anybody else. I never intimated to him [Pratt] or anybody else that Dakin had been bribed or was susceptible of being bribed."

This testimony, then, got to the heart of the whole issue. Pratt, either in anger or by intention, had twisted the events related by McHatton. Dakin might have let the issue pass but for the fact that Pratt persisted in refusing to retract his charges. Thomas Beaumont of Baton Rouge testified that Mr. Pratt had told him he had "no recollection of making such a charge, and if he did, it was in the heat of passion." Beaumont said that he related this to Dakin and that Dakin agreed to drop the whole affair if Pratt would give him a written statement to that effect; Dakin wanted to use the statement publicly to clear his name of any suspicion in the matter. Beaumont testified that he made this proposition to Pratt but received no response. Dakin had the lion by the tail and would not let go. His persistence was extraordinary or his inner hurt very deep, for the case dragged on and on.

Partially because some witnesses were out of town, requiring testimony to be taken by notary public and mailed in, and because of various court recesses, the case dragged on for about three and half years. It finally ended, unfinished, upon the death of Dakin in 1852.

Within two months after the altercation with Pratt, Dakin lost his friend and assistant, Alex Mather. The dread disease of yellow fever which raked the South in those early days snuffed out the life of young Mather in his twenty-ninth year. Dakin sadly recorded in his diary, September 21, 1848, "Alex Mather, Assistant Architect, died this evening at 10:00 of yellow fever after six days illness. He was taken sick on Saturday the 16th. at 10:00 in the morning. A better man in all the relations of life I have never met with." [45]

It does not appear that Mather was replaced. The work must have been going smoothly enough not to warrant having an assistant beyond this point. Though the problems which did arise later were not as grave as those concerning the bricks, they all had to be handled by Dakin.

The quality of bricks improved greatly after the arrival from Kentucky of Pratt's partner. James McHatton apologized for the difficulties with the bricks and the brick masons were soon working diligently again. Now it was the iron which held up construction. Dakin said, in late 1848: "The time agreed upon for finishing the brick work expired today. Constant want of iron work has prevented the brick work from progressing any faster. The Commissioners should take the iron contract from Knap & Totten and give it to some establishment that would perform its obligations agreeably to promises. . . . " Dakin had no choice but to enter a formal protest with a notary public about the failure of McHatton, Pratt, and Company to live up to the contract through no fault of their own. This was necessary in order to protect the commissioners from liability. The matter was resolved with a six-month extension of the contract.

At this time, late in 1848, the commissioners also decided to give Newton Richards the contract for the marble front and rear screen walls of the capitol. Richards trekked to Baton Rouge and announced that he would provide the best Cape Girardeau marble to be had.[46] The final product was a credit to the workmanship of this master craftsman and to Dakin's exquisite design.

About this time, Maunsel White visited General Zachary Taylor in Baton Rouge.[47] Taylor lived, not on his plantation, but at a little house near the pentagon barracks. He was the biggest celebrity in Baton Rouge; and because of his presence, and the construction of Louisiana's new capitol, the little village must have swelled with collective pride.

James Dakin also must have visited Taylor during this period, for Taylor lived but six blocks above the new capitol. Both men enjoyed the personal friendship of Maunsel White, and Dakin knew Taylor from his service in Mexico where the volunteer officers from Louisiana were frequent visitors to their fellow Louisianian's command tent. This proved to be a valuable friendship for Dakin, as it was largely through Taylor that he obtained the job as architect of the custom house.

In this same busy period of late 1848 and early 1849, Dakin found time to design a Gothic villa for Maunsel White. The latter recorded in his letterbook, on January 27, 1849: "I thank you for the sketch of the second story of the house . . . and hope you will not forget my 'villa a la mode Gothique.' " Again, on March 27, 1849: "Your letters of the 13th. and 22nd with the plan of my villa house have been duly received, and I thank you very much for the latter. It is unique and beautiful, and at more leisure, I'll speak more at large about it." [48]

It is too bad White did not "speak more at large about it" for all attempts at locating this villa have been unsuccessful. There is even uncertainty that it was built at all. White owned much property around the state: several lots in New Orleans, his sugar plantation, Deer Range in Plaquemines Parish. The villa could have been intended for any of these. It would have been very helpful to know what this Dakin-designed Gothic mansion looked like in order to compare his creativity in this area with that of his old partner, Alexander Jackson Davis. In the 1850s, Davis supplied many of the drawings and ideas for the books of Andrew Jackson Downing, the landscape architect. These books of Downing cannot be overrated in their influence on the spread of the picturesque in American residential architecture. The Gothic was the predominant style of Downing's books.[49]

Speculation about Dakin's villa for White has to include a suspicion that Afton Villa, some thirty miles south of Baton Rouge, was his creation. Louisiana's most important Gothic mansion, Afton Villa (which burned in 1963) has long taunted researchers as to whose imaginative mind created this fantasy. It is said to have been begun about 1850 for the Barrow family. The Barrows, an old Louisiana family, had been active in state politics for years, and it is very likely that Maunsel White knew them well. It is possible that White gave them Dakin's plan for the Gothic villa which had been done for him, although no evidence whatever exists to support this speculation.

In 1849, with only months to go before the target date for completion of the capitol, White was becoming nervous about it not being ready for the legislature. He wrote Dakin: "I feel much mortified to think or even anticipate that we should not have the Capitol ready for the next Legislature." He must have hounded Dakin, for he then wrote Avery: "I

regret the work progresses so slowly, and for heaven's sake, push it when the weather permits. I have too frequently urged on Dakin until at last he got restive and I have said nothing since."

Dakin, in the spring of 1849, was redoubling his efforts to finish the capitol. He was now ready to begin thinking about the interior and wrote Knap and Totten on March 9, 1849:

Herewith you will find designs for 12 cast iron clustered pillars for the New Capitol of Louisiana. We shall want them in the course of four months at the farthest. The drawings and figures and remarks thereupon will explain all that you wish to know in reference to details, etc.

We shall require     4 pillars 11 feet 5¾ inches
                         4 pillars 13 feet 4¾ inches
                         4 pillars 14 feet 1½ inches

long from the bottom of their plinths to the tops of the capitals. These castings are to form a part of the interior finish and should be made as perfect as possible, for they will be placed in situations where they will be much seen.[50]

Dakin had a minor tiff with White shortly after this over slates for the roof. Dakin recorded that Daniel Avery found a large quantity of slate sent up by White from New Orleans to be defective. Dakin, trying to press on with the work, went to New Orleans to look into the matter. While there, he bought 26,000 slates and 333 English ridge tiles. White, meanwhile, did not know of this purchase, and almost bought replacement slates himself. He sailed into Dakin when he found out what had happened:

I got here [New Orleans] yesterday by land, by water and by rail at considerable expense, hoping to find yourself or Mr. Avery or a letter, but until I had commenced this writing, I had nothing. This moment, your letter of the 29th. was handed to me, having arrived this morning, from which I learn with astonishment that you have been here, purchased the slate, went off and never once called at the office to let them know or drop me a line to advise me of your

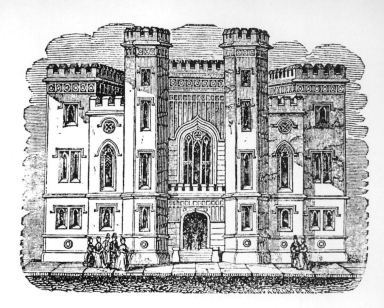

*View of the capitol as it neared completion in 1849, confirming its appearance before the fire of 1862. (From the New Orleans* Daily Delta, *November 18, 1849)*

proceedings; which course is without any excuse, inasmuch as you might have caused me to purchase the slate ... when it was easy to prevent all this with a slight verbal communication at the office—or two lines addressed to me and left there....In the future, I shall insist on nothing being done without my advice and consent. Only consider all you might have saved me, both in feelings, time and money had you acted like a man of business.[51]

The older man must have been greatly displeased by Dakin's high-handedness and lack of consideration in not advising him of his purchase. Perhaps impatience was at the root of Dakin's action, but he certainly displayed thoughtlessness in this lack of communication.

The final months of construction were hectic ones; all the loose ends seemed still to be undone and much detail required attention from Dakin. In May, he recorded: "Delivered to Mr. Avery the drawings, etc., for 8,046 lights of glass for the sashes of the new capitol." On June 6, he noted: "The slater Kenny proved to be a drunken vagabond and I cleared him out; he left this place today." On June 15: "More delay of brick work for want of iron from Knap & Totten." The usually reliable Newton Richards was running quite a bit late, and Dakin had to record a protest with a notary public "for not completing his contract for white marble for the two fronts by July 1, 1849." Dakin added, "The marble fronts not yet started from Cape Giradeau, Mo. It is expected that Mr. Richards will overrun his time by at least 60 days."

Dakin recorded a month later that "one of the East or Town Front Towers was slated," and that the first work on the roof over the senate had been started. But the biggest relief must have come on August 27, when "Marble for the fronts arrived: 111,306 lbs." On September 1, Newton Richards himself arrived for the setting of the parts. By November 11, Dakin could say with pleasure: "Gov. Johnson was

here and appeared well pleased with the new building and all matters concerned with it."

The iron columns from Pittsburgh arrived on October 26, "8 long clustered pillars, 7,105 lbs, and 4 short clustered pillars 2,957 lbs." On December 15, "Newton Richards completed the marble work, with the exception of repairing some few parts which have spalled a trifle." A week later, "Slating is so far completed as to turn rain from the roof." The building was now substantially complete and ready to house the legislature. Dakin and White had lived up to their promised deadline and the enemies of Baton Rouge as the site for a capitol were silenced, at least for a while.[52]

The most detailed and exact description ever given of the capitol was written as it neared completion. This New Orleans newspaper article spoke of it with rigorous precision and almost poetic praise. Beginning with general compliments to Louisiana architecture and citing specifically the St. Charles and St. Louis hotels, St. Patrick's Church, the then-under-construction custom house, the article goes on to a full discussion of the capitol. This author has nothing but praise for Dakin:

Such is the skillful economy of the architect, Col. Dakin—such the nature of his design—such his vigilance and activity—so perfect his knowledge (for he was an artizan [*sic*] himself) of the habits, characters, qualifications and business routine of those employed under him, in their every variety of occupation—such his general ability and rare faithfulness to the trust reposed in him, that the magnitude of his task, notwithstanding the expenses incident to the transportation of his materials—castings from Pittsburgh, marble from Missouri, sundries from New York, slates from Liverpool—added to that incurred by procuring craftsmen from all parts, he will have completed—and well completed it—at an astonishingly small cost to the State.

He has had to battle, in this work, with innumerable difficulties; difficulties, many of them, which are never encountered in contracts with private individuals, and nothing but his energy and indomitable will could lead to an issue so successful. To the lazy, the presuming, the knavish, disobedient and turbulent, his *brusque* and matter of fact ways are a marvelous sedative. To work, and work well, seems the governing maxim of his life; nonsense and insolence he will not submit to. He has, nevertheless, a kind and indulgent spirit to the honest and well-meaning.[53]

This is perhaps the best summary of Dakin's character to be found in contemporary sources. And it tells remarkably well how these characteristics served him in overcoming all the obstacles that stood in his path in the completion of the capitol. Maunsel White was proven right when he warned that there were only two men in the state who were capable of seeing a project of this proportion through. He obtained one; the other was Gallier. But perhaps even such a capable man as Gallier would not have prevailed through the difficulties that Dakin had to overcome by the strength of his will. Here the article turns to a description of the capitol:

The two facades of the edifice, looking east and west, are entirely of white marble. Its length is 187 feet 3 in.; the width of its transept is 130 feet 9 in. Of its four towers in front, the two on the east front are square—those on the west (facing the river) are octagonal, and are each 90 feet high. These towers are perforated with [windows of] lancet arches, terminating with a single trefoil and with a square headed label [moulding]. They are tastefully ornamented near the top, and immediately above the Belvedere windows, with a [wide band of] quatrefoil moulding which extends also round the transept, at the same distance below the parapets. Battlemented parapets, divided with embrasures, complete the decoration of the towers as well as of the whole line of the building at the top.

The height of the walls between the towers and transept is 64 feet. That of the other towers, also four in number, flanking each of the four angles of the transept is 77 feet. The doors and windows in both fronts . . . are in the Tudor style of Florid Gothic architecture, having four centered arches and a square heading in marble.

Nineteen feet two inches by twelve feet are the length and width

of the doorways, the arches of which are marble. The two front window frames, both marble arches, and the greatest and most expensive ornaments of this house, are each 27 feet high, by 15 feet 4 in. wide. They are divided by marble mullions . . . the finish at the top is a foliated arch trefoil. . . .

There are in each of the four towers in front, nine windows with lancet lights and square weather mouldings. On each side of the building, exclusive of the front towers, are 36 windows, besides the circular multifoils or rose windows, seven in number beneath the upper string course and between the towers and transept. . . . They are all lancet light [windows], some with, some without mullions and transoms . . . some with pointed, some with squared labels, some of unequal sizes, and these are the most beautiful of all, banded by a continuous dripstone. In short, the whole work . . . whether in general design or minuteness of detail, exhibits a variety and uniformity exquisitely picturesque and subservient alike to utility and ornament.[54]

Unfortunately, the newspaper description of the capitol, which must have been written after a personal interview with Dakin himself, did not mention the influence of specific European prototypes. It may be no coincidence that the facade bears a striking resemblance to the Clock Tower of Hampton Court in London. Of course, the characteristics of octagonal towers and pointed arch doorways were repeated many times in Tudor Gothic architecture, so that it is futile to attempt to pinpoint a specific model. We can, nevertheless, be assured that Dakin had seen views of Hampton Court and other examples of the Tudor style and used them as inspiration for the east and west fronts of his capitol.

The article's use of the term *transept* to describe the "crossing" or central wings of the capitol can be deceptive without further analysis. In the original design (as evidenced by a ground plan of the building in Dakin's own sketch and in Michael Gill's 1855 map of Baton Rouge), Dakin placed these bays, which consisted of twin square towers, about two thirds of the distance back from the river entrance, creating an analogy to a crossing in a Gothic church. Looking at the capitol today, after its restoration in 1880–82, we find the rotunda in what is apparently the same position in relation to the old transept as Dakin planned it. But the masonry bays—twin bays, as before—have been moved forward, in dead center between the end towers. The giveaway of this incongruity is the resulting asymmetrical location of the hot-house-like addition placed on the roof in 1882 to cover the upper part of the enormous cast iron fan vault in the rotunda ceiling. This added story does not line up with the rebuilt transept but with the old location as designed by Dakin.

This anomaly goes unnoticed inside, but is readily apparent from the exterior. Perhaps foundation conditions were such in the 1882 rebuilding that it was decided to retain Dakin's old foundations beneath the rotunda and yet move the transept to the central position. Or, it may have been so located as to line up the bottom steps of the circular staircase with the new enlarged entrance on the west flank. Whatever the reason, the result is not offensive, for it seems to enhance the picturesque quality of this truly unique building.[55]

Such an excellent contemporary description of the exterior deserves an equally good description of the interior. Regrettably, no complete one has been found, and no pre-Civil War views have been located. In 1862, under Union army occupation, a fire gutted the interior; thus we must rely on fragmentary pieces of evidence for a description.

The interior, it should first be noted, was finally completed in 1852, some eighteen months after Dakin left to accept the job as supervising architect of the New Orleans Custom House. He returned to Baton Rouge in late 1851 and completed the interior of the capitol. Another newspaper fortunately provides a glimpse of the interior as Dakin was finishing it in 1852: "Let us stop and stroll through the capitol. Its interior appearance is much more striking and beautiful than the exterior. Two things, however, have been shamefully neglected. . . . Light and acoustics have been wonderfully disregarded, the latter totally."[56] This article goes on to criticize the lighting deficiencies of the rotunda, and the author also ridicules the chandelier. "You look up to see the steamboat chandelier, with its four prongs and globe shades, all suspended from the top dome 75 feet above you by a twine string, looking so steamboat-like that you would not be surprised to hear the gruff voice of the mate cry out."

Another contemporary description is couched in the vitriolic language of one who detested the building. Unwittingly, he has provided those of us who *do* like it with a look at the original interior:

You enter either Chamber—they both present the same follies. All around and above you, common timber has been tortured into oak of the most excessive color and remarkable grain. This oak is made to serve many purposes.

Above, it impersonates giant beams, which pretend to support the whole superstructure, stretching down at you, here and there, a massive inverted tower, which looks across at it vis-a-vis in very arch style—and then all around everywhere, but in the greatest accumulation all over and about the Speaker's seat, this same oak is dug out into little troughs, with ornamented prows nailed to the walls, while the arch over the Speaker's chair mingles with its oak specimens of the Chinese painter's pencil. The smaller appropriations of this oak comprise curious little contrivances which seem to have been cut out for cake moulds. The construction and painting of the Speaker's and clerk's desks, I have no language for description.

But he in fact did:

Imagine that eight or ten columns of wood, some fluted and some square, and some any way, all of different sizes and lengths, and that they had, by some sudden freak, been thrown confusedly together with a great deal of other stuff—that you then put two little boys on it, one with a hatchet and augur, the other with a saw and foot adze, and let them work away at it for about a week—then get all the muddy, yellow and sickly green paint you can find; mix some lamp-black, white lead and Spanish brown, and throw it on with buckets. When it is just dry enough to be sticky and catch lint, you have a picture of the Speaker's seat.[57]

Another less than flattering description appeared in *Leslie's Illustrated* newspaper during the Civil War. This writer refers to the speaker's platform as "a complicated piece of barbaric Gothic." Pointing out that this platform is a representation of the building in miniature, the writer complains that the imposing structure makes the presiding officer himself seem insignificant, the speaker being "further concealed by the back of his chair which is some twelve feet high, turreted to 'harmonize with the surrounding architecture.'"[58]

From these descriptions, we may conclude that the ceilings of the senate and house were finished with non-load-bearing wooden vaulting, arranged in a double row of pendants, probably suspended from hammer beams. The "prows nailed to the walls" are obviously corbels from which the vaulting sprang, the beams "looking at each other vis-a-vis" are quite obviously hammer beams in the roof, the "inverted towers" are, of course, pendants, and the "cake moulds" are most likely quatrefoil and trefoil motifs. Because the exterior of the capitol resembles Hampton Court, we might well suspect that Dakin also followed, in outline, the hammer-beam construction of its main room.

This newspaper man's fuss over the speaker's chair and the timber ceiling chiefly serve to display his ignorance of Gothic architecture, but more understandable is his bewilderment by the use of polychromy. This was the coming style, and Dakin was employing polychromy for what appears to be the first time in Louisiana. It is not clear whether he used it freely elsewhere in the capitol, but he was obviously familiar with the new books of Ruskin extolling the use of color. James Gallier had just completed the new Christ Church in New Orleans, but he did not use polychromy. Dakin here displays his leadership in architecture, and it is most unfortunate that his original drawings for the interior of the capitol have never been found. They would surely have shown his inventiveness at its height.

Acceptance of the exterior of the capitol was not entirely unanimous. The vitriolic commentator on the speaker's chair didn't like the outside either: "It is the most unsightly mass that ever was built for \$250,000, and is only fit for an insane asylum. The object of the architect appears to have been to erect an edifice as *outre* in its internal shape and as inconvenient in its internal structure as possible."[59]

Some commented on the medieval associations of the capitol, saying that its worst fault was its resemblance to a feudal castle. The *Daily Delta* said, "As a capitol for a Republican state we can see neither justness of conception, propriety of taste, nor beauty of architecture in it. It is in the style of a castle of the dark ages—the age of tyranny, of Baronial oppression, of monastic superstition."[60]

These remarks must have been especially painful to Dakin, for they were made just a few months before his death. Even more disappointing was the fact that they came from the same newspaper which had provided such a favorable and detailed description of the exterior of the capitol and Dakin's labor on it just two years before. He must have wondered how the paper could have come full circle in such a short time. But he knew the critics were in the minority, and that his building was well received. Had he lived longer, he would surely have been elated to see the capitol restored to his original design thirty years later.

When the capitol was in readiness to receive the legislature, a great dedication celebration was to take place in Baton Rouge in late November, 1849. Dakin was deprived of his moment of triumph; a great fire broke out on November 24, destroying much of the downtown area and turning the gala event into a somber one for the little village.

Meanwhile, in New Orleans, the old capitol on Canal Street in State House Square could now be closed up. In June, 1850, the property facing Canal St. was sold off at high prices to be developed as stores, the commercialization of Canal Street finally erasing the last vestiges of the old capitol.[61] Just before the opening of the new capitol, a newspaper, welcoming the new and the elimination of the old, commented that "in the art . . . [of] . . . Architecture . . . the parent of all arts . . . has not Col. Dakin taxed his genius to present you an example in our magnificent State House?"[62] On January 7, 1850, Dakin tendered the capitol to the commissioners with the following letter to Maunsel White:

Dear Sir: I have the pleasure to inform you that the new Capitol of Louisiana is ready for the reception of the Legislature. We have discharged all our carpenters and joiners with the exception of seven, five of whom are at work on the stair railings, and two are hanging window sashes, etc.

The fears expressed by some gentlemen that the new edifice would not be ready for the meeting of the Legislature are now at an end, and as for the convenience and capacity of the building, it will answer for itself satisfactorily.[63]

In his diary, Dakin noted the dismissal of most of the carpenters also. His second-to-last entry reports to the commissioners that 4,039,786 bricks had been used in construction of the capitol. His journal comes to a close shortly thereafter, ending a remarkable first-person account of the construction of a major American building.[64]

## RESTORATIONS OF THE CAPITOL

Since its completion in 1852, the capitol has had several alterations made to it over the years. With the serious lighting deficiency of the rotunda, it was inevitable that the skylight would eventually be enlarged. In 1854, an excellent contractor from Baton Rouge, James McVey, was selected to do the work, and four years later, money was appropriated for the job. By November, 1858, it was noted that "an opening has been made in the roof corresponding in size to the opening in the floors of the second and third stories . . . letting in light into that center portion of the building heretofore in the dark." The writer from *Leslie's* (previously quoted) complained about this improvement also, saying that "almost the whole interior is taken up with enormous openings in the floors to let in light from the windows placed in the roof." The article exaggerated the waste of space. Each house was located at either end of the second floor, and each enjoyed as its main feature the huge tracer-ied windows done so well in marble by Newton Richards. With ample space provided there, and offices for the governor, the state library, and other state officials, the open rotunda hardly "sacrificed" the interior of the building. This article, written during the Civil War, was apparently more concerned about criticizing the South than reporting on the capitol.[65]

Even before McVey enlarged the skylight, it had been glazed with stained glass, for a viewer in 1857 said: "We admired its spacious rotunda lighted from above by a magnificent dome of stained glass." The original shape of the rotunda was elliptical, and it was unencumbered with stairs or obstructions in the center. As a result, it lent itself to great social functions, and many balls are recorded as having been held there. The capitol was a virtual center of social activity in the primitive capital of Louisiana when the legislature was not in session.[66]

It is also certain that the original color of the capitol was white, not the varying shades of brown, tan, and others used over the years. Of the verbal descriptions on this point, the best came from a writer traveling down river from Natchez. As he approached the capitol, he recorded:

We are now within sight of Baton Rouge. It is a fine looking town with a stately Capitol, towering with bastions, towers and battlements far above the other buildings. At a distance, its white appearance and bulk in the shining reflection . . . give it the look of an iceberg. . . . The architecture is Gothic and in very good taste. There is no style so beautiful for public edifices as the Gothic with its Norman or Anglo variety. We Americans copy too severely the Greek style.[67]

At the same time that James McVey was enlarging the skylight, work had begun to fulfill the dream of Maunsel White and Dr. Brashear for beautification of the grounds around the capitol. The finest expert on horticulture in the area, the nationally known Thomas Affleck, was called on to lay out plantings on the capitol grounds for a botanical garden.

In October, 1858, it was noted that "the work of ornamenting the grounds has commenced; the hill is being terraced and is to be sodded." Affleck planted trees, shrubs, and flowers of all varieties. A fountain and pool were placed at the lower end of the terrace near the river, and seats and walkways created an inviting atmosphere.[68] The capitol had entered into a period of tranquillity as it was finally being completed in its entirety. This mood was soon to be shattered by the anguish and destruction of war.

The onset of the Civil War soon found Dakin's capitol caught up in the conflict. Union forces, wisely seeing that New Orleans held the key to the heart of the Confederacy by means of the Mississippi, soon ran the blockade below New Orleans and captured it early in the war. On April 29, 1862, Admiral Farragut and General Benjamin Butler took possession of New Orleans, and another force, sent up from that city, captured Baton Rouge on May 12. The Confederates fought hard to recapture their capitol and succeeded on August 21, only to lose it again (and finally) on December 17.

On December 28 1862, a great calamity occurred to Dakin's magnificent "castle." While occupied by a contingent of Union troops, the building caught fire, and the interior was gutted. It was reported in Baton Rouge that "the loss is very heavy. Many thousands of rare and valuable books, papers and furniture of the building were destroyed. The outer walls stand in majestic defiance of the fiery ordeal they have passed through." [69]

Rumors flew fast and heavy as to how the fire began. It was blamed variously on Negro Union troops in the building, Confederates bent on creating trouble for the Union occupation forces, and other wild theories. An army board of inquiry was immediately called on January 1, 1863, to investigate the fire.[70] It was disclosed that the fire originated in the tower at the southeast corner of the capitol, where, in the basement, a stove had been placed for cooking rations for the men stationed in the building. It was speculated that because of wartime neglect to the building the flue was stopped up and the heat was transmitted to nearby wooden parts of the structure. Because there were more convenient places to start a fire deliberately than in a tower, it was determined that the fire began accidentally as a result of the cooking.

By 11 P.M., the fire was thought to be under control. The men relaxed and a hundred soldiers were posted throughout the building just as a precaution to watch for a further breakout of fire. But no one checked the upper areas of the building over and around the roof, despite an inspection having been ordered. A fire then broke out at 4 A.M. This one was worse than the first, and the interior was entirely consumed. The board of inquiry concluded that the unfamiliarity with fire precautions and the lack of inspection by the personnel assigned to the capitol was at the root of the disaster. They were labeled "wholly ignorant as to the points of danger," and everyone was exonerated.

Dakin's capitol was to remain in ruins for almost twenty years. Nothing was done for it, or the beautiful botanical gardens around it for the duration of the war. In 1865 the legislature appointed a guard to clean up and maintain what was left of the grounds. The ruinous appearance of the capitol area following the war was noticed in 1865:

After the destruction of the State House by fire... the gates leading to the grounds were left open and many of the rare trees, flowers and expensive shrubs which Mr. Thomas Affleck... planted and nursed, were either removed by persons or trampled upon by horses and cattle. The iron railings, bolts . . . as well as the seats of the terrace were either taken or broken or thrown down.

The cricket holds his feast in immortal song at the foot of the great stair case, the beetle burrows in the rubbish about the pedestal whereon stood the statue of Washington [by Hiram Powers], the bat builds his nest in the upper turrets, and the owl, with his voice of death and destruction, is their welcome guest.[71]

Evocative of the atmosphere following the destruction was the observation in *Harper's Weekly*, that "the State House still stands, a melancholy shell, and looks much more like an ancient castle than it ever had any hope of doing while perfect." But a visitor to Baton Rouge from the East caught the mood better:

The shell of the old State House of Louisiana was already in sight when we reached the deck of the ship. The white walls stand out imposingly from the beautiful terraced garden and the fine trees in front and in the rear of them. Distance has the same restoring effect upon the building as the moonlight always has with more

*An old photograph of the capitol, indicating how little the exterior was damaged by the fire of 1862. (Courtesy Louisiana Room, Louisiana State University Library)*

dilapidated ruins. From the river, the State House does not look like a ruin at all. But near at hand, it is as hollow and empty as the present Legislation of Louisiana. . . . In the garden, which slopes finely towards the river, we found . . . all the rare and costly trees that one can imagine now used to shade a few invalid horses. . . . The lower portion was once bright and cool with a fountain, the large basin of which is covered with scum. Geese and snakes thrive here admirably. Nothing is left inside the State House but the bare brick walls; even the debris seems to have been removed.

The exterior was of white stucco with marble dressings. The structure is a species of castellated Tudor Gothic, and our young country, I think, has no other ruin so fine. Near one of the front windows is the mark of a cannon ball, which no doubt struck there when the gunboats opened on Baton Rouge. In our engraving, we have given you a view of the building as it looked to us in the moonlight . . . and as it looks . . . to the traveler as he passes on the river. [72]

Horace Walpole would have been ecstatic at the sight of such a ruin. He had lived in an age when a ruin—even a sham one—was a gentleman's prized possession. But Louisiana was not elated over its ruined castle on the Mississippi. It wanted its Gothic masterpiece put back in working order.

In 1866, a team of inspectors went out to examine the capitol and report to the legislature on the feasibility of restoring it. The report was signed by James McVey, the builder who had enlarged the skylight a few years before, and F. M. Young. The report describes the building as having survived the fire and weather of four years in amazingly good shape. "Upon the minute and careful examination of the exterior walls, we find them to be free from any defect or injury from the fire or otherwise, having been built from the very best materials and of superior workmanship, except the two front octagonal towers, one of which is damaged and will have to be taken down about one-half its height." The inspectors stated that the interior

walls were slightly sprung and would have to be rebuilt. [73]

This report was a tribute to Dakin's supervision; it almost made the fight with Pratt seem worthwhile. Some parts of the building did not survive quite as well as the walls, however. The marble curtain walls on the fronts would have to be taken down and "renewed." On the other hand, the cast iron fence around the grounds was deemed still in excellent repair.

The estimate of the materials that would be required to rebuild the capitol gives us another hint of how the rotunda must have looked when finished by Dakin. It called for "four flights of stairs in the court [Rotunda]," fifty carved spandrels forming arches under the ceiling, heavy clustered ribs on the three stories of ceilings, and twelve clustered cast iron columns. The two houses also required several hundred feet each of moulded ribs for the ceiling. Much carved wood—spandrels, corbels, and the like—was also needed. The total estimate to repair the capitol came to $199,396.00.

It was generally conceded that it would be cheaper to rebuild the capitol than to erect a new one. New Orleans, however, wanted the capitol to stay there. Louisiana was then under carpetbag rule, and New Orleans could provide pleasurable entertainment for government officials. Why not accept this fringe benefit of carpetbagger rule?

After the restoration of "Bourbon" rule in 1877, the legislature was ready to return to its old capitol and restore Dakin's building. But it wanted Uncle Sam to pay for it. A joint resolution of the Louisiana legislature in 1877 required its representatives in Congress to request an appropriation to restore the capitol. Accordingly, a bill was presented in Washington on December 10, 1877, requesting that $175,000 be appropriated to help Louisiana rebuild its capitol, "said building having been partially destroyed by fire while under the control and in the custody of the U.S. military authorities, and while being occupied by Federal troops during the late war." [74]

The bill was shunted off to the Committee on War Claims, where it died. The federal government was not in the mood to pay for the restoration of a rebel capitol. It was clear that the state would have to assume the entire burden of restoring the capitol. The decision to move the seat of government back to Baton Rouge was made finally in the Constitutional Convention of 1879, with the country legislators voting yea and the city nay. It was stipulated that the city of Baton Rouge place in the state treasury $35,000 to help defray the cost of restoring the capitol. [75] By the spring of 1880, Governor Wiltz had appointed the distinguished New Orleans architect, William Freret, to the position of architect for the restoration of the capitol.

Freret was probably Louisiana's best architect of this period. The son of William Freret, a former mayor of New Orleans, he was born in New Orleans in 1833 and educated there. He completed his architectural education in France, and before the Civil War, worked for the city of New Orleans as a drainage engineer. He later became the state engineer. Freret distinguished himself as a military engineer for the Confederacy in the Civil War. After the war was over, he proved his ability to work in the Gothic style by designing several buildings for the city of New Orleans from the funds of the John McDonough estate. Most of the McDonough schools are still in use at this writing. Not long after completing the restoration of the Louisiana capitol, Freret was named by President Grover Cleveland as United States Supervising Architect for the Treasury Department and was involved in the construction of many federal buildings around the country. [76]

A new state house commission met in New Orleans on May 15, 1880, to take up the matter of designs for the restoration of the capitol. The commission spent most of its time haggling over what amounted to an artistic desecration of the building. A senator pointed out that it was his interpretation of the law that a report of a legislative joint committee had recommended that a mansard roof be put on the capitol. [77] Freret, with his plans already on the table, was taken aback and replied emphatically that he would *not* put a mansard roof on a Gothic building, particularly a castellated one. He followed this up with a statement that he would not allow his name as an architect to be connected with such a structure. The senator persisted that this was what he believed was the law, and Freret, faced with an impasse, said that perhaps a small mansard roof—invisible from the sides—might be worked into the plan. The matter was later somehow resolved, probably with a more liberal interpretation of the committee report, and Freret did not have to compromise his artistic taste; no mansard roof was placed on the building.

The condition of the capitol was of extreme importance, it having lain unattended in the elements for twenty years. A team of inspectors, comprised of four men who, it was said, had been "employed in constructing the old capitol," James McVey, J. W. Brown, Oliver Potts, and R. H. Burke, gave a generally favorable appraisal of its condition, "affirming the propriety of retaining the walls in their present height, simply repairing or removing the slight existing defective work." They concluded that it would be a needless waste to demolish existing walls, especially the exterior ones. [78]

However, William Freret's plans, presented earlier, included changes which would "elevate the central portion" and "effect . . . a larger additional entrance . . . connecting with the central portion, where he has constructed a dome of iron and glass, rich in tracery, In the centre of the area covered by the dome is a large circular staircase." This was all to be done while "retaining, as much as possible, the old lines and appearance of the building." It was therefore Freret's desire to enlarge the central block of the building by adding one more story and rearranging the interior. This would necessitate giving less consideration to the inspection report just mentioned than to an earlier one done by unknown parties for the joint legislative committee. It was less optimistic about the interior walls, reporting that they were "almost completely demolished and will have to be taken down to the line of the basement floor. The marble work around the principal openings, as well as the granite steps, have been greatly damaged and will have to be renewed." The inspectors also considered the exterior walls and the octagonal towers to be in poor condition. They estimated the cost of repairing the capitol at $180,000.[79] Eventually, the more optimistic report proved more accurate, and the building was substantially preserved, though Freret did implement his plan for enlarging the center. Shortly before restoration was completed, the state house commission reported:

After mature deliberation and careful inspection, assisted by competent experts (architects & builders), it was determined to utilize and preserve the old structure as far as was practicable. The walls, originally built with great care and solidity, indicated such a state of preservation and strength that it was deemed futile to demolish them.

Taking this as our basis, we proceeded to make such additions and alterations as would tend to effect the object comtemplated by the Act of the Legislature. An additional story was given to the building, thereby adding increased capacity.... For additional ventilation and increased light, a new entrance of large and commanding appearance has been made, connecting with and leading to the central hall, where again more light is obtained from the colored glass of the enriched gothic dome which covered [sic] the principal stairway and court.[80]

So, a serious fire and twenty years of lying unattended in the weather had left Dakin's building damaged but not beyond repair. It had given promise enough to three committees of inspectors to warrant their recommendation to restore it. The survival of the capitol through such difficulties demonstrates James Dakin's abilities in the supervision of the construction of his buildings. It is unfortunate that he did not live until 1880; he might have had the unusual opportunity of aiding in the restoration of his masterpiece. Had he done so, Dakin would have been seventy-four years old, not so very great an age in view of the fact that his old partner Alexander Jackson Davis was still alive and was to live on until 1892.

Of the many suppliers and contractors who worked on the capitol, the building reports show that the principal ones were Shakspeare and Company of New Orleans, who supplied the iron (it was owned by the mayor of the city); Kursheedt and Bienvenu of New Orleans, who "renewed" the marble and granite; and J. C. Kiddell for plastering and other work.[81]

William Freret was amply rewarded for his part in the restoration. He was paid $1,500 for plans and specifications and an annual fee of $2,500 per year for his services as supervising architect. With such a small fee, he was not expected to live in Baton Rouge and superintend the construction, although Dakin had been required to do so with only $3,000 compensation. Instead, Major Thompson E. Bird, of East Baton Rouge Parish, a well-respected planter (just as Maunsel White had been) was chosen as superintendent, and his main duty was to see to the proper payment of contractors in disbursing the state's funds.[82]

There can be no question that Freret's most spectacular contribution to the capitol reconstruction was the design of the rotunda. He created a massive cast iron vault which springs from a central iron column, around which winds a spiral staircase (also of iron) to the second floor, where the house and senate chambers are located. The eye is carried upward to a kaleidoscope of stained glass panes set above and around the ribs of the fan. On a bright, sunny day, standing beneath it is like standing under a huge, stained glass umbrella! (Plate 11)

To accomplish this effect, Freret had to erect on the roof, a sort of "hot house" with many panes of glass to admit the light necessary to illuminate his "fan" and to house its upper portions. It has the adverse effect, on the exterior, of increasing the height of the central portion considerably, with a whole floor already having been added, thus distorting the original proportions intended by Dakin. (The asymetrical placing of this glass house over the dome was discussed in the section about the original design.) For the slender windows of this "hot house," Freret employed Venetian Gothic arches, adding yet another variety of window styles to the profusion selected by Dakin.

The rotunda, or transept, as it was called in 1849, was entirely done over by Freret, substituting for the old wooden Gothic elements, cast iron replacements. This included the fifty spandrels for the rotunda mentioned in the 1866 report.

The concept of a central fan vault in a round or polygonal room was unquestionably borrowed by Freret from the chapter houses in medieval Gothic ecclesiastical architecture. No specific one can be found as a source, the idea being freely adapted to include a spiral staircase around the supporting column. It was a superb choice for the rotunda, one Dakin himself would have greatly admired, especially with its heavy emphasis on cast iron.

In the houses, Freret employed traceried Tudor spandrels over the spectator galleries, also in cast iron. The ceilings apparently were not done over in the hammer-beam Hampton Court fashion, but this is uncertain, for they were redone many times and now feature a very un-nineteenth century material, acoustical tile.

Besides placing the glass house on the roof, Freret disturbed the exterior appearance and proportions in other ways—not to the good. He added large cast iron cylindrical turrets atop the four main towers. They were finely traceried, and surely well intentioned, but served to "gild the lily." The same results came from another Freret innovation: the adding of bartizan turrets at every upper corner of the newly redone central portion.

The result of all this Gothicizing evoked a devastating outburst from Mark Twain in his *Life on the Mississippi:*

Baton Rouge was clothed in flowers. . . . The magnolia trees in the Capitol grounds were lovely and fragrant. . . . Sir Walter Scott is probably responsible for the Capitol building; for it is not conceivable that this little sham castle would ever have been built if he had not run the people mad a couple of generations ago, with his medieval romances. The South has not yet recovered from the debilitating influence of his books. . . .

It is pathetic enough that a whitewashed castle, with turrets and things—materials all ungenuine within and without—should ever have been built in this otherwise honorable place; but it is much more pathetic to see this architectural falsehood undergoing restoration and perpetualization in our day, when it would have been so easy to let dynamite finish what a charitable fire began, and then devote this restoration money to the building of something genuine.[83]

Twain may partially be excused for his vehemence, for he wrote his book *after* the cast iron turrets and bartizan towers had been added. It had, indeed, been over-Gothicized. However correct Twain's taste may have been, his grounds for objection indicate how poorly he read the southern mind, especially Louisiana's. He expected the South to give up its sense of chivalry and gentility which,

*Louisiana State Capitol, ca. 1900, after restoration. Note the dark color of the capitol, which was originally white, and the cast iron turrets added by William Freret in 1880. (Courtesy Library of Congress)*

during Reconstruction, was about all it had left. After the war, Louisiana wanted everything put back just as it had been before, including its former capitol—*especially* its capitol—for it did, indeed, carry connotations of the chivalry of antebellum times.

Twain's comments are undermined anyway by the fact that he himself lived in a Gothic house. His home in Hartford, Connecticut, was built in 1873–74 in an exaggerated high Victorian Gothic style. Did Twain think that the zig-zag patterns of brick across his walls or the garish colored tiles on his roof were more "genuine" than Dakin's capitol? It is unfortunate that Twain's comments are almost always quoted when the Louisiana capitol is mentioned.[84]

Like his predecessor, Freret found himself pushing to finish in time for the opening of the legislature which was scheduled for May, 1882. The work faltered many times and reportedly stopped altogether once in April of 1881 for want of material.[85] How similar this situation was to Dakin's! The workers were spurred on later that year and by November appeared to be head and head with the schedule. Freret made his deadline and the capitol was ready on time to receive the legislature on May 8, 1882. His restoration was favorably accepted—Twain notwithstanding—for the national architecture magazine, *American Architect and Building News,* had several nice things to say about it. "One finds . . . [Baton Rouge] . . . possessed of a capitol that does not consist of a columned facade, pediment and dome, but is assertive of independent characteristics [These had been Dakin's and White's feelings almost a half century before]. Evidently the newer building conforms to the general plan of the former one. It is in excellent condition . . . and is so satisfactory . . . that it will be long years before Louisiana considers the subject of building another."[86]

This was a prophetic observation. Except for the wise removal of the cast iron turrets and bartizan towers in 1907, the capitol has remained virtually untouched and in sound condition from that time.[87] It was only because Huey Long, in 1931, restless and eager to make changes of all kinds in Louisiana, had erected a new skyscraper capitol, that the old one was replaced. The new capitol is a very fine building in its own right and eminently worthy of its function as Louisiana's state house. Its greater size has enabled expansion of state facilities which the smaller old capitol could not have provided for the future. The old capitol became obsolete more by its small size than by its arrangements.

The old capitol has been restored many times (it is now used as an art gallery and meeting place for war veterans), proving that Louisiana has no intention of giving up Dakin's beautiful castle on the Mississippi. It would not be too much to say that this is a holdover of the same feelings that Mark Twain objected to. A sense of antebellum gentility pervades the old capitol grounds. Louisiana has decided it can have its modernity and its antiquity side by side. As the *Picayune* put it in 1922, "Because of the architectural beauty [of the capitol] at Baton Rouge, it is doubtful if that edifice ever will be torn down."[88]

## THE CAPITOL'S ELUSIVE WASHINGTON STATUE

No story of the Louisiana capitol would be considered complete without relating the peregrination of the somewhat mysterious statue by Hiram Powers which was commissioned for the capitol. Houdon's striking statue of George Washington, which then stood in the Virginia state capitol, attracted Louisiana officials in 1848, and they determined to have a duplicate of the great figure of Washington for the new Louisiana capitol, then just under construction.

*Current view of Louisiana State Capitol.*

By the end of the year, thinking in bigger terms, they had decided against a copy and resolved to have an original.[89]

Negotiations were begun with the most important American sculptor of his day, Hiram Powers, to obtain a statue of Washington for the new capitol's rotunda. It was not a classical Washington that Powers agreed to give Louisiana—Greenough had done him in a toga like a Roman patrician—but instead (in the words of Powers himself):

I am representing Washington in the citizen's dress of his time, standing six feet five inches high, larger than life, in order that the statue may have the appearance of life size where it is to stand alone and on its pedestal in a large room. He seems as meditating, holding the farewell address in one hand, while he leans with the right arm upon a column composed of rods bound together, at the foot of which I have placed two emblems of husbandry, the sickle and the pruning tool. . . . I have preferred to represent him as a citizen. . . . I suppose Washington to have been the greatest, when, by voluntary act, he did all he could to make himself least.[90]

This is the only known extant description of the statue, and no view of it has ever been found. Notwithstanding its size, estimated at over two tons, Powers' statue has remained an elusive one for scholars. The accuracy of Powers' depiction of Washington's garb is unimpeachable, for it was based on the president's own clothing. Powers sent a messenger to the Patent Office, where the clothes were preserved in 1849, to obtain exact measurements. He also obtained copies of the bust by Houdon and the portraits of Peale and Trumbull, enabling him to portray Washington with the greatest accuracy possible in those days before the photograph.[91]

Dakin was to have sent a plan of the interior of his capitol to Powers so that he could visualize it in place, but this was apparently never done.[92] The architect did not live to see the statue, for it was not until January, 1855, that the statue arrived in Baton Rouge, three years after Dakin's death. It remained unpacked for almost a year until a suitable pedestal could be provided. Powers had conceived his statue for a large room, but in Baton Rouge it was thought too heavy for the floor of the rotunda. Instead, a separate enclosure was erected on the capitol grounds to accept the statue.[93]

The dedication took place January 4, 1856, with the governor and suitable dignitaries on hand. Washington's Farewell Address was read, and a ball followed in the capitol rotunda. But the statue's enclosure ignited a heated discussion. It was called variously a cage, a temple, a pagoda, and even a stable.[94] A Baton Rouge writer complained that one "greatly underestimates [Powers'] ability as an artist to think he would ever have consented to have it cooped up in a frame building." But Powers himself had given instructions as to its placement:

Hands ought not to touch the naked marble, and there should be a railing round the statue to keep people at a sufficient distance or some will handle it and ruin the surface. The light for the statue should be considerably above its head, and to cast the necessary shadow for expression, you should see the shade of the nose upon the upper lip. Sculpture is expressionless without a proper light. I am anxious, of course, that a work on which I have taken so much pains should be as gratifying as possible to those who have done me so much honor.[95]

The much maligned pagoda lasted until 1858. James McVey began the move indoors in December, 1858, when workmen began cutting away the floor of the rotunda to make the foundation for the statue. It was not placed in the center, as one might expect, but rather in a niche at the head of the "Grand Stairway" where it was somewhat hidden from view.[96]

The statue languished in the shadows for a time, until it

was carried off during the Civil War. When Baton Rouge fell on May 12, 1862, General Butler, knowing the Confederates would try to retake Baton Rouge, ordered the statue and much of the state library moved to New Orleans for safe-keeping. He had the Powers statue packed up and shipped to Washington because he did not want to "suffer the marble image of the Father of this country to remain among savages, guerrillas and thieving rebels." He said "it is of no possible use to secessionists." Butler had unwittingly saved the statue from destruction in the December, 1862, fire which gutted the interior of the capitol.[97]

The statue arrived in Washington in November, 1862, in the custody of the Quartermaster General. He had it sent over to the national Capitol where it stood on display in the rotunda for about two years. It was moved again in 1864, this time to the Patent Office where it stayed until long after the Civil War.[98]

Like Dakin's capitol, the statue symbolized happier days in Louisiana before the war, and the legislature agitated for its return. On March 2, 1869, it was boxed up and sent back to Louisiana. Because the old capitol was in ruins, the statue was placed in what was known as the Octagonal Building at the New Orleans Fair Grounds. It attracted considerable attention and was regarded as the high point of the exhibition. A plaque was placed on the base, reading: "Powers Statue of Washington . . . Returned to the State of Louisiana by order of Pres. Johnson through the influence of Sen. Kellog." The statue had at last come home to rest. Had Washington himself slept in so many beds? But it was not to be dormant for long. A month before the 1871 fair was to open, a fire broke out, destroying the Octagonal Building. The remains of the statue were found in the ruins, its marble charred and crumbled. The statue's remnants are said to have been carried out to the lower reaches of the Mississippi below New Orleans and dumped overboard, ending its last journey.[99] Its odyssey must be one of the most involved and unhappy ones in the history of American art.

*New Orleans Custom House, front elevation (First plan, 1846).*

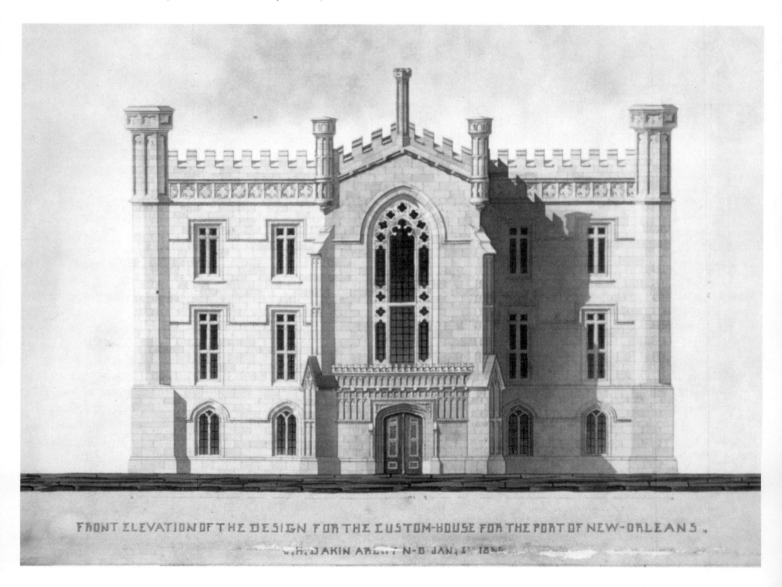

*New Orleans Custom House, side elevation (First plan, 1846).*

FLANK ELEVATION OF A DESIGN FOR A CUSTOM-HOUSE FOR THE PORT OF NEW-ORLEANS.

J.H. DAKIN ARCH'T. N.O. JAN. 1st 1846.

*New Orleans Custom House (floor plan). Longitudinal section.*

time another act of Congress was passed on March 3, 1847, appropriating $100,000 for foundation excavations and other purposes. Dakin, meanwhile, had competed for and won the job of designing the Louisiana capitol on May 4, 1847. He now found himself torn between the attractions of two jobs. One he already had, the other he wanted even more than the capitol. Though a state capitol was about as prestigious a project as an architect could hope to obtain in his time, the federal job was even more prestigious—and more lucrative.

Dakin submitted another set of plans for the Custom House on June 22, 1847.[8] He also saw some of the other drawings submitted at the time and commented on them in his "capitol diary":

June 26, 1847. Delivered to D[enis] Prieur at the Custom House, my Design for the New Custom House to be erected in New Orleans. Saw a number of designs by various architects, and to my mind, there was scarcely one entitled to the least consideration, both on account of taste and arrangements. I was astonished by the bad taste and worse arrangements of Mr. Gallier's plan. His Principal Room was in the center of the square surrounded by buildings, giving no chance for light or air. I consider the whole of them a lot of rubbish, to speak plain. I also delivered to Mr. Prieur a letter printed [it was indeed printed] to the Secretary of the Treasury and to himself explaining my designs.[9]

It is interesting that of all the plans Dakin saw, he singled out Gallier's for criticism. Gallier's plan, preserved at Tulane University, is rather undistinguished. Gallier's placement of the main business room in the center was also part of A. T. Wood's plan. Could this have been one of the ideas that Gallier says Wood "borrowed" from him?

Dakin alluded to his second plan in his June 26, 1847, entry; this design was in the Greek Revival style. Dakin's Gothic building was probably too much for the government's taste, so he retreated to the safer Greek style. In his printed letter, Dakin proposed that the front of the building face, not Canal Street but the river. This would have made the main facade on New Levee Street (now North Peters). Dakin further proposed that the land between the Custom House and the edge of the Mississippi River—about one block then, before the river shifted—be entirely cleared, providing a grand view of the Custom House from the river. He hedged on this point, however, and stated that, if required, the front could be changed to Canal Street.

His plan called for the Corinthian order, with three blind porticos on Canal Street and one blind portico on Customhouse Street (now Iberville). From this plan, we see that Wood's design also bears features of another architect's drawings, for Dakin's three blind porticos on Canal and one on Iberville are incorporated into Wood's final plan.

This Corinthian design of Dakin's was one of his most grandly conceived plans. His original drawing shows a sprawling two-story colonnade across the front, consisting of twenty-eight columns rising from the second-story level, above a rusticated first floor. Its center portico contains eight columns, two smaller porticos at either side contain six each, and the recessed areas in between contain eight. The central portion was pedimented, and the two end pavilions were flat roofed, with a row of antefixae on the cornice of the roof between the center and side portions.

However extravagant the front elevation, the E-shaped floor plan was extremely well laid out. The recessed portions of the facade were really loggias through which the public could pass to reach an open courtyard directly in the rear. The building in the front was to be the Post Office, and the rear section behind the arcade and courtyard was the Custom House area. Behind this section was another courtyard leading to the United States District Court on Decatur Street. The warehouse for use by the Custom House was

CUSTOM HOUSE, NEW ORLEANS.

*New Orleans Custom House, front elevation. Second of three plans
submitted by James Dakin, 1847.*

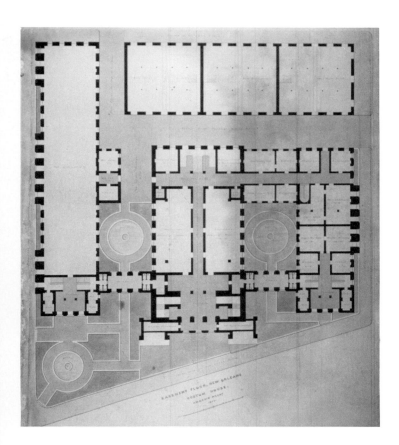

*Floor plan of Dakin's second design for New Orleans Custom House.*

placed on the Canal Street side and could be reached by an L-shaped courtyard. This plan provided all the air and light that Dakin insisted upon so strenuously.

A day after dropping off these plans at the commissioner's office in New Orleans, Dakin returned to Baton Rouge to lay out the site for the new capitol. He recorded shortly afterward in his diary that Mr. Prieur was mailing the Custom House designs to Washington on July 8. A day later, Dakin copied into his diary, two letters of introduction to the authorities in Washington, one from Governor Isaac Johnson of Louisiana and one from A. D. Crossman, mayor of New Orleans. Both letters praised Dakin's character and his professional skill.

On July 14, 1847, as noted previously, Dakin departed with his family for Pittsburgh. Spending only one day there, he left for Washington on July 29, arriving in Baltimore on the thirtieth. (His trunk was sent to Washington, and he, like many travelers before and since, had to wait for his belongings to return.)

On August 2, 1847, he left Baltimore for Washington at 6:30 A.M. and arrived there two hours later. He records that he did not find Secretary of the Treasury Walker or "Dr. Gwynn," both of whom were at Rockaway, Long Island, at the Marine Pavilion Dakin had designed some fifteen years before. (The reference here is to William M. Gwinn, a commissioner for the erection of the Custom House.)

For some unspecified reason, Dakin returned to Baltimore a day later and went on to Philadelphia, staying there only one day. (It would be interesting to know why he made this brief trip. Could Thomas U. Walter have been there, awaiting a friendly call?) Dakin then set out for Rockaway, where he finally saw Walker and Gwinn on August 4. He writes: "August 5. Studied new designs for Custom House in morning, and at 2:30, started for New

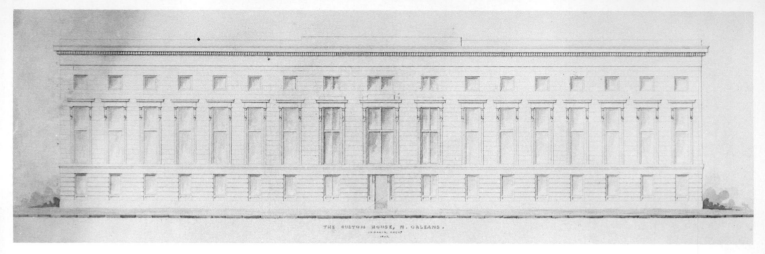

*New Orleans Custom House, front elevation. Third of three plans submitted by James Dakin, 1847.*

York for purpose of making out my drawings and arrived at Clinton Hall at 5:00 PM.'' This was where he had had his office from 1833 to 1835; he probably borrowed office space there to work on his plans.

Dakin records that he drew an entirely new design the next morning, this time ''making the building perfectly plain and dispensing with all ornamental works.'' This design was in response to Mr. Walker's determination to have a building ''planned and erected solely for business purposes.'' Dakin acknowledged the validity of Walker's arguments and commented that ''Mr. Gallier's designs were not considered as being in any manner suited for the purpose and object desired.'' Dakin goes on to say that ''Mr. Wood's design was a most foolish thing for any man having the least pretension to architectural skill. The entire area of the square was covered, having no means of ventilation or air for the interiors, except by means of a skylight over the General Business Room which was in the center of the dense mass of building. His plan would have made a tolerable Mausoleum or Tomb for an Egyptian King.''

After completing his new designs Dakin met with Walker, Gwinn, and other officials. They were, Dakin records, ''unanimous in expressing their decided opinion in favor of my design as being much superior to all others, and these gentlemen advised Mr. Walker to adopt my suggestions in regard to light and ventilation, etc. I made two plans, one was to have a building in the center, with a passage all around it [ground plan sketched in here] and the other to have an open court in the centre instead of a building. The latter plan will be adopted as it will also give room for reception of goods.'' [10]

The original drawings for this revision indicate that Dakin redid his plan in a very plain Greek Revival style. It was rusticated on the first floor, as is Wood's plan (Did

Wood get this from Dakin's third design?), with unpedimented windows having modillion brackets just under the lintels. The roof was flat, with only dentils under the cornice and a low blocking course on top for decoration.

The shape of Custom House Square was irregular, creating a serious aesthetic design problem because of the awkward angle at Canal and New Levee streets. (The other three corners were ninety degrees.) In his first Greek Revival version, done in New Orleans, Dakin had ignored the angle, squaring his building and placing a fountain on the little triangular piece of troublesome land. But now, he followed the irregular site in an obvious attempt to satisfy Secretary Walker's desire to utilize as much of the land as possible. To obviate the problem, he turned to a style which was more modular and capable of withstanding such harsh treatment. Basically Greek Revival, it had the feel of the Italian Palazzo style.

His revised plan indicates a passageway through the square from New Levee to Decatur Street and a courtyard in the middle. This provided the light and air he insisted upon. His post office was on the second floor, on the Decatur Street side, again as in Wood's final plan. The District Court was directly above it, on the third floor. Wood's plan was also so arranged.

On August 18, 1847, he records that he ''saw the Bonded Warehouse in New York with Bogardus and Dr. Gwinn.'' This was the famous cast iron warehouse that James Bogardus had just completed, the first all metal building in the United States. This visit must have had a profound effect on Dakin's thinking as an architect, for though he had planned his Louisiana capitol with some metal parts, he was later to go much further in proposing the use of cast iron, further than any architect of his time had gone for a major building.

A notation in his diary the day after his visit to Bo-

*Earliest known view of the New Orleans Custom House, February, 1848, signed "A. T. Wood, Architect." (From New Orleans* Daily Delta, *February 13, 1848)*

gardus' warehouse indicates that something had happened in the decision making over the Custom House. Dakin wrote: "I cannot see anything in the way of success in all this matter unless it be my political opinion which I hardly think will be considered." Resigned to the victory of A. T. Wood, Dakin left New York a few days later, on August 26, arriving in Washington on August 28. While in New York, though, he had "procured two plans or modes of heating the State House with hot air." (This contradicts the restoration commission's report which said that there was no provision for heating).[11] By October, he was back in Baton Rouge to begin in earnest on the capitol.

It is readily apparent from Dakin's diary and Gallier's autobiography that the government's practice in the 1840s and 1850s of selecting and developing a final plan for a public building was hardly in keeping with what is considered today to be professional ethics. The showing of one man's design to another competing architect and the mongrelization of the best features of several plans was not fair to any of the competitors. Even worse was calling the final result one architect's work.[12]

Because A. T. Wood's competition drawings for the New Orleans Custom House have not been found and on the strength of Gallier's complaints over the selection procedure, it is reasonable to assume that some features of Wood's final plan were "borrowed" from other designs. Dakin may also have contributed something (unwillingly) to the final plan, both verbally on his visit to New York and through his three versions of the Custom House design.

The earliest revelation of the final plan for the Custom House came on February 13, 1848, when a New Orleans newspaper ran a five column-wide cut of the design. A. T. Wood was credited as the architect.[13] It featured a rusticated first floor, as did Dakin's second and third plans, a solid mass of building with no courtyard, as did Gallier's plan, and was in a composite style which included details of the Greek and Egyptian styles and the modularity of Dakin's third plan.

The facade on Canal Street was somewhat Egyptianized by the use of four free-standing columns with lotus capitals, but fluted in the Doric style. They stood in a shallow portico in the center. Two false porticos were placed near the outer ends of the facade (as in Dakin's second plan) and four square Doric-inspired pilasters shaped the portico. Dakin's comment that the building would "make a tolerable mausoleum or tomb for an Egyptian king" was quite appropriate.

The roof line was originally flat, with very low triangular pediments placed over the two false porticos and a large blocking course above the central one. Modillion brackets set under the cornice produced a kind of triglyph effect. Years later, long after Wood's death, a triangular Greek pediment was placed over the central portico, which, combined with the square Doric pilasters, the fluted columns and the "triglyphs," further shoved the design of the Custom House into the realm of the Greek rather than the Egyptian Revival. Small wonder that Talbot Hamlin referred to the designer as "an architect only by courtesy," and said, "It is a huge rather gaunt, granite mass, with exterior detail unlike any ancient work whatsoever, although it probably represents a rather uneducated person's idea of Egyptian." Hamlin went on to say, however, that "somehow, the whole, even its awkwardness, perhaps even in its downright ugliness, has a kind of power, a sort of forthright arrogance, that is impressive if only as an expression of the bold pride of New Orleans in the cotton-boom days."[14]

While James Dakin was back in Baton Rouge, hard at work on his capitol, A. T. Wood began construction of the Custom House. On January 27, 1848, the First Municipality of the city of New Orleans—the Creole section—had responded to the appropriations and selection of a plan by the federal government by donating the entire block on Canal Street to the United States for the purpose of erecting a custom house.[15] In that same year, 1848, there came to light some of the considerations which supposedly figured in the selection of the plans. A letter from Secretary of the Treasury Walker was published in the New Orleans papers which indicated why Dakin's designs had no chance of winning the competition.

Walker stated that the government "wants a plain and substantial building, avoiding all unnecessary expense and ornament, simple and unostentatious . . . avoiding everything merely calculated for display. A building of an ostentatious or ornamental character . . . would be less useful, inasmuch as a large portion . . . would be unnecessarily occupied by courtyards, steps, porticos or pillars, thus, to that extent, wasting the space intended for useful purposes, rendering the entrance less accessible, obscuring the light and interrupting the ventilation of the building."[16]

How Walker had come full circle since Dakin spoke to him in New York! Or had he misled Dakin into believing his plan for more light and air was the better one? Whatever the circumstances, it was certainly questionable reasoning for Walker to state that a building with courtyards and porticos would be less well ventilated and lighted than one which covered an entire city block.

With the government committed to Wood's massive pile, the demolishers set to work on the old Custom House in June of 1848.[17] By October, Colonel William Turnbull had arrived to commence his foundations for the Custom House (Wood was not assigned this part of the job). Turnbull had served in the Mexican War as a topographical engineer, and he was still a career Army officer in the Engineers corps.[18]

His foundations were of the kind Latrobe had disdained—a mat of cypress logs. Trenches were dug seven feet deep and eighteen feet across, and cypress logs a foot square were tightly laid in. Hydraulic cement then was poured in to fill up the trough, upon which was laid a foundation of bricks. They were laid in inverted arches to equalize the load and produce even settlement. (In 1926, these logs were examined and no decay was found.)[19]

By the end of 1849, most of the granite blocks of the first floor were set in place over these foundations. They weighed from five to twenty tons each, but heavy cranes made their handling relatively easy. In January, 1850, Wood left for Washington to obtain more appropriations from Congress to continue the work. This was a trip which was to cost him his job.

While in Washington, some time before May, 1850, Wood had been engaged in putting together contracts for the Custom House with Secretary Meredith. On May 4, 1850, Meredith notified the commissioners in New Orleans that Wood had been discharged as architect.[20] He said that Wood had added to a general contract a contract for granite which had not been approved. Meredith had told Wood not to make contracts on his own, and when he found the unapproved contract on his desk with others for his signature, he fired Wood. In a very long and convoluted letter (as always, published in the newspapers), Wood replied; but Meredith held to the discharge.[21]

James Dakin, then in Baton Rouge nearing completion of his capitol, heard of the dismissal and wrote his friend, President Zachary Taylor, on May 22, 1850, requesting the job as architect of the Custom House.[22]

The next day, Dakin also wrote Secretary of the Treasury Meredith for the position, giving as references President Taylor and Congressman C. M. Conrad of the House of Representatives. The letter to Zachary Taylor must have had the desired effect, for on June 6, 1850, Meredith wrote the commissioners of the Custom House in New Orleans for an opinion of Dakin, who, he said, "has been strongly recommended." Their reply on June 14, 1850 (from Samuel J. Peters and John W. Crockett), stated: "Mr. Dakin is a highly respectable man and an accomplished architect, but is not considered as *practical* as Mr. Gallier, whom we have recommended. Mr. Gallier, in our opinion, and in the opinion of this Community, is without a rival. But Mr. Dakin, we conceive, ranks next to him, and we have no doubt the work could be safely entrusted to his hands." [23]

Peters wrote a separate letter to Congressman Conrad about the question of Dakin or Gallier. He stated that the commissioners had "written [Meredith] in high esteem of Mr. Dakin, but nevertheless express a preference for Mr. Gallier." Dakin would have been mentioned as a candidate, but the commissioners "supposed his engagement at Baton Rouge, where he is employed on the New State House would render it impossible for him to accede to it." [24]

A little later during that summer of 1850, after the dismissal of Wood and before the naming of a replacement, Dakin went to the East again, probably to see Zachary Taylor. It is certain that he visited New York, for Alexander Jackson Davis records in his diary for July 27, 1850: "Mr. Dakin called and reported on Louisiana, etc." [25] Dakin also visited Washington that month and may or may not have been able to see President Taylor before his death on July 9. But Dakin lost no time in seeing Congressman C. M. Conrad of New Orleans who wrote the Secretary of the Treasury that Dakin was coming to see him. He told the Secretary: "I repeat to you what I said on previous occasions, that Mr. Dakin is universally considered with us the most accomplished architect in the State and is highly esteemed and respected as a citizen. The late President knew him well, Mr. Dakin having commanded a regiment of volunteers which he raised mainly by his personal industries during the late war and served under the immediate command of Gen. Taylor." [26]

Three days later, on July 20, 1850, Dakin was named by Meredith as superintending architect of the Custom House. The contacts, letters, and recommendations had achieved the desired effect. New Orleans newspapers—the *Picayune,* the *Delta,* and the *Crescent*—and the Baton Rouge *Gazette* were all enthusiastic that the position had gone to Dakin. [27]

The *Delta,* though happy over the choice, did express some regret that the original architect would not be allowed to finish the building. Responding to the *Delta's* reservation, the *Crescent* commented:

Our contemporary contends that "no man is so able to complete a building as he who designed it." This is true under ordinary circumstances but we might imagine many ways in which the most skillful architect might render himself incapable of carrying out his own design. For instance, he might prove recreant, leave his post, and from drunkenness, render himself incapable of attending to his duties, repeatedly for weeks together, during which the building might be ruined. We should be very sorry to see any injustice to Mr. Wood, but from what we know of the case, we should think it would be indiscreet in the friends of that gentleman to press this matter. [28]

This thinly veiled allusion to Wood's personal problem was borne out in other places, particularly in a letter to the commissioners in January, 1852, from Lewis E. Reynolds, Dakin's immediate successor at the Custom House.

Dakin took charge on August 12, 1850, after concluding his business in Baton Rouge. Only the interior detailing on the capitol remained to be completed, and Daniel Avery was to supervise that work. Dakin did not move his family to New Orleans at this time, choosing instead to commute between New Orleans and Baton Rouge by steamboat. After his inspection of the Custom House he reported on the progress, saying that the work had reached "to the springing of the first tier [floor] of groined arches." Thus, when he assumed the job, only the foundations, the arch work, and setting of stone of the ground floor had been completed.[29]

Dakin was never satisfied with the floor plan of the Custom House as designed by Wood. His chief objection continued to be the utter lack of light and ventilation in the interior rooms and offices. He was hardly on the job a month when he devised alterations to counteract this defect of light and air and the archaic use of groined arches for the interior. He immediately prepared a pamphlet, directed to the commissioners, which he had printed and distributed. The newspapers quoted from it, making known his proposed changes.

The pamphlet, dated September 21, 1850, made suggestions for two major changes.[30] The first was to modify the floor plan, and the other was to use a cast iron interior instead of groined brick arches. He said that the central placement of the Collector's General Business Room was a serious error. The interior of the building would be cut off from light and air. "It could be lighted sufficiently through its roof, but at the same time a volume of heat would be admitted at least eight months in each year that would be intolerable." Dakin went on to say, "The proper ventilation of this room as now located must depend entirely upon mechanical or artificial means. . . . The air must necessarily become heated and vitiated in its passage amongst human beings and merchandise." He pointed out that ventilation

by artificial means would "involve great cost," and that there were many other rooms and passageways which were likewise without air or light.

He then said that "to correct these errors and objections, I propose to move the 'Collector's Room' forward so as to front directly on Canal St. and open the center of the mass of the edifice by an uncovered court." After making these changes, "no mechanical or artificial means [of ventilation] will be required."

Dakin also proposed digging a cellar under the open courtyard for storage of wines and liquors. He suggested placing glass "bulls' eyes" in the pavement for lighting these areas.

Dakin's other major suggestion was the use of cast iron instead of masonry arches to support the four floors. He said that "a system of groined arching and massive piers will involve great time and expense." He pointed out that "the practice of turning arches over a story for the support of a floor above, unless for military purposes, has long been . . . obsolete in countries where iron is abundant. In England, for instance, arched floors or ceilings have become very rare for any purpose whatsoever, and in all public and commercial buildings for some years past, iron has been substituted because of its greater economy and . . . strength and convenience to the structure and at the same time occupying much less space." Dakin also calculated that the outside walls, as then designed, would not be able to hold the strong lateral thrust of groined vaulting.

This suggestion for the use of iron was amazing for its time. Had Dakin's recommendations been carried out, this would have been the earliest known instance of cast iron being used in a substantial portion of a major American building. By 1850, Bogardus' little warehouse and a small library had already been built with iron, but it would not be for some years after Dakin's proposals that the Harper's Building in New York would be erected with an iron frame.[31] His proposing this new material for the largest building in the United States again demonstrates that Dakin deserves to rank among America's finest and most imaginative architects. Oddly, six years later, the head of the Treasury Department's architectural section, Captain A. H. Bowman, was to claim for his 1856 plans for federal buildings, that "the introduction of wrought iron beams and girders in these Edifices, instead of the groined arches as formerly used, is, I believe, wholly new." He made this claim, despite his joining the department just two years after Dakin's departure and the hubbub over his changes, as well as a voluminous report made by the Treasury Department at that time. This must have been a case of "convenient memory."[32]

Anticipating much opposition to his changes, Dakin had appended to his pamphlet several dozen letters of endorsement from various persons approving his changes. Among these letter writers were architect Lewis E. Reynolds, Postmaster Michel Musson, whose office would be located in the building, Collector of Customs Daniel O. Hincks, who agreed that the whole community approved of Dakin's changes, except for "a few persons who have been misled by the representations of the late architect, Mr. Wood." The commissioners added, "We ... declare that in our deliberate judgment, the edifice, if constructed according to the original design, would tumble into ruins of its own weight before it could be completed ... the cost [using Dakin's revisions] would be reduced by three hundred thousand dollars, and [the building] would be completed and ready for use three years sooner. ... We have deemed it best to send Mr. Dakin to Washington to lay his plan before the Department in person"

The New Orleans newspapers thoroughly agreed with these changes and urged their adoption. But Dakin had stirred up a hornet's nest of opposition from the Creoles of the First Municipality. They charged indignantly that to move the business room to the Canal Street front would give an advantage to the Second Municipality and that business in the First Municipality would suffer as a result. They further stated that they had donated the square of land based on the assumption that Wood's plan of placing the business room in the center would be the permanent arrangement. Dakin appeared before their city council but in vain.[33]

The newspapers were dumbfounded by the objections to the changes. The *Picayune* said, "We must acknowledge our incapability to discover what the many advantages the First Municipality would derive from that particular plan of the building [Wood's] and which it would lose to the new one. ... We should think that so long as there is free access to the Collector's Room from streets all around the building—all of which, it should be remembered, are in the First Municipality—it would matter little whether the main business room be on the first or second floor or on the roof."[34] The *Picayune* proceeded to admonish the First Municipality for its sectional attitude. This was the same trait which years before had caused the city to be split into three municipalities. Despite all appeals to reason, the Council of the First Municipality angrily passed, by an eleven to one vote, a resolution against Dakin's change. So adamant were they that they also approved a memorial to the Secretary of the Treasury objecting to the changes.[35]

A. T. Wood saw his opportunity and jumped into the battle shortly afterwards with a letter to the papers—as always—in retaliation against Dakin's pamphlet.[36] Wood was, of course, stung by Dakin's remarks about the "serious error" in the placement of the Collector's Room. He repeated the same charges of the First Municipality Council that the donation of the ground was predicated on using his original plan. Wood wrote:

Col. Dakin comes forward bravely, yet meekly, firmly, yet modestly with a remedy for the 'defects and architectural deficiencies' . . . and a lesson of instruction not only to myself, but to all architects capable of reflection. This gentlemanly architect for the construction does not, certainly, attempt to detract from my credit by a reference to the foundation of St. Patrick's Church in Camp St. or the block of buildings known as Gasquet Row in Camp St., near St. Joseph — or from my calculations to the correctness of his, on the three houses [Union Terrace] opposite the old State House in Canal St., and numerous other examples in this city. But it might be inferred by others less charitable than himself, that the deficiencies pointed to by him in my plan might, if not intentionally, seriously injure my reputation as an architect, and therefore would only be warrantable under a conscientious discharge of his duties and a strict regard to truth. It would be unfair to presume Mr. D. would intentionally do me an injustice or reflect a discredit, that might affect me in obtaining a livelihood by my profession. Therefore, I am constrained to the belief that he is totally ignorant of the building now under his supervision.[37]

Wood, defending his masonry arches, cited buildings which had utilized them, such as the national Capitol and three other federal buildings in Washington, as well as Girard College in Philadelphia and the Custom Houses of London, New York, and Boston. However, most — at least four — if not all, were built some fifteen to twenty years before, when cast iron was little heard of in American building construction. It is hardly probable that Town and Davis (New York Custom House), Thomas U. Walter (Girard College), and the architects of these other buildings would have so designed them in 1850. Ammi B. Young, architect of the Boston Custom House in 1837, would himself be in New Orleans in a year to repudiate the use of

groined arches, as we shall see. Wood was clearly behind the times and resented Dakin's using the latest methods.

Wood ended his letter solemnly defying anyone to refute his arguments. He furthermore warned the Secretary of the Treasury "that the proposed alterations will be attended with great hazard, while I protest against any departure from my original plan as a violation of many of the contracts . . . and an unwarrantable insult and injury offered to my name and professional reputation."

What Wood lacked in architectural ability, he made up for in political *savvy*. He was clearly playing on the strong feelings in the French section against the moving of the room. By making his original design seem sacrosanct, he might get his old job back and possibly strike a blow at Dakin, who had "dared" to tamper with his plan. Wood, taking Dakin's pamphlet partly as a personal attack, had responded in kind. The references to St. Patrick's Church and the other buildings were his attempt to in turn discredit Dakin. But Wood was in prison at the time of the St. Patrick's Church incident, and would have had, of necessity, only hearsay information.

About 1834, A. T. Wood and his former partner, George Clarkson, had severed relations. On July 27, 1835, the two had engaged in a fight in which Clarkson was killed. The newspapers said, "Clarkson had Wood down and wouldn't let him go," whereupon "a blow was audible," and Clarkson received a wound in the chest from which he died shortly thereafter. In 1836, Wood was tried and sentenced to six years in the Louisiana State Penitentiary at Baton Rouge.[38] Ironically, while there, Wood was used to supervise the construction of an addition to the Penitentiary; he was released about 1842.[39] A special act of the legislature had to be passed in 1850 to restore "the civil and political rights of Alexander Thompson Wood, who was convicted in

1836 of the crime of manslaughter.''[40] In doing so, the legislature was rather sympathetic, noting that the crime was possibly in self-defense and that part of the convicting jury considered it justifiable homicide; all had recommended clemency.

The allusion to Gasquet Row certainly indicates that Wood got his information garbled. Here the testimony of William Gasquet himself in the Baton Rouge slander case negates Wood's allegations. Gasquet, it will be remembered, said he "was well satisfied with his [Dakin's] efforts . . . that I know of no one I would sooner have to superintend a building for me." Dakin had in fact done over twenty-five buildings for Gasquet.

Wood's other gibe, about Union Terrace, was correct in the sense that Dakin lost money on the job, as we saw in the bankruptcy records. But there is no way of knowing whether the loss was from a cost over-run he did not calculate for or as a result of the Panic of 1837. What is important however, is that William Gasquet was one of the four owners of Union Terrace and came back to Dakin again and again.

The issue of changing the Custom House plans smouldered for a while. It would soon heat up again when Dakin obtained the backing of an old friend, Isaiah Rogers. Rogers, often called the father of the American hotel for his designs for the Tremont House and the Astor House, had been asked around 1850 to design the Battle House in Mobile (which he did) and to prepare alterations for the St. Louis Hotel in New Orleans. While he was in New Orleans for these purposes, he visited Dakin who asked him to observe and comment upon the situation at the Custom House.

It was also at this time that the St. Charles Hotel burned to the ground, leaving the city of New Orleans in a state of shock. Rogers was asked to do the plans for the reconstruction of the St. Charles; the city simply could not do without its great old St. Charles, and it wanted the man who built more important hotels than anyone else to do it. Though Rogers ultimately declined to be the architect for the hotel, he did draw some plans for its design, roughly following the original design of Gallier and Dakin for the exterior. The interior design of the second St. Charles Hotel should definitely be credited to Rogers.

For a reason still unknown, William Strickland, then building the capitol of Tennessee, was also in New Orleans at the same time as Isaiah Rogers, and he too called on Dakin upon arriving. Their conversations have not been recorded in detail, but Rogers has left a diary which gives some description of the meetings among these men and the matters concerning the hotels and the Custom House.[41]

Rogers, arriving from Cincinnati, where he had established his office in 1848, recorded several meetings with Dakin and one with the commissioners of the Custom House. Of the latter meeting, Rogers wrote: "Saw some of them [the commissioners] and talked over the subject. They appear to be in a bad fix with the building. They wished me to give them in writing my views of Dakin's report." Rogers then left New Orleans for Louisville. While in Louisville he prepared the message he had promised, and on February 13, he returned to New Orleans, just a few days after the St. Charles had burned. Rogers' journal entries reveal his activities in late February and early March:

February 14, New Orleans. Took a look at the ruins of the St. Charles Hotel.
February 25, New Orleans. Saw Mr. Dakin. Had a talk with him. Mr. Dakin and Mr. Strickland called on me in the evening. Had a long talk with them on architecture and various subjects.

*Isaiah Rogers, father of the American hotel, who sided with Dakin in the Custom House controversy. (From* The American Architect, *May 3, 1911)*

March 1, New Orleans. Commenced plan of the St. Charles Hotel and outlined first floor nearly.

March 5, New Orleans. Finished plans of St. Charles Hotel in all the day.

In his last entry Rogers records a hurried departure from New Orleans: "March 14, New Orleans. Had a long talk with the directors of the St. Charles Hotel. Told them I could not stop any longer in the city and requested them to release me from making any further plans of the hotel. After some consultation, they concluded to release me and wished me to name a price for my services so far. I declined . . . but they insisted on making me some compensation and named $300. . . ."[42]

His diary entries clearly show that Isaiah Rogers was the real designer of the second St. Charles Hotel. He followed rather closely the exterior outline of the first one as designed by Gallier and Dakin. The few changes made to the exterior included the substitution on the ground floor of twin granite piers for the store area instead of the austere front of the Gallier and Dakin plan. Also added were dentils in the pediment which had formerly been very plain. The coming ornate styles of the 1850s brought accompanying pediments over the windows supported by brackets. The great dome of the first hotel was thought superfluous, and since it was quite expensive it was dispensed with.

Rogers complied with the request of Dakin and the Custom House commissioners during his short return trip to Louisville in January, 1851. He sent the following letter to the commissioners:

Having been requested to give my opinion of the plan and suggested improvements by Mr. Dakin, Architect, and having examined the original plan and perused the pamphlet containing those suggestions, I take this opportunity to say that I concur with his views. His arrangement for the large room is certainly very much better than the original, and the courtyard opening in the center, is, in my estimation, indispensible for so large a building, both for light and ventilation. I am only surprised that any person should have conceived of an arrangement for a building of the magnitude of the Custom House—divided into so many apartments—many of them not opening onto the Streets, but depending on other apartments, themselves not too well lighted and ventilated, for light and air. And all this, I am informed, is by a professional architect!

With the humble position I occupy in the profession as an Architect, I feel regret and mortification that any one should make so sad a mistake for a building of that magnitude, as is too evident from an examination of the plans. It certainly reflects severely on the architects of this country if we cannot get Public Buildings designed with more fitness for their use than that of the Custom House at New Orleans. The large business room, as suggested by Mr. Dakin, may be made a splendid affair, both to comfortable arrangements, business and appearance.

The approach should be to land in the center by a double staircase, leaving the entire of the walls for business purposes—the public accommodations around the staircase in the center—I think this is one of Mr. Dakin's plans for entering the large room. [This was correct.]

In regard to the suggestions of Mr. Dakin in reference to a cellar under the building, it would be, in most places, considered indispensable. But in New Orleans, it can only be done in one way that I can suggest, and that is to make a counter vault for all the partitions and walls to rest on, which, if done, would, I think, render the building much more secure from settling. As the foundation is now, I should have misgivings of its sufficient strength to support the great weight of those massive walls on such a formation as the City of New Orleans appears to be.[43]

Regrettably, Rogers did not comment on Dakin's proposal for using cast iron instead of groined arches, but his statement, "I concur with his views," carries with it the approval of this old master. Very soon Rogers himself would begin to use cast iron extensively in his hotels.

Perhaps the real significance of Rogers' letter is its demonstration of the principles set forth in the constitution of the American Institution of Architects, of which Rogers and Dakin were founding members. In denouncing the floor plan of the Custom House, he expresses "regret and mortification that any one should make so sad a mistake." He further states that "it certainly reflects severely on the architects of this country." The American Institution of Architects did not function widely for the reasons previously cited, but its members obviously fought individually to maintain certain standards and principles. Its significance as a forerunner to the American Institute of Architects can, perhaps, be better judged by the force with which architectural pioneers like Rogers insisted on better performance from those in the profession.

Besides Isaiah Rogers, another major architect tacitly sided with Dakin's position. Thomas U. Walter, in Washington in January, 1851, was asked by the Treasury Department to propose other floor plans for the Custom House. He reported: "I have rearranged the interior . . . retaining the Collector's Room in the centre, and although many of the objections of the original plan are obviated, I am still not satisfied with it [nor had been Rogers and Dakin, because of the intrinsic fault of the lack of a courtyard]; I have therefore made another design in which the apartments of the [District] Court are placed on the shortest front . . . [and a courtyard in the center] but it has occurred to me that there might be some objection to such a change . . . of which I am not aware."

The last remarks may have been prophetic, for the placement of the Collector's Room was to be the chief issue. Walter, in his second plan (the one with the courtyard), had unknowingly committed the grievous sin of moving the room to the Canal Street front.[44]

The use of iron, curiously, did not seem to create much of

a furor, although Dakin did get into a long discussion with the Treasury Department over the shape of the proposed iron beams. American experimentation with building materials as to their load-bearing characteristics was in its infancy, so that it is odd, but not surprising, that it was suggested to Dakin that the iron beams be shaped like an inverted U. Dakin somehow knew—perhaps because of a friendship with Bogardus—that the most efficient shape for cast iron beams was an I. Dakin's knowledge of the preferred shape of iron members is interesting, in view of his remoteness from the experimentations with iron.[45]

As it became apparent to Dakin that he would have a difficult time persuading the government to impose his changes over all objections, he proposed, in early 1851, that an impartial review board of engineers and architects be named to decide the issue.[46] The idea lay dormant in the files of the United States government for most of 1851, but later events, involving politics rather than architecture, became so chaotic that the issue had to be implemented before the year was out. The battle against the changes shifted from the Council of the First Municipality to the United States Senate.

The French municipality had a friend in Congress, Senator Pierre Soule. In a forceful drive in the Senate, Soule attempted to get an amendment passed to the country's general appropriations bill for 1851–1852, requiring that "no material departure be made from the original plan" of the New Orleans Custom House, and that "the main business room shall remain as contemplated in the same plan."[47] It seems absurd that such a minute trifle as the placement of a room should hold the attention of the United States Senate for debate, but it did. It is even more absurd that the First Municipality should carry its sectional feelings all the way to Congress to have its imagined wrongs redressed.

Soule's amendment, offered on March 3, 1851, had previously been acted upon unfavorably in committee. Senator Davis of Massachusetts remarked that "a majority [of the committee] came to the conclusion not to recommend it. I do not see how it is possible for a Department [Treasury] to carry on the business in a proper way unless they can be clothed with some discretion. It is quite impossible that a great building, which is to cost some $3,000,000, can be erected unless there is some discretion given to the Department."[48]

Soule, probably sensing that the Senate couldn't care less about the placement of a room in a building, cast the issue into a political mould. He pointed out that "while the building was in progress ... a change took place in the administration of the country, and the fate of the building had to pass into other hands. No sooner had the Commissioners now in office been invested with the power of managing the great undertaking, than it became evident that all their ingenuity and adroitness would be directed towards a single object, the perverting of the intentions of the original designers of the structure.... The Custom House [was] to turn its back, as it were, on the Municipality which had donated the ground whereon it was being erected"[49]

Soule should have been laughed off the floor of the Senate after this speech, but he had worked up the chamber along political lines; and the Democrats were ready to strike a blow at the Whig administration of Millard Fillmore. One amendment was added, requiring the restoration of A. T. Wood as architect, but it got no support; and another requiring the nomination of the architect by the president, with the advice and consent of Senate, was voted upon. The make-up of the Senate was then thirty-five Democrats, twenty-five Whigs, and two of other parties.[50] A vote was taken, and factionalism prevailed, both nationally and at the New Orleans level. Thus Soule succeeded.

In compliance with this new act, President Fillmore nominated James Dakin on March 12, 1851.[51] The Senate went into executive session behind closed doors that day and emerged with a rejection of Dakin, without comment. Obviously, Soule continued to retain his hold on the Senate. Fillmore then nominated James Gallier on the next day, and he was approved.[52] Soule had succeeded in ousting Dakin and his changes in the plan. Gallier, on the other hand, had proposed, like A. T. Wood (or Wood had stolen from him), the idea that there be no central courtyard, thereby permitting the business room to be a few feet closer to the First Municipality than in Dakin's plan. Gallier was, of course, acceptable to Soule and the French faction for this reason.

However, Gallier upset their plans and declined the nomination. In a letter from Barre, Massachusetts, dated April 10, 1851, Gallier returned the nomination papers to the Secretary of the Treasury with his regrets. If we infer correctly from his autobiography, he had already retired from active participation in business because of his failing eyesight. He had, in fact, since the spring of 1850, remarried and spent most of his time traveling throughout Europe. Perhaps also he saw the turmoil ahead for the Custom House and wisely wanted no part of it. With his refusal, the Creole municipality was back where it had started.[53]

Dakin continued as acting superintendent until a suitable replacement could be found. The new law did not go into effect until June, 1851; and A. T. Wood, previously on the outside looking in, was back in contention again. He went to Washington and bombarded the Treasury Department and the commissioners with letters protesting any changes being made.[54]

By September 1, 1851, Dakin was thoroughly disgusted with the entire situation; he handed in his resignation, despite the fact that no permanent architect had been selected. Addressing himself to Secretary of the Treasury Thomas Corwin, Dakin wrote:

Dear Sir:

As Superintending Architect of the new Custom House, New Orleans, I have the honor to address you, tendering my resignation of the title and appointment as above named. Circumstances connected with the erection of said new Custom House are such that were it possible to continue me, I should feel little pride or ambition in the service belonging to my appointment: therefore, it would be difficult for me to discharge my duties with that fervor and interest that I ought to feel. Besides, I have reason to believe that the authorities in Washington feel some little embarrassment in relation to the affairs of this edifice, and that I am or have been the unintentional cause of some of that embarrassment. I most sincerely honor and respect the motives of the President and yourself in the premises.

Be pleased to accept this, my resignation, and oblige

Your obedient servant and friend,
James H. Dakin, Architect[55]

It was obvious to Dakin that the only way in which he could be approved as supervising architect would be to acquiesce to Wood's original plan. This, as a professional, he could not do.

There are probably not many instances in the history of American architecture in which a man resigned an important post rather than compromise what he believed in. Undoubtedly, Dakin could have retained his post if he had met with the Creoles and placated them by putting the business room in the center. And he surely would have had to compromise his plan of using cast iron instead of groined arches because it deviated from the original design. But Dakin was an uncompromising man, and if patience was not among his virtues, tenacity surely was. His professionalism cost him his job at the Custom House.

Just before Dakin's resignation, the commissioners, who were probably advised of it beforehand, were searching about for a successor. In a letter to the Secretary of the Treasury, it is mentioned that James Gallier, Jr., had been recommended for the post: "Though a young man not quite thirty, he is theoretically and practically one of the finest Architects in the country, and certainly ranks next to his father and Mr. Dakin in this community." This letter goes on, however, to recommend "Major Beauregard of this city . . . [who] has long and actively engaged in superintending the erection of fortifications" [56] It is not known what happened to the suggestion of James Gallier, Jr., for the post. It may well be that he, like his father, foresaw continued political wrangling over the Custom House and wanted no part of it. He was in ten years to distinguish himself with the construction of the French Opera House. Notwithstanding young Gallier's achievements, the next appointment went (on an interim basis while Congress was not in session) to Lewis E. Reynolds. [57] Unfortunately, A. T. Wood was also given some sort of advisory status to ensure that his original plan was followed. This resulted in constant conflict with Reynolds, who deserved a better fate. Reynolds was one of the best architects to follow the Dakin and Gallier period in New Orleans. He designed a great Garden District mansion, the 1856 Buckner-Soule house at 1410 Jackson Avenue, as well as the Factors Building, the facade of which is a great composition in ornamental cast iron. In the more elaborate style of the late 1850s, this building still stands, almost in its original condition and in use since 1858. [58]

With the controversy still raging over the drastic changes in the plans for the Custom House, the Treasury Department finally agreed to implement Dakin's suggestion that an impartial board of examiners be called to decide on a course of action. It was called on November 15, 1851, and lasted a month. The distinguished group of examiners who heard the evidence included Major William H. Chase, a United States Army engineer who was well acquainted with local problems of construction; [59] Major P. G. T. Beauregard; Adolphus Heiman, a Nashville architect who was one of Strickland's competitors for the Tennessee capitol and who built a suspension bridge in 1850 over the Cumberland River at Nashville; [60] Lewis E. Reynolds, the interim supervising architect of the Custom House; and Ammi B. Young, a Boston architect who was one of the co-founders of the American Institution of Architects with Dakin, Rogers, and others. [61] Heiman was probably a substitue for William Strickland, who declined to serve. Strickland may have suggested Heiman, his contemporary in Nashville. [62] Heiman came a long distance for this hearing, as did Ammi Young. Every effort was made to give full opportunity to hear both sides fairly.

Dakin, who had been seriously ill in Baton Rouge for almost a month, came down for the hearings on November 18, and testified. [63] Wood also had his say and, in fact, attended almost every day for the month the hearing lasted.

By December 15, the board of examiners had reached a conclusion. The points that Dakin had made a year previously: (1) that the business room should be moved to the Canal Street front and the center opened up for light and air; (2) that cast iron should be substituted for groined arches; and (3) that the walls were inadequate to withstand the lateral load of the groined arches were *all* agreed to unanimously by the five-man board. [64]

The irony was that Dakin, who had been proven correct by this panel, had been ousted because of his advocacy of these very changes. It must nevertheless have given Dakin much satisfaction to see the result.

*New Orleans Custom House, Main Business Room, probably by A. T. Wood, James Dakin, and Ammi B. Young. (Courtesy Library of Congress)*

Another danger was foreseen by the board, thanks to some experiments made for the hearings. They found, through test borings, that the soil of New Orleans varied in its "compressibility"; that is, its density varied from place to place, making an evenness of settlement difficult to achieve, even with matting. The board concluded that the system of inverted arches in the foundations of the Custom House would equalize the settlement only if it were on soil of equal "compressibility."[65] This meant that the lateral thrust of the groined arches was even more dangerous, and the use of iron vertical members, with no outward thrust, was the best solution. The examiners stated that even this was no guarantee against uneven settlement.

The board prepared two sets of plans to send to Washington with the report. One showed the business room in the center (A. T. Wood signed these, although he did not draw them), with cast iron substituted for groined arches. The other set, unsigned, placed the business room on Canal Street. The plans were drawn on November 20 by an unknown architect.[66]

This leads to the problem of the authorship of the "great hall"—the Business Room. It has long been considered one of the most impressive rooms in American Greek Revival architecture.[67] It features fourteen Corinthian columns, forty-one feet high, with capitals which include the heads of Mercury, god of commerce, and Luna, goddess of the moon, whose symbol, the crescent, alludes to the "Crescent City"—New Orleans.

Because Wood's original plans have never been found, these 1851 plans are the earliest known. The first, based on Wood's placement of the room, shows Corinthian columns and an entablature much like the one executed, that is, with a row of anthemia similar to the Choragic Monument of Lysicrates. But the other plan, based on Dakin's changes, also called for Corinthian columns. Unfortunately, it is only given as a floor plan and not a section. It is quite possible that Dakin had designed this room, and that the plan sent to Washington (signed, but not drawn by Wood) was based on this design. Without more facts it is impossible to determine who designed the Business Room. It is presently certain only that the Corinthian plan existed when Dakin departed the job and that the earliest plan was signed but not drawn by Wood, it being but a composite of the suggested changes of the board of examiners.[68]

Lewis Reynolds was the next victim of the Custom House. President Fillmore nominated him on December 16, 1851, the day after the report of the examiners was mailed to the Treasury Department. The Senate again went into executive session, and Senator Soule, from the Committee of Commerce to whom the nomination had been referred, reported that the Senate had rejected Reynolds.[69] The report was received by the Treasury Department, and after a period of about two months, it decided to go ahead with Wood's plan anyway. The First Municipality and its senator had apparently been too much for them.[70]

Reynolds stayed on as acting superintendent for a while, squabbling with the agressive Wood; then by September, 1852, Thomas K. Wharton, long the clerk of the works and second-string supervising architect took charge temporarily. In May, 1853, Major Beauregard succeeded him as the official supervising architect. A. T. Wood died in 1854, so that Beauregard worked now with little impairment, but in conformity with Wood's plan.[71]

Ammi Young and Captain Bowman of the Treasury Department in Washington took charge of the government's buildings and cooperated with local architects like Beauregard who were on the spot supervising construction. Beauregard remained at the Custom House until December,

1860, when he was appointed Superintendent at West Point. In a matter of days, the Civil War broke out, and Beauregard resigned to become a Confederate soldier.

After this time, John Roy and Wharton shared the superintendence with many others, the work dragging on until 1881 when it was considered finished. At different periods, there were complaints about dampness and uneven or excessive sinking.[72] In 1870, the Treasury's architect, A. B. Mullett, said that he did not believe that "*any* expenditure . . . would result in providing a suitable, creditable or convenient building."[73] Because of sinking, masonry was removed and iron substituted to lighten it; a whole story was even removed for this reason.[74] The present cornice and pediment is of cast iron for lightness.

The real losers over the Custom House were not Dakin or the other architects, but the business community of New Orleans. Because of petty politics and stubbornness in refusing to take Dakin's and the board of examiners' advice, New Orleans had to wait thirty years for a usable Custom House.

# 11
# THE END IN
# BATON ROUGE

IN HIS LAST MAJOR ACT AS AN ARCHITECT, JAMES DAKIN HAD repudiated the un-architectural plan of Wood, rather than give in to its mediocrity. This act of courage cost him his job, and he then sought work elsewhere. He found it in his home city, Baton Rouge, where finishing touches were still going on at his new state house. He was rehired by the commissioners and set to work completing the interior.

By February 17, 1852, the commissioners for the capitol—still Maunsel White, Daniel Avery, and Walter Brashear—considered the capitol substantially complete. Their report to the state on that date was a virtual tendering of the building to the state. It noted that only "joiner's work in the third story and the painting in that, and the first, is all that remains unfinished in the principal building." [1] It was at that time that the beautiful cast iron fence around the capitol was conceived. The report stated:

We consider it our duty to recommend to the Legislature that provision be made for a permanent enclosure of the public grounds. The present fence was put up for temporary purposes and is now so dilapidated that a new one is required.... One made of iron would, in our opinion, be in the end, the most economical. Its first cost would be about the same as that of a brick wall, and considerably greater than one made of wood; but on the other hand, it would be more permanent than either.... Patterns of appropriate height, weight and design have been offered to us in anticipation of your favorable action. [2]

Thus a design was made at the time when Dakin had returned to the capitol. The fence has long been attributed to him, but this report makes it appear almost certain that it was his design. Not to be overlooked is the fact that Maunsel White, who always championed Dakin's causes, was still head of the commissioners.

The fence is hardly less interesting than the capitol itself. It is a mixture of political symbols and architectural motifs—both Gothic and Greek—pleasingly combined into a beautiful work; yet it also accomplishes well its main purpose of protecting the capitol grounds. Standing about six feet high, its fence posts form pointed arches separated by tiny trefoils. Every sixteenth post is a heavy line post that is a reproduction of the clustered Gothic pillars Dakin had used in the rotunda of the capitol. Linking the posts at the base is a course of quatrefoil moulding, duplicating the string course of moulding on the capitol building just under the parapet and complementing the latter by its opposite position at the bottom of the fence. Set atop this quatrefoil moulding at the lower edge of the fence are anthemia, rising alternately short and tall, between the posts. On the top of the fence is a row of fleurs de lis, symbolizing the French ancestry of Louisiana. On each of the heavier line posts stands a seed pod of the magnolia tree, apparently symbolizing the fecundity of the rich soil of the agricultural South.

Atop the main gate posts are large iron eagles, with wings outstretched, representing the American influence in Louisiana. The end posts of the swinging gates (so heavy they must move on rollers) are a representation of fasces, from the top of which arises a hatchet, symbolizing the strength of the union. The design is truly ingenious; Dakin seems to have outdone himself here.

This elaborate fence did not come cheaply. Two years after the report of 1852 the legislature loosened its purse strings to appropriate $21,630 to build it. It is said that the John Hill Foundry of Baton Rouge manufactured the fence, which was not finished until 1855. It has been renewed many times since then, but always in the same pattern. [3] The fence was shortened somewhat in length when the street in front of the capitol was widened in the 1950s and the fountain at the foot of the hill is said to have been removed at the same time.

*Louisiana State Capitol, Baton Rouge, 1847. Note the eagle, magnolia seed pod, and fleur-de-lis on the cast iron fence. Quatrefoil motif on fence matches course on capitol below parapet.*

In the last months of his life, Dakin also completed a commission he had received from the legislature in 1850 to create a memorial tablet in memory of General Philemon Thomas. He is known as the "liberator of Baton Rouge," because he led a group of Baton Rouge residents in overthrowing the Spanish garrison there in 1810. This act freed the West Florida parishes from foreign domination, whereupon a little independent nation was formed (the Republic of West Florida); it shortly joined with the union and became part of the Territory of Louisiana. The old warrior, Thomas, had died in Baton Rouge (he is buried in the National Cemetery) three years before Dakin received this commission, and the legislature wanted to remember in some way this now undeservedly obscure patriot.

Dakin had been provided $500 to make a plan for and to erect a tablet to Thomas in the Senate chamber of his capitol. In what turned out to be the last public communication known to have been written by Dakin, he sent a brief letter to the commissioners for the capitol concerning the memorial:

Architect's Office, New Capitol
Baton Rouge, January 27, 1852.
I have the honor to inform you that I have complied with the requisitions of the State. . . . The said tablet is in its place in the Senate Chamber. About twelve months ago, I made the design for the tablet and called upon Messrs. John Stroud & Co. of New Orleans [marble workers] . . . to furnish the work according to the design and my directions. . . .

Your humble servant,
James H. Dakin, Architect[4]

The tablet was destroyed in the fire of 1862 and no view of it has been found. The legislature thought so much of Thomas that, as soon as the capitol was restored after the war, a second appropriation was made in 1884 to erect another tablet in the senate. It too has disappeared.[5]

It should also be mentioned that a duplicate of the 1852 tablet was erected in the senate in 1857 in memory of John H. Harmonson, a distinguished Congressman from Louisiana who died in 1850. His tablet probably suffered the same fate in the disastrous fire of 1862.[6]

That spring of 1852 was a difficult one for Dakin. Already ill, and destined to live for only a few months more, he had to endure the criticism of those few but vociferous newspaper writers who objected to the interior of his capitol. It was also at this time, during the libel suit against Pratt which was still dragging on, that A. T. Wood was asked to give testimony against Dakin. One would have expected an extreme statement from Wood, but he, perhaps seeing Dakin was a dying man, or afraid of upsetting his precarious role as "advisor" on the Custom House job, limited himself to the facts about that building: that Dakin had been rejected for the Custom House job simply because "he was opposed to the original plan and also because he was in the employ of the State of Louisiana."[7]

Dakin's final illness had apparently begun in the fall of 1851. His expense voucher to the federal government for his trip from Baton Rouge to New Orleans to testify before the board of examiners of the Custom House (and his request for pay for the month of October) lists:[6]

| | |
|---|---|
| Two Physicians' bills, 19 days each | 80.00 |
| Cupper | 10.00 |
| Nurse's bill, 19 days at | |
| $5 per diem | 70.00 |
| Medicines | 10.00 |

He had trouble in submitting the voucher through the commissioners at the Custom House who thought it excessive; thus he wrote to Secretary of the Treasury Thomas Corwin on December 12, 1851:

Dear Sir:

On the 1st. October last, as Architect of the New Custom House at New Orleans, I applied to the active Commissioner of that Edifice, Col. J. W. Crockett, for leave of absence for a few days for the purpose of visiting my family at Baton Rouge. Col. Crockett replied thus: 'There is nothing of any consequence doing on the works of the New Building and nothing that requires your presence; therefore you have my consent to be absent as long as you please.' On the strength of this permission, I left New Orleans with the intention of returning in the course of 10 or 15 days. A day or two before I had intended to return to New Orleans, I was taken alarmingly sick and was confined to my bed the balance of the month. When I presented my bill against the Treasury Department, Col. Crockett readily signed. Samuel J. Paters, Esq., declined because I had been absent the whole of the month of October.

I hope, Sir, you will not consider my misfortune a crime but authorize my bill $248 to be paid and greatly oblige your

Sincere and Humble Servant,
Jas. H. Dakin[9]

Despite this letter, the government refused to pay the voucher. Dakin had tried to save the government hundreds of thousand of dollars by revising the Custom House plan only to receive this reward.[10]

On May 13, 1852, James Dakin died at his home in Baton Rouge. A story in the family has it that he died of an intestinal ailment caused by eating spoiled food, although the newspapers said he died of a "long and painful illness." [11] The exact cause is unknown, but it may possibly have been related to something that began during his service in Mexico, where many internal ailments took their toll on the lives of the American soldiers.

The newspapers gave his death rather extensive write-ups. At least six newspaper obituaries have been located. The New Orleans *Picayune* gave his death prominent attention:

We regret to see announced in the Baton Rouge papers the death of our former fellow-townsman, Col. James H. Dakin, which sad event took place at the deceased's residence in the Parish of West [they must have meant East] Baton Rouge, on Thursday evening last, after a long and painful illness. The funeral took place last Saturday and was attended with Masonic honors and ceremonies.

Col. Dakin was long and well known in this city, where he resided many years. His talent as an architect was principally evidenced in the plans for and superintendence of the Verandah Hotel, the Arsenal of the Artillery Batallion, and St. Patrick's Church—all in this city. He was also at one time the popular commander of a large and fine volunteer corps which he raised himself in this city and which was called... the "Louisiana Volunteer Regiment." The regiment... was noted for its discipline and soldierly appearance, whilst under the command of its tall and manly looking leader. . . .

The deceased leaves to regret his loss a family and a large circle of friends.[12]

Dakin's death at forty-six ended a career which, though it must be called a success, was certainly destined to have been even greater. He deserves far more fame than he has received. His creativity was at full strength—his plans for the Custom House and the Louisiana capitol reveal this—and his skill as an artist and draftsman remained undiminished at the time of his death. With the death of Dakin in 1852 and the virtual retirement of Gallier in 1850, the era of the early Greek Revival in Louisiana was ended. It was now left to Henry Howard, Lewis Reynolds, Gallier, Jr., and others to carry on what the older men had begun.

All attempts to locate Dakin's grave have been fruitless. He was probably buried in the Baton Rouge city burial ground and later reinterred in the Girod Street Cemetery in New Orleans. Both cemeteries have been destroyed and there are no burial records. A notation of inscriptions in the Girod Cemetery, made in the 1930s, has been found for a tomb of a James H. Dakin; but Dakin had a grandson whose name was identical, and this may have been his grave. However, it is more than likely that the first James Dakin was buried in this tomb.[13]

Dakin possessed a personal library of over 250 books, probably mostly architectural, which, according to his estate's inventory record, was not sold after his death.[14] Some individual volumes have turned up in New Orleans. One was Charles Dakin's copy of the Lafever *Beauties of Modern Architecture* and another was a presentation copy by Lewis E. Reynolds of his book on stairway construction. Both are stamped "Fisk Library, New Orleans," which was an early library whose holdings were later divided up between the Howard-Tilton and New Orleans Public libraries. The survival of Dakin's library intact would have been an invaluable source of information on contributions to his creativity.

Dakin's widow did not have an easy time of it after her husband's death. Left with two young children, her main asset was a small plantation Dakin had purchased in Baton Rouge in December, 1848, near Ward's Creek and Claycut Road. To assist her in these matters, the court appointed members to "family meetings," there being no relatives of her real family in the area. (Included in their number was James McVey, contractor for the enlargement of the skylight of the capitol.)

The estate records show that it took six years to sell the plantation. Georgianna Dakin did make a small profit in the end, selling it for four thousand dollars, a thousand more than her husband had paid for it. Of the three slaves, two were sold, and the third, a man named Hardy, remained in the employ of the Dakins long after emancipation.[15] Dakin's widow also benefitted from a small appropriation by the Louisiana legislature for $932 in 1855, the same year it appropriated money for the capitol fence. The act was entitled "For the Relief of Georgiana Dakin."[16]

Dakin's two children married within a few years after his death. Mary Caroline married Arthur W. Hyatt in Baton Rouge on July 14, 1855. Charles James Dakin married Julia Chase on February 14, 1860. Arthur Hyatt had been editor and publisher of the Baton Rouge *Comet* until early 1852 when he entered the commercial printing business. Charles James Dakin later worked for him and became well known as a printer.

It is unfortunate that Dakin did not live long enough to apprentice his son in his office, as Gallier did. James Dakin's legacy in architecture has to be measured instead by his tutorship of Henry Howard, by his influence through the Lafever books, and his insistence on high professional standards. The most striking example of the latter is his virtual self-immolation over changing the Custom House plan.

If Dakin needs a monument, he has several in his buildings. They are his greatest legacy to us. All display the quality Dakin fought during his whole life to promote—professionalism.

# NOTES

## NOTES TO CHAPTER 1

1 Albert H. Dakin, *Descendants of Thomas Dakin of Concord, Mass.* (Rutland, Vt., 1948), 110–11. The month, day, and place could not be confirmed in official sources. Confirmed were the year and state; for James, *Seventh U.S. Census*, 1850, for East Baton Rouge Parish, La.; for Charles, his gravestone in the Catholic Cemetery, St. Gabriel, La.

2 Dakin, *Descendants*, 9–11.

3 Office of the Secretary of the State of New York, *Calendar of Historical Manuscripts Relating to the War of the Revolution* (Albany, 1868), I, 79; James A. Roberts, *New York in the Revolution as Colony and State* (Albany, 1898), 248; Dakin, *Descendants*, 30.

4 Interview with Kathyrine Regan, summer, 1965.

5 Letter in possession of James Dakin's great-granddaughter, Mrs. Blanche W. King, New Orleans.

6 *Ibid.*

7 Dakin, *Descendants*, 110–11. The tomb of Dakin's parents and grandparents is at Spencer's Corners, two miles north of Millerton, New York.

8 Jane B. Davies, "A. J. Davis' Projects for a Patent Office Building, 1832–34," *Journal of the Society of Architectural Historians* (October, 1965), 231. For illustration of Town bridge truss, see Don Gifford (ed.), *Literature of Architecture* (New York, 1966), 301–305.

9 Kathyrine Regan (great-granddaughter of James H. Dakin), biography of James H. Dakin (MS in Howard-Tilton Memorial Library, New Orleans).

10 Ithiel Town to Isaac Damon *et al.*, October 17, 1827, cited in Roger Hale Newton, *Town and Davis, Architects* (New York, 1942), 93; Karl S. Putnam, *The Northampton Book* (Northampton, Mass., 1954), 148; Northampton *Daily-Hampshire Gazette*, July 22, 1970, p. 4; Vincent Scully, "American Houses: Thomas Jefferson to Frank Lloyd Wright," in Edgar Kaufman, Jr. (ed.), *The Rise of an American Architecture* (New York, 1970), 164.

11 Davies, "A. J. Davis' Projects," 239–40.

12 *Ibid.*, 245–46.

13 Talbot Hamlin, *Greek Revival Architecture in America* (London, 1944), 151, 344.

14 John A. Kouwenhoven, *Made in America*, retitled *The Arts in Modern American Civilization* (New York, 1967), 54, 59.

15 Hamlin, *Greek Revival Architecture*, 151, 344.

16 Jacob Landy, *The Architecture of Minard Lafever* (New York, 1970), 218, 283, n.8.

17 Kouwenhoven, *The Arts in Modern American Civilization*, 54, 59.

18 Theodore S. Fay, *Views in New York and Its Environs . . . Drawings Taken on the Spot Expressly for this Work, by Dakin, Architect. . . .* (New York, 1831).

19 Hamlin, *Greek Revival*, 143; Adolph K. Placzek, Avery Library, Columbia University, to author, October 27, 1966.

20 Town, Davis, and Dakin, Architects, Financial Records, 1832–1835 (MS in Avery Library, Columbia University, New York).

21 *Ibid., passim;* Long Island *Daily Press*, December 9, 1935; *The Marine Pavilion,* Historical Collections of the Borough of Queens, I, 173 (Copy in Queens Borough Public Library, Jamaica, N.Y.).

22 Philip Hone, *Diary of Philip Hone* (New York, 1927), I, 174.

23 James Early, *Romanticism and American Architecture* (New York, 1965), 36.

24 Hone, *Diary of Philip Hone,* I, 174.

25 Regina M. Kellerman, "La Grange Terrace: The Question of Authorship," report given before Society of Architectural Historians, New York, January 29, 1966 (La Grange Terrace was also called Lafayette Terrace); Regina M. Kellerman to author, January 7, 1971; Fay, *Views in New York,* 46.

26 Regan biography of Dakin; Charles James Dakin to editor, New Orleans *Daily Picayune,* July 17, 1900, p. 12.

27 New Orleans *Vieux Carre Courier,* October 27, 1967, p. 7; Samuel Wilson, Jr., original draft of article, later excerpted for New Orleans *States,* October 24, 1953, p. 26; Succession of George Clarkson, New Orleans Civil District Court, 1835; Town, Davis, and Dakin, Financial Records.

28 See Chapter 9, n.17.

29 *Acts of Louisiana Legislature,* 1828, No. 24, February 28, 1828; Notarial acts of William Christy, notary, May, 1833, in New Orleans Notarial Archives. (All notarial acts cited hereinafter are located in New Orleans Notarial Archives.)

30 Eliza Ripley, *Social Life in Old New Orleans* (New York, 1912), 90, 167–72.

31 A. J. Davis Day Book, I, August 4, 1830 (MS in New York Public Library).

32 Original drawing in A. J. Davis Collection, IV (24, 66.1402), folio 144, Metropolitan Museum of Art, New York.

33 A. J. Davis Journal, June 6, 1832 (MS in Metropolitan Museum of Art, New York); act before Felix de Armas, notary, May 17, 1832, sale by John Ursin de la Villebeuve to Anthony Rasch; Conveyance Book 37, folio 207, Orleans Parish, sale to Joseph L. Wibray.

34 Davis Journal, entry between September 1, 1833, and November 1, 1833; Act before William Christy, notary, January 27, 1834.

35 Building Contract between Jacob Levy Florance and Alexander T. Wood, act before William Christy, notary, January 27, 1834.

36 Original drawing, dated 1832, by James H. Dakin, Dakin Collection, New Orleans Public Library. The drawing matches perfectly an 1891 photograph of the Washington Street Methodist Episcopal Church in

the Long Island Historical Society collection; in the photograph, a plaque over the door reads "Erected 1832." This identification was made by the Long Island Historical Society, to which the author extends his gratitude.

37 Dakin Collection; Town, Davis, and Dakin, Financial Records, entry between August 15, 1833, and October, 1833.

38 Town, Davis, and Dakin, Financial Records, settlement of November 1, 1833; Glenn Patton, "Chapel in the Sky," *Architectural Review* (March, 1969), 177–80.

39 Three letters from James H. Dakin to A. J. Davis, in Davis Papers, Box 1, Miscellaneous, New York Public Library.

40 Minutes of the Board of Trustees of New York University, 1829–1864 (MS at New York University; microfilm copy in author's possession).

41 New York *American,* May 27, 1837, quoted in LeRoy E. Kimball, "The Old University Building and the Society's Years on Washington Square," *New York Historical Society Quarterly* (July, 1948), 158–61.

42 Kimball, "Old University Building," 154.

43 Unsigned watercolor of chapel at New York Historical Society; Oxford Cathedral lithograph in Dakin Collection; Patton, "Chapel in the Sky," 178.

44 Patton, "Chapel in the Sky," 178.

## NOTES TO CHAPTER 2

1 Original drawings by James H. Dakin, Dakin Collection; James H. Dakin to T. B. Biglow, December 9, 1834, bill for one hundred dollars for the church plans, in Archives of First Presbyterian Church, Troy, N.Y.

2 Invoices for marble, approved by Dakin, in Archives of First Presbyterian Church, Troy, N.Y.

3 *First Presbyterian Church of Troy, New York: Historical Resume of 125 Progressive Years, 1791–1966* (Troy, N.Y., 1966), 17.

4 Original painting by James H. Dakin, Dakin Collection; Jacob Landy, "The Washington Monument Project in New York," *Journal of the Society of Architectural Historians* (December, 1969), 291–97; Jacob Landy to author, February 10, 1970.

5 Dakin Collection.

6 Attribution to Shryock made in Elizabeth Shryock Field, "Gideon Shryock, His Life and Works," *Kentucky State Historical Society Register* (April, 1952), 126.

7 Dakin Collection.

8 Talbot Hamlin, "The A.I.A. Meets in Kentucky," *Pencil Points* (May, 1940), 286.

9 Clay Lancaster, "Gideon Shryock and John McMurty, Architect and Builder of Kentucky," *Art Quarterly* (Autumn, 1943), 264–65. See also Clay Lancaster, *Antebellum Houses of the Blue Grass Country* (Lexington, Ky., 1961), 82–84.

10 *William Kay and Tubman Lawes* vs. *Bank of Louisville,* Louisville Chancery Court, Case No. 793, filed December 31, 1837.

11 *Dakin and Dakin, Architects,* vs. *President, Directors, and Company of the Bank of Louisville,* Parish Court, Orleans Parish, New Orleans, Docket No. 9317, filed February 27, 1837.

12 *Acts of the Kentucky Legislature,* February 2, 1833; short biography of Snead in *Louisville, Past and Present: Its Industrial History* (Louisville, 1875), 113–14; reference to Bank of the United States in Sabri M. Akural and William C. Mallaliau, "Kentucky Banks in Crisis Decade, 1833–44," *Kentucky State Historical Society Register* (October, 1967), 296; reference to Bank of Louisville extension onto sidewalk in Minute Book, Meetings of Mayor and Council, Louisville Board of Administrators, April 27, 1835, in Louisville City Hall.

13 John S. Snead to James H. Dakin, February 29, 1836, in lawsuit file, *Dakin and Dakin* vs. *Bank of Louisville.*

14 Minute Book, Louisville Board of Administrators, November 16, 1835, in which the financial committee report notes its acceptance of Shryock's proposal to erect a new courthouse in Louisville.

15 Completion date of 1837 given in *Louisville City Directory,* 1838–39, Appendix, 9; *Kay and Lawes* vs. *Bank of Louisville.*

16 *Kay and Lawes* vs. *Bank of Louisville.*

17 *Dakin and Dakin* vs. *Bank of Louisville.*

18 Landy, *The Architecture of Minard Lafever,* 50.

19 Plate 1, Front Door, and Plate 5, Details of Plate 1, employ the same treatment of the central acroterion and swirls of vine on their cornices. The acroterion and swirls were repeated several times more: Plate 6, Parlor Window, Plate 13, Sliding Doors, with accompanying elevation on Plate 14, and Plate 19, Parlor Door. These constitute a substantial number of plates influenced by the Bank of Louisville facade by James Dakin. Minard Lafever, *The Beauties of Modern Architecture* (2nd ed.; New York, 1968).

20 *Ibid.,* Plate 32.

21 Clay Lancaster, "Builders' Guide and Plan Books and American Architecture," *Magazine of Art* (January, 1948), 18, 19; adaptation of Plate 63 also noted in Lancaster, *Antebellum Houses of Bluegrass Country,* 83; Hamlin, *Greek Revival,* 354.

22 *A Noble Landmark of New York: The Fifth Avenue Presbyterian Church, 1808–1958* (New York, 1960), 13.

23 Minutes of the Board of Trustees, Duane Street Presbyterian Church (MS on file at successor congregation, Fifth Avenue Presbyterian Church, New York); special thanks to Miss Elfreida Kraege for transcripts; original drawings by James H. Dakin, Dakin Collection.

24 Minutes of the Board of Trustees, Duane Street Presbyterian Church.
25 Old engraving in *A Noble Landmark,* 43.
26 A. J. Davis to Reverend Cyrus Mason, March, 1834, in A. J. Davis Collection, "Letter Book," 105, noted by Landy, *Minard Lafever,* 258 n. 12.
27 Minutes of the Board of Trustees, Duane Street Presbyterian Church. Dakin must have turned over supervision to another architect, for he had left New York in the fall of 1835.
28 *Ibid.*
29 Reverend Dr. Samuel Miller, *Sketch of the Early History of the First Presbyterian Church* (New York, 1937), 39, 45. The church was taken down and rebuilt in Jersey City, N.J. See New Orleans *Daily Picayune,* May 31, 1845, p. 1.
30 Dakin Collection.
31 *Ibid.* These drawings coincide exactly with two illustrations at New York Historical Society: August Will, 1898, and unknown artist, *ca.* 1850. A brief history is in Theodore Savage, *The Presbyterian Church in New York* (New York, 1949), 144–51.
32 Dakin Collection. Municipal Archives and Records Center, City of New York, to the author, December 4, 1970; Richard Carrott to author, January 24, 1967.

## NOTES TO CHAPTER 3

1 James Gallier, *The Autobiography of James Gallier, Architect* (Paris, 1864), 18–19.
2 Town, Davis, and Dakin, Financial Records.
3 Gallier, *Autobiography,* 19–21.
4 *Ibid.,* 21. Original drawings of Mobile City Hall in Labrot (Gallier) Collection, Howard-Tilton Memorial Library, New Orleans, and in Dakin Collection.
5 Gallier, *Autobiography,* 33–34; original drawings in Labrot (Gallier) Collection, dated December 30, 1834.
6 Joseph H. Ingraham, *The South-west* (New York, 1835), 145–46; Benjamin H. B. Latrobe, *Impressions Concerning New Orleans,* ed. Samuel Wilson, Jr. (New York, 1951), 97 n.15.
7 B. M. Norman, *Norman's New Orleans* (New Orleans, 1845), 99.
8 All original drawings in Labrot (Gallier) Collection.
9 *Historical Epitome* (New Orleans, 1840), 318. An excellent illustrated guidebook to New Orleans.
10 Building contract, act before William Christy, notary, July 30, 1835; New Orleans *Daily Picayune,* March 2, 1837, p. 4; New Orleans *Bee,* March, 14, 1842, p. 2.

## NOTES TO CHAPTER 4

1 James H. Dakin to Mrs. James H. Dakin, November 23, 1835, in possession of Mrs. Blanche W. King, New Orleans.
2 New Orleans *Bee,* November 18, 1835, p. 2.
3 Gallier, *Autobiography,* 27.
4 New Orleans *Daily Crescent,* November 26, 1849, p. 2.
5 Gallier, *Autobiography,* 27.
6 *Norman's New Orleans,* 141.
7 *New Orleans City Directory,* 1838, pp. 321 and vii (Errata).
8 *Norman's New Orleans,* 161; original drawings in Labrot (Gallier) Collection, Dakin Collection, and Historic New Orleans Collection.
9 Building contract, act before Jules Mossy, notary, filed March 30, 1835; *Norman's New Orleans,* 138.
10 New Orleans *Times Picayune,* July 5, 1959, Sec. 2, p. 9, and November 15, 1959, Sec. 2, p. 14.
11 New Orleans *Bee,* April 21, 1835, p. 2; sale by Hagan, act before H. B. Cenas, notary, May 1, 1835; New Orleans *Bee,* October 2, 1835, p. 2; building contract, act before William Boswell, notary, December 4, 1835.
12 *Historical Epitome,* 331.
13 Gallier, *Autobiography,* 23.
14 *Norman's New Orleans,* 141; dome effect compared to London's St. Paul's Cathedral in New Orleans *Daily Delta,* January 19, 1851, p. 2, and in Thomas L. Nichols, *Forty Years of American Life* (London, 1874), 230.
15 New Orleans *Daily Picayune,* February 9, 1837, p. 2, and February 16, 1837, p. 2; New Orleans *Daily True American,* February 25, 1837, p. 2; *Norman's New Orleans,* 137. Joseph Clohecy, foreman, New Orleans *Daily Delta,* August 1, 1847, p. 2.
16 New Orleans *Daily Picayune,* February 7, 1846, p. 2.
17 New Orleans *Daily Delta,* January 19, 1851, p. 2. Molten lead endangered escaping children, noted in New Orleans *Daily Picayune,* April 11, 1898, p. 12.

## NOTES TO CHAPTER 5

1 Building contract between James Gallier and William Nott, act before H. B. Cenas, notary, November 21, 1835.
2 Copartnership agreement between James H. Dakin and Charles B. Dakin, dated December 24, 1835, act before H. B. Cenas, notary, recorded August 16, 1836.
3 Mobile *Daily Commercial Register,* December 31, 1835, passenger arrivals, p. 2.
4 Letter from James H. Dakin, in Louisiana House of Representatives, *Journal,* 1836, 2nd Sess., 38.

35 Vestry Minutes, Christ Church, Mobile.

36 *Mobile City Directory*, 1837.

37 Margaret Rose Ingate, "Mobile Ironwork," *Antiques* (September, 1967), 355.

38 Elliptical ceiling mentioned in Vestry Minutes, Christ Church, May 30, 1838.

39 Brantley, *Banking*, I, 72–73.

40 New Orleans *Daily Picayune*, August 16, 1839, p. 2.

41 Brantley, *Banking*, I, 86–87; Caldwell Delaney (ed.), *Craighead's Mobile* (Mobile, 1968), 81–85.

42 New Orleans *Daily Picayune*, November 30, 1839, p. 2.

43 Mobile *Daily Commercial Register*, February 15, 1840, p. 2, cited in Brantley, *Banking*, II, 387 n.54.

44 Passenger lists of ships arriving in the United States, National Archives, Washington, D.C., Reel 18, List 185.

45 New Orleans *Daily Picayune*, July 17, 1900, p. 12.

## NOTES TO CHAPTER 7

1 *Dictionary of American Biography, s. v.*, Warren Stone.

2 Building contract between Dakin and Dakin and Drs. Warren Stone and William E. Kennedy, act before H. B. Cenas, notary, February 8, 1839.

3 Act before H. B. Cenas, notary, December 26, 1838.

4 New Orleans *Daily Picayune*, August 8, 1839, p. 2; *New Orleans City Directory*, 1842, p. 163; John Duffy (ed.), *The Rudolph Matas History of Medicine in Louisiana* (Baton Rouge, 1958–62), II, 229–30; New Orleans *Daily Picayune*, May 22, 1852, p. 4.

5 Cited in Duffy (ed.), *Matas History*, II, 520.

6 New Orleans *Louisiana Courier*, August 17, 1830, p. 1.

7 *Acts of Louisiana Legislature*, February 25, 1836.

8 Minute Book, First Municipality, City of New Orleans, December 18, 1837.

9 *Acts of Louisiana Legislature*, No. 30, March 14, 1839.

10 *New Orleans City Directory*, 1838, p. 258.

11 Samuel Wilson, Jr., *A Guide to the Architecture of New Orleans, 1699–1959* (New York, 1959), 12.

12 Original drawing in Dakin Collection.

13 Matthew Baigell, "John Haviland in Philadelphia, 1818–1826," *Journal of the Society of Architectural Historians* (October, 1966), 206.

14 Building contract between Dakin and Dakin and State of Louisiana, act before F. Grima, notary, July 1, 1839.

15 *Ibid.*

16 New Orleans *Daily Picayune*, October 3, 1839, p. 2.

17 New Orleans *Republican*, November 12, 1873, p. 1.

18 Minute Book, Louisiana State Museum Board, February 18, 1914.

19 Gallier, *Autobiography*, 28.

20 Roger Baudier, "St. Patrick of New Orleans, 1833–1958," in Charles L. Dufour (ed.), *St. Patrick's of New Orleans, 1833–1958* (New Orleans, 1958), 55–95.

21 *Norman's New Orleans*, 95.

22 Act before H. B. Cenas, notary, June 6, 1838.

23 Act before D. L. McCay, notary, April 23, 1838.

24 Act before H. B. Cenas, notary, June 6, 1838.

25 Original drawing of longitudinal section by James H. Dakin in Louisiana State Museum.

26 Act before H. B. Cenas, notary, June 6, 1838.

27 *Ibid.*

28 Original drawing in Dakin Collection.

29 New Orleans *Daily Picayune*, May 18, 1838, p. 2.

30 *St. Patrick's Church* vs. *Dakin and Dakin*, Commercial Court of New Orleans, Docket No. 1145, filed October 11, 1839; appealed by James Dakin, Supreme Court of Louisiana, Docket No. 3988, filed November 30, 1839. (Photocopies of significant documents in author's possession.)

31 *Ibid.*; Re Collins: Act before H. B. Cenas, notary, May 4, 1836; Clohecy, see ch. 4, n. 15.

32 Act before H. B. Cenas, notary, October 1, 1839.

33 *St. Patrick's Church* vs. *Dakin and Dakin*.

34 *Robinson's Reports:* 1 Robinson 202.

35 From tableau of assets in bankruptcy case, *Creditors of James H. Dakin* vs. *James H. Dakin*, Parish Court, Orleans Parish, Docket No. 14,114, filed July 16, 1841.

36 New Orleans *Daily Picayune*, November 27, 1855, p. 3 (italics mine).

37 Gallier's drawings are in Louisiana State Museum.

38 New Orleans *Louisiana Courier*, April 2, 1839, p. 3.

39 New Orleans *Daily Picayune*, August 14, 1839, p. 2.

40 *Ibid.*, October 18, 1839, p. 2, October 26, 1839, p. 1; Succession of Richard Owen Pritchard, New Orleans Civil District Court, Docket No. 249, filed October 22, 1839. Death certificate therein contains statement by James W. Zacharie that Pritchard drowned by "falling over board" the steamer *Brilliant.*

41 Stephen A. Caldwell, *A Banking History of Louisiana* (Baton Rouge, 1935), 61–64.

42 New Orleans *Daily Picayune*, May 21, 1842, p. 2, May 22, 1842, p. 2.

43 *Creditors of James H. Dakin* vs. *James H. Dakin*.

44 New Orleans *Bee*, July 5, 1842, p. 2.

45 Cast iron was supplied by John G. Tibbets of New York City.

46 Journal of Michel Douradou Bringier, Bringier Papers, Louisiana State University Library Archives.

47 Marriage contract, dated May 31, 1839, described in Succession of Duncan Kenner, New Orleans Civil District Court, Docket No. 21,664.

48 *Creditors of James H. Dakin* vs. *James H. Dakin*.

49 *Ibid.*

50 Obituaries: Alexander Baggett in New Orleans *Times*, November 10,

1865, p. 6; Benedict Baggett in New Orleans *Daily Picayune,* October 3, 1866, p. 4.

51 *Creditors of James H. Dakin* vs. *James H. Dakin.*

52 Dakin Collection.

53 *Sixth U.S. Census,* for New Orleans, Second Municipality, 100; Dakin, *Descendants,* 111.

54 New Orleans *Daily Picayune,* June 21, 1842, p. 2; Tombstone Inscription Index, Girod Street Cemetery, compiled by Daughters of the American Revolution, in Louisiana State Museum Library.

55 Original drawing, Dakin Collection.

## NOTES TO CHAPTER 8

1 John M. Keating, *History of Memphis and Shelby County, Tennessee* (Syracuse, N.Y., 1888), II, 223–26.

2 Dakin Collection.

3 Memphis *Evening Scimitar,* October 1, 1900, p. 8.

4 Quoted in Shields McIlwaine, *Memphis Down in Dixie* (New York, 1948), 89.

5 New Orleans *Bee,* September 29, 1834, p. 1.

6 *Acts of Louisiana Legislature,* 1835, April 2, 1835.

7 Louisiana *Senate Journal,* February 12, 1836, p. 37; Louisiana *House Journal,* January 26, 1837, p. 25; Louisiana *Senate Journal,* February 6, 1838, p. 35. Various buildings were used by the Medical College prior to 1843, *e.g.,* the class of 1836 graduated in Reverend Clapp's church on St. Charles Street, with the address given by the dean in Latin. See *Proceedings,* Medical College Faculty, entry of April 2, 1836 (MS in Dean's Office, Tulane University Medical School).

8 *Proceedings,* Medical College Faculty, February 27, 1842; financed by the faculty, *ibid.,* entry of May 30, 1847.

9 *Acts of Louisiana Legislature,* 1843, No. 62, March 22, 1843.

10 *Norman's New Orleans,* 168–69.

11 *Proceedings,* Medical College Faculty, May 5, 1843; New Orleans *Commercial Bulletin,* October 14, 1843, p. 3.

12 New Orleans *Lafayette City Advertiser,* November 12, 1842, p. 1; New Orleans *Daily Picayune,* April 14, 1843, p. 1.

13 A. T. Wood to the editor, New Orleans *Bee,* October 18, 1850, p. 1. Exhaustive research shows that Gasquet owned only the northeast side of Camp and St. Joseph streets.

14 Re corner Camp and St. Joseph streets: Conveyance Book 23, folio 340, Orleans Parish, March 27, 1838, Gasquet sale to Parish and resale in Conveyance Book 31, folio 334, June 3, 1842. Re property with acroterion on doorway: Act before John F. Coffey, notary, July 7, 1877, and *Victor Choppin* vs. *Walter Cox and Company,* Fifth Civil District Court, New Orleans, Docket No. 15,247, containing earlier acquisition also by

*Daniel Parish* vs. *Walter Cox,* in Third District Court. *New Orleans City Directory,* 1838, lists "Gasquet, Parish & Co., importers."

15 Building contract, act before Jules Mossy, notary, December 2, 1843, Robert Seaton, builder, and James H. Dakin, architect and superintendent.

16 T. P. Thompson, "Early Financing in New Orleans—The Story of the Canal Bank, 1831–1915," *Louisiana Historical Society Publications,* VII (1913–14), 28, 43. Thomas Ewing Dabney, *One Hundred Years of the Canal Bank, 1831–1931* (New Orleans, 1931), 9.

17 View in *Historical Epitome,* 323.

18 Dabney, *One Hundred Years,* 14; Thompson, "Early Financing," 42. Norman's map of New Orleans, 1845 (copy at Howard-Tilton Memorial Library), shows bank at site of Dakin building.

19 Canal Bank ownership of land for same site in act before G. A. Stringer, notary, May 12, 1831, and act before L. T. Caire, notary, January 19, 1847.

20 In building contract cited in note 15 above.

21 Kimball and James' *Business Directory for the Mississippi Valley, 1844* (Cincinnati, 1844), 434. Regan, manuscript biography of Dakin, mentions alleged work in Cincinnati and St. Louis. A cryptic entry in New Orleans *Bee.* June 19, 1839, p. 2—passenger arrivals, "on Steamboat Alton . . . from St. Louis . . . Messr. Deacon *(sic)* . . . "—may link Dakin to St. Louis, but a passenger on this boat could have come from Cincinnati and gotten aboard at Cairo, Illinois.

22 James H. Dakin to Samuel D. Morgan, June 15, 1844, in papers of Board of Commissioners for Tennessee State Capitol, in Tennessee State Library and Archives, Nashville.

23 Nell S. Mahoney, "William Strickland and the Building of Tennessee's Capitol, 1845–54," *Tennessee Historical Quarterly* (June, 1945), 105–106; Clayton B. Dekle, "The Tennessee State Capitol," *Tennessee Historical Quarterly* (Fall, 1966), 213–38.

24 Building contract before William Christy, notary, January 24, 1844.

25 Original drawings, Dakin Collection.

26 New Orleans *Daily Picayune,* February 17, 1850, p. 2.

27 Building contract, act before William Christy, notary, January 17, 1844.

28 Dakin Collection.

29 Regan, manuscript biography of Dakin.

30 Testimony given by Conrey, in *James H. Dakin* vs. *William Pratt,* Sixth District Court, East Baton Rouge Parish, filed October 23, 1848.

31 In Plan Book 52, folio 57, New Orleans Notarial Archives.

32 Act before A. Baudoin, notary, February 24, 1853.

33 "Biographical Sketch of Henry Howard, Architect," in Samuel Wilson, Jr. (ed.), *Henry Howard, Architect: An Exhibition of Photographs of His Work by Clarence John Laughlin* (New Orleans, 1952).

34 Samuel M. Green, *American Art* (New York, 1966), 208–209.

35 Obituary in New Orleans *Daily Picayune,* November 20, 1888, p. 2.

36 Maunsel White to James H. Dakin, May 31, 1848, in Maunsel White Letter Book, Southern Historical Collection, University of North Carolina Library, Chapel Hill (microfilm in author's possession).

37 Conversation with Mrs. Celestine Koen Ross, July, 1971, who resided in the house.

38 New Orleans *States,* December 14, 1924, Feature Section.

39 Assessment Rolls, Second Municipality, 1842–47, New Orleans, in sub-basement of New Orleans Public Library.

40 Act before H. B. Cenas, notary, November 18, 1842.

41 Wilson (ed.), *Henry Howard,* in autobiographical section.

42 *New Orleans City Directory,* 1838, p. 258.

43 New Orleans *Commercial Bulletin,* February 25, 1843, p. 2. With military interests holding much of his attention, Dakin turned his creativity to a design for a tent, which he patented May 30, 1842. It was, as Dakin said in the patent, "somewhat similar to the folding up and expansion of a common umbrella." The superstructure was contained entirely in a cone-shaped frame at the top and could either be suspended from above by a pulley or supported by an upright rod in the center, with the canvas sides hanging from the superstructure and "secured . . . by pins as in the . . . manner for military tents." Whether Dakin earned any monetary return for his idea is not known. U. S. Patent No. 2,655.

44 Minute Book, Louisiana Volunteer Company (MS in possession of Mrs. Blanche W. King, New Orleans).

45 New Orleans *Commercial Bulletin,* October 5, 1843, p. 2. Not all his early military experiences were pleasant. On February 25, 1844, Dakin led his men in the funeral procession of Daniel H. Twogood, a militia colonel and his old builder friend, who had been killed when attacked by a man at a political rally. New Orleans *Daily Tropic,* February 26, 1844, p. 2, and New Orleans *Daily Picayune,* March 23, 1844, p. 2.

46 New Orleans *Daily Picayune,* April 10, 1845, p. 2.

47 *Ibid.,* April 11, 1845, p. 2.

48 General Taylor to Governor of Louisiana, April 26, 1836, quoted in Thomas Bangs Thorpe, *Our Army on the Rio Grande* (Philadelphia, 1846), 41; New Orleans *Daily Delta,* May 3, 1846, p. 2.

49 Taylor's and Arista's initial strength discussed in Otis A. Singletary, *The Mexican War* (Chicago, 1960), 11, 13. Louisiana volunteers total strength, cited in Bernadette Rogan, "Louisiana's Part in the Mexican War" (M.A. thesis, Tulane University, 1939), 244. Eventually, the total of all volunteers reached over twenty thousand men, noted in Charles L. Dufour, *The Mexican War* (New York, 1968), 97.

50 New Orleans *Daily Delta,* May 20, 1846, p. 2, and June 5, 1846, p. 1.

51 Ezra L. Warner, *Generals in Gray* (Baton Rouge, 1964), 27. Albert Blanchard Diary (Typescript in Louisiana Room, Louisiana State University Library, Baton Rouge).

52 Blanchard Diary, May 20, 21, and 29, 1846.

53 New Orleans *Daily Delta,* June 5, 1846, p. 1, reporting news of May 31, 1846.

54 New Orleans *Daily Picayune,* May 23, 1852, p. 2.

55 Baton Rouge *Gazette,* May 29, 1852, p. 2.

56 H. W. Kostmayer, "The Tulane School of Medicine: 1834–1960," *Bulletin of Tulane University Medical Faculty* (August, 1961), 223.

57 *Acts of Louisiana Legislature,* 1847, No. 147, April 22, 1847.

58 Building contract, act before H. B. Cenas, notary, June 25, 1847.

59 Ground plan in E. Robinson, *Map of New Orleans* (New York, 1883). Front elevation in New Orleans *Daily Delta,* February 28, 1848, p. 1. Original drawing of front elevation by James H. Dakin, Dakin Collection (reverse marked in pencil, "Phillipa St.," contemporary name of University Place, showing oblique angle of Phillipa and Common streets).

60 Illustration in Green, *American Art,* Plate 3-22.

61 Davies, "A. J. Davis' Projects," 237.

62 New Orleans *Daily Delta,* February 28, 1848, p. 1; New Orleans *Daily Picayune,* September 20, 1855, p. 2, and September 21, 1855, p. 2; A. E. Fossier, "History of Medical Education in New Orleans," *Annals of Medical History* (1934), p. 350; *Acts of Louisiana Legislature,* 1855, No. 137, March 14, 1855.

63 New Orleans *Daily Delta,* February 28, 1848, p. 1.

64 *New Orleans Medical and Surgical Journal* (May 1, 1848), 800; *Hazard's Review* (November 6, 1830), 293.

65 Fossier, "History of Medical Education," 350. For an 1852 view, see *New Orleans City Directory,* 1852, Ad "C."

66 Fossier, "History of Medical Education," 435.

67 Illustration in *Harper's Weekly* (April 21, 1866), 241.

68 New Orleans *Daily States,* March 27, 1898, p. 3; New Orleans *Times-Democrat,* March 23, 1898, p. 3.

## NOTES TO CHAPTER 9

1 Federal Writers Project, *Georgia* (New York, 1940), 392–93; George G. Smith, *The Story of Georgia* (Baltimore, 1901), 257.

2 Newton, *Town and Davis,* 119; Wayne Andrews, "American Gothic," *American Heritage* (October, 1971), 97.

3 New Orleans *Daily Tropic,* August 11, 1846, p. 2.

4 New Orleans *Daily Delta,* November 28, 1849, p. 2.

5 *Acts of Louisiana Legislature,* 1846, No. 3, March 9, 1846.

6 Baton Rouge's population in 1850 was: Whites, 2,562; Free Colored, 251; Slaves, 1,092—totaling 3,905 (from *Seventh U.S. Census,* 1850). See also, New Orleans *Daily Picayune,* April 1, 1843, p. 2.

7 Maurice Ries, *160 Years of Tabasco Sauce* (Avery Island, La., 1968), 6. Maunsel White Sauce mentioned in New Orleans *Daily Picayune*, April 8, 1869, p. 2, and June 24, 1890, p. 6. Tabasco peppers grown by White in 1849, mentioned in White to Joseph Bracewell, April 4, 1849, in Maunsel White Letterbook, Southern Historical Collection, University of North Carolina Library, Chapel Hill (microfilm of portions in author's possession).

8 Clement Eaton, *The Mind of the Old South* (Baton Rouge, 1964), 69–89. An excellent engraving of White from *De Bow's Review* is included.

9 Maunsel White's letterbook also contains letters to Andrew Jackson and Zachary Taylor. White's prestige in New Orleans during this era is probably underestimated by historians.

10 *Acts of Louisiana Legislature*, 1847, No. 10, January 21, 1847.

11 James H. Dakin to Commissioners for the Erection of the State House, January 26, 1847, in James H. Dakin Diary for the construction of the capitol, Louisiana State University Library Archives.

12 Louisiana *Senate Journal*, 1847, April 9, 1847, pp. 34–35.

13 Official Debates of Louisiana Senate, 1847, in *Louisiana Courier*, April 10, 1847, p. 2. The army base site is probably where the 1931 capitol was constructed.

14 Senate Debates, in *Louisiana Courier*, April 12, 1847, p. 2.

15 *Ibid.*, April 14, 1847, p. 2.

16 The *Courier* blasted Kenner for his deprecating remarks about a "cabinet man" and quoted Vitruvius to counter him, *Louisiana Courier*, May 24, 1847, p. 3. Concurring with the *Courier* was the Baton Rouge *Democratic Advocate*, June 2, 1847, p. 1.

17 New Orleans *Commercial Bulletin*, April 16, 1847, p. 2. None of these plans have been found.

18 *Louisiana Courier*, April 17, 1847, p. 2.

19 New Orleans *Daily Delta*, May 6, 1847, p. 2.

20 Louisiana *Senate Journal*, 1847, April 21, 1847, p. 70.

21 Dakin Diary, May 4, 1847.

22 Dekle, "Tennessee State Capitol," 220.

23 *Acts of Louisiana Legislature*, 1847, No. 257, May 3, 1847; *Ibid.*, 1846, No. 3, March 9, 1846.

24 Minutes of Baton Rouge Board of Selectmen, Baton Rouge City Record Book A, 271, in East Baton Rouge Courthouse Building.

25 *Ibid.*, September 21, 1847, p. 279.

26 Dakin Diary, June 27, 1847; Baton Rouge *Democratic Advocate*, June 2, 1847, p. 2.

27 *Acts of Louisiana Legislature*, 1844, No. 79, March 25, 1844; *Annual Report; of Louisiana State Penitentiary, 1844* (copy in Howard-Tilton Memorial Library); New Orleans *Daily Picayune*, October 18, 1844, p. 2.

28 Dakin Diary, July 14, 1847.

29 *Ibid.*, July 28, 1847. Knap and Totten were known in New Orleans. See

New Orleans *Daily Delta*, September 23, 1846, p. 2.

30 White Letterbook, September 6, 1847.

31 Maunsel White to James H. Dakin, September 8, 1847.

32 Dakin Diary, October 7, 1847. *Cincinnati City Directory*, 1849–50, lists "Caroline Dakin, boarding house, s. side Court St., between Race & Elm." Her last known appearance in records is a February 3, 1873, sale of Texas land left over from Dakin's bankruptcy, signed in New Orleans, "Mrs. Caroline Belcher Dakin," and recorded in San Patricio County Courthouse, Texas, Abstract 107–109. A family story has it that her daughter, Georgianna, married a "Dr. Talbot." Cited in Dakin, *Descendants*, 111.

33 See n. 6 above for population statistics.

34 Baton Rouge *Democratic Advocate*, November 3, 1847, p. 2, November 10, 1847, pp. 1, 2; Baton Rouge *Comet*, November 4, 1847, p. 1; New Orleans *Commercial Times*, November 10, 1847, p. 2.

35 Dakin Diary, February 16, 1848.

36 *Acts of Louisiana Legislature*, 1848, No. 182, March 16, 1848.

37 White to Dakin, White Letterbook, May 31, 1848.

38 *Ibid.* June 7, 1848.

39 *Ibid.*, June 26, 1848.

40 Associated Press (Louisiana Mail Service) story by T. J. Adams, *ca.* 1930, "Troubles of Man Who Directed Building of Old State Capitol, Told as New One Nears Reality." (MS in files of Baton Rouge *State Times*, LA 815; newspaper clipping of this was in possession of Albert Dakin, author of Dakin descendant book). Also, see "Diary Reveals Insight Into Early American Architecture," *Architect and Engineer* (August, 1938), 24, and Baton Rouge *State Times*, May 16, 1932.

41 Dakin Diary, August 3, 1848.

42 White Letterbook, August 18, 1848.

43 *Ibid.*, August 28, 1848.

44 *James H. Dakin* vs. *William Pratt*, Sixth District Court, East Baton Rouge, Probate Docket No. 319, filed October 23, 1848.

45 Dakin Diary, September 21, 1848. Mather was buried in Catholic Cemetery, Baton Rouge, September 26, 1848 (St. Joseph Cathedral Records, Archives of the Diocese of Baton Rouge).

46 Dakin Diary, December 22, 1848.

47 White Letterbook, December 27, 1848.

48 *Ibid.*, January 27, March 27, 1849.

49 In this period, a splendid X-shaped Gothic house was erected in New Orleans and is still standing on South Carrollton Avenue and Freret Street. It was built for Nathanial Wilkinson, the officer of the Canal Bank with whom Dakin served on the committee to obtain a statue of Franklin from Hiram Powers. The architect has never been identified. New Orleans *Daily Picayune*, April 24, 1844, p. 2, April 30, 1844, p. 2, May 1, 1844, p. 2; New Orleans *Daily Tropic*, April 30, 1844, p. 2, May 4,

1844, p. 2. See New Orleans *Daily Crescent*, November 29, 1850, p. 1, and act before William Christy, notary, February 19, 1850. Photos in *Diverse Fab* (New Orleans, 1967).

50 James H. Dakin to Knap and Totten, March 9, 1849, in Dakin Diary.

51 In Maunsel White Papers, May 24, 1849.

52 Dakin Diary, May, 1849, through November, 1849, *passim*.

53 New Orleans *Daily Delta*, November 18, 1849, p. 1.

54 *Ibid.*

55 Special thanks to Henry Krotzer of Koch and Wilson, Architects, for pointing out this asymmetry.

56 New Orleans *Daily Crescent*, February 12, 1852, p. 2.

57 New Orleans *Daily Delta*, February 13, 1852, p. 1.

58 *Leslie's Illustrated*, May 24, 1862, p. 84.

59 New Orleans *Daily Delta*, February 13, 1852, p. 1.

60 *Ibid.*, February 29, 1852, p. 2.

61 *Ibid.*, June 16, 1850, p. 2.

62 *Ibid.*, December 16, 1849, p. 2.

63 *Ibid.*, January 10, 1850, p. 2.

64 Dakin Diary, January 7, 1850; last entry in diary is dated January 10, 1850. In February, Dakin advertised his new invention, a bagasse drier. Baton Rouge *Gazette*, February 16, 1850, p. 3, February 23, 1850, p. 3. U.S. patent no. 7,375; it was not successful.

65 *Acts of Louisiana Legislature*, 1854, No. 209, March 18, 1854; Baton Rouge *Weekly Gazette*, May 21, 1857, p. 7; Baton Rouge *Gazette and Comet*, November 10, 1858, p. 2; *Leslie's Illustrated*, May 24, 1862, p. 84. McVey described himself as a builder in his ad in *Louisiana Statistical Register* (Baton Rouge, 1855), in Louisiana State Supreme Court Library, New Orleans.

66 Baton Rouge *Weekly Gazette and Comet*, July 19, 1857, quoted in Baton Rouge *State Times*, July 19, 1957. See also New Orleans *Daily Delta*, July 18, 1852, p. 1; June 15, 1850, and Baton Rouge *Gazette*, February 23, 1850, p. 1. The capitol was also used for important events such as the Constitutional Convention of 1852, in New Orleans *Daily Delta*, July 15, 1852, p. 2. For rotunda's elliptical shape, see Baton Rouge *Weekly Comet*, February 11, 1855, p. 3, March 4, 1855, p. 1.

67 Baton Rouge *Daily Advocate*, July 13, 1855, p. 1.

68 New Orleans *Daily Crescent*, October 2, 1858, p. 1; Baton Rouge *Weekly Gazette and Comet*, March 25, 1864, p. 1.

69 New Orleans *Daily Delta*, January 1, 1863, p. 3.

70 *The War of the Rebellion; A Compilation of the Official Records of the Union and Confederate Armies* (Washington, 1880–1901), Ser. I, Vol. XV, 630–33.

71 Baton Rouge *Weekly Gazette and Comet*, March 25, 1864, p. 1.

72 *Harper's Weekly*, September 8, 1866, p. 566; *Every Saturday*, August 5, 1871, pp. 140–42.

73 Report of Committee on Examination of Damages to the Public Build-

ings at Baton Rouge, December 20, 1866 (Copy courtesy of George Leake, American Institute of Architects, New Orleans). See also New Orleans *Bee*, February 2, 1866, p. 2, and Baton Rouge *Tri-Weekly Advocate*, September 6, 1865, p. 2.

74 *House Documents*, 45th Cong., 2nd Sess., No. 2021, December 10, 1877.

75 New Orleans *Daily Picayune*, July 2, 1879, p. 2. A previous referendum called by the state resulted in Baton Rouge being selected. See Baton Rouge *Louisiana Capitolian*, February 8, 1879, p. 1.

76 New Orleans *Daily Picayune*, December 6, 1911, p. 11; New Orleans *Times Democrat*, July 21, 1887, p. 1; *Journal of the Constitutional Convention*, 1879, p. 153; New Orleans *Times*, May 22, 1880, p. 4; New Orleans *Vieux Carre Courier*, July 7, 1967, p. 2; Henry and Elsie Withey, *Biographical Dictionary of American Architects (Deceased)* (Los Angeles, 1956), 223.

77 Committee report in Louisiana *Senate Journal*, February 23, 1880, p. 126; New Orleans *Daily Picayune*, February 23, 1880, p. 1; New Orleans *Democrat*, May 16, 1880, p. 3. The report suggested digging the basement to a more useful depth and said it found no provision for heating and plumbing, which is in conflict with Dakin's diary entry of August 26, 1847, in which he records that while in New York, he "procured two plans or modes for heating the State House with hot air."

78 Inspectors report, New Orleans *Daily Picayune*, May 29, 1880, p. 2. Potts mentioned in Baton Rouge *Tri-Weekly Capitolian*, May 27, 1880, p. 3.

79 Louisiana *Senate Journal*, 1880, February 23, 1880, p. 126.

80 Report of State House Commission, November 20, 1881 (bound with *Messages of the Governor*, 1881, at Howard-Tilton Memorial Library, New Orleans).

81 *Ibid.*

82 *Daily Picayune*, July 2, 1880, p. 2; Baton Rouge *Tri-Weekly Capitolian*, May 18, 1880, p. 3.

83 Mark Twain, *Life on the Mississippi*. Chapter 40.

84 See photo of Mark Twain house in Edith C. Salsbury (ed.), *Suzy and Mark Twain* (New York, 1965), 173. Also Henry-Russell Hitchcock, "Ruskin and American Architecture," in Sir John Summerson (ed.), *Concerning Architecture* (Baltimore, 1968), 198.

85 Baton Rouge *Weekly Advocate*, April 1, 1881, p. 2.

86 Arthur H. Noll, "Louisiana's Capitol," *American Architect and Building News*, December 6, 1890.

87 After a fire in 1906, the turrets were removed. See Allison Owen editorial, *Architectural Art and Its Allies*, I (June, 1906), 8, and Thomas McManus, *The Campaigning Grounds of Louisiana* (Baton Rouge, 1907?), n. p. (in Louisiana State University Library, Louisiana Department). Photos in New Orleans *Times Democrat*, March 20, 1909, show capitol before and after the turrets were removed.

88 New Orleans *Daily Picayune*, June 11, 1922, p. 3.

89 Address by Governor Isaac Johnson to Legislature, in *Senate Journal 1848*, January 18, 1848, p. 10; *Acts of Louisiana Legislature*, 1848, No. 110, March 16, 1848.

90 Hiram Powers to Secretary of State Charles Gayarre, June 8, 1852, quoted in *Louisiana Historical Quarterly* (July, 1919), 272; New Orleans *Daily Crescent*, January 8, 1856, p. 2.

91 New Orleans *Daily Delta*, November 5, 1849, p. 2. New Orleans *Daily Crescent*, January 8, 1856, p. 2.

92 Baton Rouge *Weekly Gazette and Comet*, December 28, 1858, p. 2.

93 Baton Rouge *Weekly Comet*, February 11, 1855, p. 3. *Acts of Louisiana Legislature*, 1855, No. 146, March 14, 1855, appropriated $15,000 for enclosure. Baton Rouge *Weekly Comet*, June 22, 1855, p. 2.

94 Baton Rouge *Weekly Advocate*, February 23, 1856, p. 2. New Orleans *Daily Crescent*, January 8, 1856, p. 2 on unveiling. Baton Rouge *Weekly Comet*, September 23, 1855, p. 1; New Orleans *Daily Crescent*, October 2, 1858, p. 1.

95 New Orleans *Daily Crescent*, January 8, 1856, p. 2.

96 Baton Rouge *Weekly Gazette and Comet*, July 19, 1857, quoted in Baton Rouge *State Times*, July 19, 1957; Baton Rouge *Weekly Gazette and Comet*, December 28, 1858, p. 2; New Orleans *Daily Crescent*, October 2, 1858, p. 1; *Leslie's Illustrated*, May 24, 1862, p. 84.

97 *Daily Picayune*, August 24, 1862, p. 4; New Orleans *Daily Delta*, August 23, 1862, p. 2.

98 Washington *Post*, February 18, 1951. Letter from J. George Stewart, Architect of the Capitol, Washington, D.C., March 27, 1969, says statue arrived in Washington by November 11, 1862, and displayed in the Rotunda, January, 1863.

99 New Orleans *Daily Picayune*, March 2, 1869, p. 1, April 7, 1869, pp. 1, 2; New Orleans *Deutsche Zeitung*, April 7, 1869, p. 8; New Orleans *Times*, March 6, 1871, p. 1; Baton Rouge *State Times*, February 22, 1960.

## NOTES TO CHAPTER 10

1 E. Merton Coulter, *The South During Reconstruction* (Baton Rouge, 1947), 253.

2 Latrobe, *Impressions Concerning New Orleans*, ed. Wilson, xiv.

3 New Orleans *Bee*, May 20, 1835, p. 2.

4 Lawrence Wodehouse, "The Federal Government as Architectural Client," (unpublished MS; excerpts supplied to this writer and gratefully acknowledged).

5 Gallier, *Autobiography*, 39.

6 New Orleans *Daily Delta*, June 5, 1847, p. 2; Dakin Diary, June 26, 1847, and July 8, 1847.

7 Original drawings, Dakin Collection.

8 James H. Dakin to Secretary of Treasury, June 22, 1847, in Record Group 121, Records of Public Buildings Service, National Archives, Washington, D.C.

9 Dakin Diary, June 26, 1847. Consistent with his comments in his diary, Dakin stressed the desirability of light and air in his letter to the Treasury, June 22, 1847.

10 Dakin Diary. One official was John Frazee whom Dakin knew from their work on the First Presbyterian Church at Troy. See Chapter 2, n. 3.

11 See Chapter 9, n. 77.

12 This point is well made in Wodehouse, "The Federal Government as Architectural Client."

13 New Orleans *Daily Delta*, February 13, 1848, p. 1.

14 Hamlin, *Greek Revival*, 230. Wood was born in England in 1799 (Sexton's Burial Records, Cypress Grove Cemetery, New Orleans, October 10, 1854), and first appears in known records in Longworth's *New York City Directory* in 1831; he is listed until 1833, when he went to New Orleans. His architectural abilities must remain in doubt, in view of the fact that he and George Clarkson bought plans from Dakin for their building ventures. See Chapter 1, n. 27. To his credit, he designed the first building for the State Seminary of Learning (now LSU). See *Annual Report of Board of Supervisors*, 1857, p. 21, and succession of A. T. Wood, No. 8,245, Civil District Court, New Orleans, filed 1854.

15 Conveyance Office Record Book 44, folio 334, Parish of Orleans, January 27, 1848.

16 New Orleans *Daily Delta*, February 13, 1848, p. 1.

17 New Orleans *Commercial Times*, June 20, 1848, p. 2.

18 New Orleans *Daily Crescent*, October 2, 1848, p. 2; Cadmus M. Wilcox, *History of the Mexican War* (Washington, 1892), 615.

19 Communication No. 52, Commissioners for the Erection of the Custom House to Secretary of the Treasury, November, 1850, quoted in Stanley C. Arthur, *A History of the United States Custom House, New Orleans* (New Orleans, 1940), 30, 47. The letterbook referred to by Arthur in his bibliography (item No. 3) could not be located.

20 New Orleans *Daily Delta*, June 14, 1850, p. 2.

21 *Ibid.*, June 21, 1850, p. 2, and June 22, 1850, p. 4.

22 James H. Dakin to President Zachary Taylor, May 23, 1850, in Record Group 56, General Records, Treasury Department National Archives.

23 Commissioners for the Erection of the Custom House to Secretary of the Treasury, June 14, 1850, *ibid.* Dakin was called "an architect of the highest order and skill" in New Orleans *Democrat*, September 1, 1880, p. 1.

24 S. J. Peters to Congressman C. M. Conrad, June 15, 1850, in Record Group 56, General Records, Treasury Department, National Archives.

25 A. J. Davis Day Book, July 27, 1850, p. 412.

26 In Record Group 56, General Records, Treasury Department, National Archives.

27 In Record Group 56, Miscellaneous Letters, XIV, Treasury Department, National Archives; New Orleans *Daily Picayune,* July 30, 1850, p. 2; Baton Rouge *Gazette,* August 3, 1850, p. 2.

28 New Orleans *Daily Crescent,* August 1, 1850, p. 2; Lewis E. Reynolds to Commissioners for New Custom House, January 5, 1852, in Record Group 121, Records of Public Building Service, National Archives.

29 Avery was compensated as superintendant of the capitol, in *Acts of Louisiana Legislature,* 1850, No. 269, March 21, 1850. Report of the Works, from James H. Dakin, Superintendant of the Custom House, August 31, 1850, in Record Group 121, Records of Public Buildings Service, National Archives.

30 Incomplete copy at Howard-Tilton Memorial Library Archives. Complete copy in Samuel Wilson, Jr., Collection (courtesy of Mr. Wilson).

31 Further research may uncover an earlier building, but as cited in Carl W. Condit, *American Building Art: The Nineteenth Century* (New York, 1960), the first major American building with an iron frame was the Harper and Brothers Printing Company building in New York dating from 1854. My definition deliberately excludes the Travers Library in Paterson, N.J., which, though earlier (1846), cannot be compared in size or importance to the New Orleans Custom House. Dakin's 1850 report (see n. 30 above) suggested these changes: "I have proposed the substitution of iron floors, etc., instead of brick arched floors, and also shown that the exterior walls as now erected are, in my judgment, entirely insufficient to withstand the thrust of the arches against them, and that extraordinary means must be employed to ensure perfect safety in the structure. I have omitted to mention that the above system of iron flooring will have an effect to anchor and tie the walls of the edifice in every direction, and that there will be no lateral or horizontal pressure against them in the least degree." (Report by Dakin to Commissioners of the Custom House, in the New Orleans *Bee,* October 11, 1850, p. 1.) Carl Condit states that as of 1972 the Harper building is the earliest known constructed with an iron frame. Dr. Condit to author, December 8, 1972. See Chapter 11, n. 14.

32 Lawrence Wodehouse, "Ammi B. Young, 1798–1874," *Journal of the Society of Architectural Historians* (December, 1966), 277.

33 New Orleans *Bee,* October 11, 1850, p. 1; New Orleans *Daily Delta,* October 12, 1850, p. 2.

34 New Orleans *Daily Picayune,* October 6, 1850, p. 2.

35 New Orleans *Bee,* October 5, 1850, p. 1; Minutes of the First Municipality, October 4, 1850 (MS in New Orleans Public Library).

36 New Orleans *Bee,* October 18, 1850, p. 1.

37 *Ibid.*

38 *Louisiana Courier,* July 28, 1835, p. 3, August 7, 1835, p. 5, and August 11, 1835, p. 3.

39 Debates of Senate, bound in *Senate Journal,* 1850, February 21, 1850, p. 54.

40 *Acts of the Louisiana Legislature,* 1850, No. 124, March 16, 1850.

41 Rogers diary, typescript copy generously supplied this writer by Mr. Denys Peter Myers. Original MS placed by Mr. Myers in Avery Library. Information about the Battle House, St. Louis Hotel, and Hamilton County Courthouse in letter from Mr. Myers of July 15, 1968.

42 *Ibid.;* New Orleans *Daily Picayune,* April 19, 1894, p. 10.

43 Quoted in Dakin pamphlet (see n. 30 above).

44 Photocopy of letter and drawing courtesy of Lawrence Wodehouse. Originals in National Archives.

45 James H. Dakin to William L. Hodge, Assistant Treasurer of the United States, January 4, 1851, in Record Group 121, Public Buildings Service, National Archives. He mentions Thomas U. Walter as having offered suggestions regarding ventilation.

46 James H. Dakin to Commissioners of Custom House, January 9, 1851, in Record Group 121, Public Buildings Service, National Archives.

47 *Congressional Globe* [now *Record*], 31st. Cong., 2nd Sess., 1850–51, March 3, 1851, p. 821.

48 *Ibid.,* 822. The committee hearings could not be located.

49 *Ibid.*

50 Richard B. Morris (ed.), *Encyclopedia of American History* (New York, 1961), 426.

51 United States, *Statutes at Large,* 1851–1855, 31st. Cong., 2nd Sess. Act of March 8, 1851, p. 609.

52 United States Senate, *Journal of Executive Proceedings,* 1848–52, VIII, 333, 335.

53 James Gallier to W. L. Hodge, April 10, 1851, in Record Group 56, General Records, Treasury Department, National Archives.

54 Arthur, *History of the Custom House,* 37.

55 New Orleans *Daily Picayune,* September 3, 1851, p. 2.

56 Commissioners of the Custom House to Thomas Corwin, Secretary of the Treasury, August 29, 1851, in Record Group 56, General Records, Treasury Department, National Archives.

57 New Orleans *Deutsche Zeitung,* October 26, 1851, p. 2.

58 See chapter, "*Wood vs. Reynolds,*" in Arthur, *History of the Custom House,* 38–39, and note 28 above. Reynolds mentioned in Wilson, *Guide to New Orleans Architecture,* 97, 123.

59 General George W. Cullum, *Biographical Register of United States Army Officers* (Boston, 1891), 155. Dakin had recommended Chase in January, 1851, in his letter to Commissioners, cited in note 46 above.

60 Francis B. Heitman, *Historical Register of United States Army* (Washington, 1903), II, 54; Alfred L. Crabb, *Nashville: Personality of a City* (Indianapolis, 1960), 37, 46, 55; Withey, *Biographical Register,* 276.

61 Wodehouse, "Ammi Young"; Hamlin, *Greek Revival.*
62 Wodehouse, "Federal Government as Client," 15. Strickland may have gone to New Orleans with regard to the Custom House when he, Dakin, and Rogers met on February 25, 1851.
63 Expense Voucher, James H. Dakin to Treasury Department, December 10, 1851, in Record Group 217, General Accounting Office Records, National Archives.
64 Report of Special Commission of Inspectors to Secretary of the Treasury, December 15, 1851, in Record Group 121, Public Buildings Service, National Archives.
65 *Ibid.*
66 Original drawings in Record Group 121, Public Buildings Service, National Archives.
67 Hamlin used a view as his frontispiece for *Greek Revival Architecture in America* and discussed it on page 230.
68 The drawing based on Dakin's floor plan uses concentric rings as a symbol for the business room columns, a device employed to differentiate Doric columns (one ring) from pedestal type columns, *i.e.*, Ionic and Corinthian. Because of the great height contemplated for the room, Corinthian, the taller order, was undoubtedly intended.
69 Reynolds recommended by Commissioners of Custom House in their letter to Secretary of Treasury, October 9, 1851, in Record Group 56, Head of Bureaus Application Files, Treasury Department, National Archives. His nomination by President Fillmore and rejection by Senate in U.S. Senate, *Journal of Executive Proceedings* 1848–52, 32nd Cong., VIII, 340, 449, 609.
70 New Orleans *Daily Delta*, March 21, 1852, p. 8.
71 Wharton's status in Arthur, *History of Custom House*, 39, 40. Beauregard named, in New Orleans *Daily Picayune*, May 5, 1853, p. 2. Wood died October 9, 1854, at age fifty-five. Obituary in New Orleans *Daily Picayune*, October 9, 1854, p. 2. Wharton said of him: "He had no equal in the profession — he was a thoroughly practical architect — confident and self reliant — bold and daring in construction — of which abundant evidence is the grand edifice he leaves incomplete but which will stand as an imperishable monument to his talents and architectural genius." Quoted by Samuel Wilson, Jr., in *A Century of Architecture in New Orleans, 1857–1957* (New Orleans, 1957), n. p. This lavish praise was undeserved by a man whose building had such deficiencies as those noted by Isaiah Rogers and James Dakin, especially the use of archaic groined arches, the passageways which are poorly laid out, ad infinitum, and a man who, just a few years before, was buying plans from Dakin. Even a casual visitor to the Custom House will observe and be dismayed by the irregular layout of the main business room which does not line up with the main (Canal Street) staircase. This is but one of several anomalies of Wood's "masterpiece."

72 New Orleans *Times*, March 15, 1866, p. 14.
73 U.S. Treasury, *Report*, 1870, p. 297.
74 New Orleans *Daily Picayune*, February 23, 1871, p. 4; Arthur, *History of Custom House*, 49.

## NOTES TO CHAPTER 11

1 *Report of the Commissioners of Public Buildings*, February 17, 1852 (Copy in Vertical Files, Howard-Tilton Memorial Library).
2 *Ibid.*
3 *Acts of Louisiana Legislature,* 1854, No. 228, March 16, 1854; Baton Rouge *Weekly Comet*, September 23, 1855, p. 1. *Louisiana Federal Writers' Project, Old State Capitol* (Baton Rouge, 1940), 5 (Copy in Vertical Files, Baton Rouge Public Library); Baton Rouge *Daily Comet*, January 4, 1856, p. 2; Baton Rouge *State Times*, February 1, 1932. An unsubstantiated story persists that after the 1880 restoration, interior furnishings were obtained which were originally intended for Emperor Maximillian of Mexico. This may have been based on the gift of two chairs from Mexico by General Persifor F. Smith in 1850. See *Messages of Governor Walker of Louisiana, 1852,* 49 (Copy in Huntington Library, San Marino, Calif.).
4 *Report of Commissioners*, 1852, pp. 1, 5.
5 *Acts of Louisiana Legislature*, 1884, No. 49, July 5, 1884; New Orleans *Daily Picayune*, June 19, 1884, 3.
6 *Acts of Louisiana Legislature*, 1857, No. 43, February 28, 1857.
7 *James Dakin* vs. *William Pratt.*
8 See Chapter 10, n. 63.
9 James H. Dakin to Secretary of Treasury Corwin, December 12, 1851, in Record Group 121, Records of Public Buildings Service, National Archives.
10 Attorney for Dakin's widow, Amos W. Bell of Baton Rouge, requested payment because Dakin left his wife "in straitened circumstances," but she was not reimbursed. A. W. Bell to Secretary Corwin, January 22, 1853, in Record Group 121, Records of Public Buildings Service, National Archives.
11 Regan, manuscript biography of Dakin.
12 New Orleans *Daily Picayune*, May 18, 1852, p. 2.
13 *Acts of Louisiana Legislature*, 1852, No. 224, March 17, 1852. It formally requested permission to use the army base. Tombstone inscriptions, Girod Street Cemetery Index in Louisiana State Museum Library.
14 Succession of James H. Dakin, Probate No. 274, East Baton Rouge Courthouse, filed July 31, 1852. As this goes to press, Dakin's copy of Thomas Tredgold, *Practical Essay on the Strength of Cast Iron…* (London, 1842), has been found in the New Orleans Public Library.
15 Interview with Miss Kathyrine Regan, June, 1970.
16 *Acts of Louisiana Legislature*, 1855, No. 187, March 15, 1855.

# SELECTED
# BIBLIOGRAPHY

This partial listing of sources includes those which were used most extensively in the writing of this book. Comments on their value are included where appropriate.

Arthur, Stanley C. *A History of the United States Custom House, New Orleans.* New Orleans, 1940. Not complete, but the best single source of information.

Baigell, Matthew. "John Haviland in Philadelphia, 1818–1826." *Journal of Society of Architectural Historians* (October, 1966), 197–208.

Blanchard, Albert. "Diary." Typescript copy in Louisiana Room, Louisiana State University Library.

Brantley, William H., Jr. *Banking in Alabama.* 2 vols. Birmingham, Alabama, 1961.

———. "Henry Hitchcock of Mobile, 1816–1839." *Alabama Review* (January, 1952), 3–39. An excellent biography.

Buckingham, J. S. *The Slave States of America.* 2 vols. London, 1842.

Condit, Carl W. *American Building Art: The Nineteenth Century.* New York, 1960.

Dakin, Albert H. *Descendants of Thomas Dakin of Concord, Massachusetts.* Rutland, Vermont, 1948. A copy is in the Library of Congress.

Dakin, Charles B. Mobile Account (or Receipt) Book. Manuscript owned by Mrs. Beryl Trenchard Patin, New Orleans.

Dakin, James H. Collection. New Orleans Public Library. This collection contains 181 original drawings and 38 lithographs.

———. "Louisiana State Capitol Diary." Manuscript in Louisiana State University Library, Archives Department.

———. *To the Commissioners for the Erection of a New Custom House in New Orleans.* New Orleans, 1830.

Davies, Jane B. "A. J. Davis' Projects for a Patent Office Building, 1832–34." *Journal of Society of Architectural Historians* (October, 1965), 229–51. The most accurate and useful piece ever written on Town, Davis, and Dakin.

Davis, Alexander Jackson. "Day Book," Vol. 1. Manuscript in the New York Public Library.

———. "Day Book," Vol. 2. Manuscript in Avery Library, Columbia University.

———. "Diary" or "Journal." Manuscript in Metropolitan Museum of Art, New York.

———. "Papers, Letter Book and Miscellaneous Letters." Manuscripts in New York Public Library.

———. "Papers." Manuscripts in New-York Historical Society.

Dufour, Charles L., ed. *St. Patricks of New Orleans, 1833–1958.* New Orleans, 1958.

Early, James. *Romanticism and American Architecture.* New York, 1965.

Eaton, Clement. *The Mind of the Old South.* Baton Rouge, 1964. Contains an excellent short biography of Maunsel White.

Fay, Thomas S. *Views in New York and its Environs. . . .* New York, 1831. Very rare. Complete copy in Library of Congress and nearly complete one in New-York Historical Society.

Fossier, A. E. "History of Medical Education in New Orleans." *Annals of Medical History* (1934), 320–52; 427–47.

Gallier, James. *Autobiography of James Gallier.* Paris, 1864.

Gilchrist, Agnes A. *William Strickland, Architect and Engineer.* Philadelphia, 1950.

Green, Samuel M. *American Art.* New York, 1966.

Hall, A. Oakey. *The Manhattaner in New Orleans.* New York, 1851.

Hamlin, Talbot. *Greek Revival Architecture in America.* London, 1944. Still remarkably thorough and accurate. *Historical Epitome of the State of Louisiana. . . .* New Orleans, 1840. An early guidebook to New Orleans.

Hone, Philip. *Diary of Philip Hone.* 2 vols. New York, 1927.

Howard, Henry. "Autobiography," in *Henry Howard, Architect: An Exhibition of Photographs of His Work. . . .* Edited by Samuel Wilson, Jr. New Orleans, 1952. This autobiography, transcribed from the original, is more accurate than that in *Jewell's Crescent City.*

Jewell, Edwin L., ed. *Jewell's Crescent City.* New Orleans, 1873.

Kimball, LeRoy E. "The Old University Building and the Society's Years on Washington Square." *New-York Historical Society Quarterly* (July, 1948), 149–219.

Kouwenhoven, John A. *Made in America,* retitled *The Arts in Modern American Civilization.* New York, 1967.

Landy, Jacob. *The Architecture of Minard Lafever.* New York, 1970. An excellent book which stops short of an analysis of Lafever's books, a topic in itself.

———. "The Washington Monument Project in New York." *Journal of Society of Architectural Historians* (December, 1969), 291–97.

Medical College of Louisiana. "Proceedings and Minutes of the

Faculty." Manuscript in Dean's office, Tulane University Medical School.

Newton, Roger Hale. *Town and Davis, Architects*. New York, 1942. This book is not as useful as Jane Davies' article cited above.

*A Noble Landmark of New York: The Fifth Avenue Presbyterian Church, 1808–1958*. New York, 1960.

Noll, Arthur H. "Louisiana's Capitol." *American Architect and Building News* (December 6, 1890), 145–46.

Norman, B. M. *Norman's New Orleans*. New Orleans, 1845. The very best of the early guidebooks to New Orleans.

Patton, Glenn. "Chapel in the Sky." *Architectural Review* (March, 1969), 177–80.

Powers, Hiram. "Letters to Secretary of State Charles Gayarre." *Louisiana Historical Quarterly* (July, 1919), 272. These relate to his Washington statue for the Louisiana capitol. The original letters are in a letter book of Gayarre, called "Order Book," in the basement of the Louisiana Supreme Court Library, New Orleans.

Regan, Kathyrine. "Biography of James H. Dakin." Manuscript in Manuscripts Division, Howard-Tilton Library, Tulane University. Prepared in 1942.

Ripley, Eliza. *Social Life In Old New Orleans*. New York, 1912.

Rogers, Isaiah. "Diary." Manuscript in Avery Library, Columbia University.

St. Patrick's Church Supreme Court Case. Resume in *Robinson's Reports (1 Robinson 202)*. Copy in Louisiana Supreme Court Library, New Orleans.

Savage, Theodore. *The Presbyterian Church in New York*. New York, 1949.

Scully, Vincent. "American Houses: Thomas Jefferson to Frank Lloyd Wright," in *Rise of an American Architecture*, edited by Edgar Kaufman. New York, 1970.

Town, Davis, and Dakin. "Financial Records." Manuscript at Avery Library, Columbia University.

University of Louisiana. "Minute Book of the Board of Administrators. Manuscript in Dean's office, Tulane Medical School.

White, Maunsel. "Papers, Letter Books, etc." Manuscripts in Southern Historical Collection, Louis Round Wilson Library, University of North Carolina at Chapel Hill.

Wilson, Samuel, Jr. *A Guide to Architecture of New Orleans, 1699–1959*. New York, 1959.

———. *Building Contract Index*. Manuscript in Manuscripts Division, Howard-Tilton Library, Tulane University. This card index, prepared from the New Orleans Notarial Archives, was generously donated by Mr. Wilson and is an invaluable tool. It does not purport to be a complete listing of all early contracts in the Notarial Archives, but was informally compiled at random.

Wodehouse, Lawrence. "Ammi B. Young, 1798–1874." *Journal of Society of Architectural Historians* (December, 1966), 268–80.

# INDEX